AMERICAN CATHOLICS, AMERICAN CULTURE: TRADITION AND RESISTANCE

AMERICAN CATHOLICS IN THE PUBLIC SQUARE
Edited by Margaret O'Brien Steinfels

The American Catholics in the Public Square series is a joint effort between Sheed & Ward and the Commonweal Foundation with special funding from The Pew Charitable Trusts. The result of a three-year study sponsored by Pew aimed at understanding the contributions to U.S. civic life of the Catholic, Jewish, mainline and evangelical Protestant, African-American, Latino, and Muslim communities in the United States, the two volumes in this series gather selected essays from the Commonweal Colloquia and the joint meetings organized by the Commonweal Foundation and The Faith and Reason Institute, a conservative think tank in Washington. Participants in the Commonweal Colloquia and the joint meetings—leading Catholic scholars, journalists, lawyers, business and labor leaders, novelists and poets, church administrators and lobbyists, activists, policymakers, and politicians—produced approximately forty-five essays presented at ten meetings that brought together over two hundred and fifty participants. The two volumes in the American Catholics in the Public Square series address many of the most critical issues now facing the Catholic Church in the United States by drawing from the four goals of the colloquia—to identify, assess, and critique the distinctive elements in Catholicism's approach to civic life; to generate concrete analyses and recommendations for strengthening Catholic civic engagement; to encompass a broad spectrum of political and social views of Catholics to encourage dialogue between Catholic leaders, religious and secular media, and political thinkers; to reexamine the long-standing Catholic belief in the obligation to promote the common good and to clarify how Catholics may work better with those holding other religious or philosophical convictions toward revitalizing both the religious environment and civic participation in the American republic.

Volumes in the American Catholics in the Public Square Series

American Catholics and Civic Engagement: A Distinctive Voice
American Catholics, American Culture: Tradition and Resistance

AMERICAN CATHOLCS, AMERICAN CULTURE: TRADITION AND RESISTANCE

Volume 2

American Catholics in the Public Square

Edited by
MARGARET O'BRIEN STEINFELS

A SHEED & WARD BOOK

ROWMAN & LITTLEFIELD PUBLISHERS, INC.

Lanham • Boulder • New York • Toronto • Oxford

A SHEED & WARD BOOK

ROWMAN & LITTLEFIELD PUBLISHERS, INC.

Published in the United States of America
by Rowman & Littlefield Publishers, Inc.
A wholly owned subsidiary of The Rowman & Littlefield Publishing Group, Inc.
4501 Forbes Boulevard, Suite 200, Lanham, Maryland 20706
www.rowmanlittlefield.com

PO Box 317
Oxford
OX2 9RU, UK

British Library Cataloguing in Publication Information Available

Library of Congress Cataloging-in-Publication Data

American Catholics, American Culture : tradition and resistance / edited
by Margaret O'Brien Steinfels.
  p. cm. — (American Catholics in the public square series ; v. 2)
  Includes bibliographical references and index.
  ISBN 0-7425-3160-0 (alk. paper)—ISBN 0-7425-3161-9 (pbk. : alk.
paper)
  1. Christian sociology—United States. 2. Christian
sociology—Catholic Church. I. Steinfels, Margaret O'Brien, 1941– II.
Series.
  BX1406.3 .A485 2004
  261.8'088'282—dc22

                                                    2003019713

Printed in the United States of America

∞™ The paper used in this publication meets the minimum requirements of
American National Standard for Information Sciences—Permanence of Paper for
Printed Library Materials, ANSI/NISO Z39.48-1992.

CONTENTS

PREFACE

American Catholics in the Public Square was a three-year project (2000–2002) supported by a grant from The Pew Charitable Trusts. It was part of a Pew-funded family of studies aimed at understanding the contributions to U.S. civic life of the Catholic, Jewish, mainline and evangelical Protestant, African-American, Latino, and Muslim communities in the United States.

The Catholic study was undertaken jointly by the Commonweal Foundation, which publishes *Commonweal* magazine, and The Faith and Reason Institute, a conservative think tank in Washington. The two partners in this enterprise conducted much of it in parallel but separate tracks addressing various aspects of Catholic social thought, of the church's institutional activities, and of individual Catholics' presence in politics and civil society. The Latino project was organized independently and includes both Catholic and evangelical partners. The two volumes in this series gather selected essays from the Commonweal Colloquia and the joint meetings organized by the Commonweal Foundation and The Faith and Reason Institute. The publications of The Faith and Reason Institute are available from its Washington office.

American Catholics in the Public Square was designed to examine and explore Catholic participation in the nation's civic life. Its four major goals were:

1. To identify the distinctive elements in Catholicism's approach to civic life; to explore the strengths and weaknesses of this tradition in the American context; to discover how (and how successfully) this tradition is being transmitted; to identify obstacles within the Catholic church itself and the Catholic community to a more robust

and distinctive Catholic presence in the public square; and to analyze both receptivity and resistances in the larger American culture to the Catholic presence.

2. To generate concrete analyses and recommendations for strengthening Catholic civic engagement—not in an attempt to devise a platform or simple formulas, but simply as a way to gather a range of ideas about current practices and imaginative possibilities that Catholic leaders in various spheres can evaluate, adapt, adopt, or discard as they see fit.

3. To encompass a broad spectrum of political and social views of Catholics so as to encourage dialogue between sectors of a large and diverse church who often do not come into significant contact with one another and to open up lines of inquiry that will capture the attention of Catholic leaders, religious and secular media, and political thinkers in a way that could extend the discussion well beyond this project.

4. To reexamine the long-standing Catholic belief in the obligation to promote the common good and to clarify how Catholics may work better with those holding other religious or philosophical convictions toward revitalizing both the religious environment and civic participation in the American republic.

Participants in the Commonweal Colloquia and the joint meetings—leading Catholic scholars, journalists, lawyers, business and labor leaders, novelists and poets, church administrators and lobbyists, activists, policy makers and politicians—produced approximately forty-five essays presented at ten meetings that brought together over two hundred and fifty participants. Each meeting included three to five presentations, two appointed respondents for each, and extended discussions with invited participants (many of the responses and discussions are available at the Web site: www.catholicsinpublicsquare.org). The project's findings address many of the most critical and neuralgic issues now facing the Catholic Church in the United States. Public attention to the church's handling of sexual abuse cases will undoubtedly have an impact on both the church's role in public life and that of individual Catholics visibly trying to relate their civic responsibilities to their faith.

Those essays and responses not published in these volumes are available at www.catholicsinpublicsquare.org.

ACKNOWLEDGMENTS

American Catholics in the Public Square would not have succeeded without the spirit of solidarity, cooperation, and sense of the common good so often spoken about in these pages and at our meetings. The *Commonweal* staff, which puts out the magazine every two weeks, pitched in on all phases of the project, beginning, middle, and end. Special thanks go to Paul Baumann and Grant Gallicho, who attended every meeting, even the difficult ones. Successive business managers, first, Gregory Wilpert helped construct the budget and, then, Paul Kane kept us on budget and in the black. Tiina Aleman, production editor and Web mistress, created the project's website and made the copy for this book as digitized as possible—and she put out the magazine, too! John Garvey generously assisted with the copyediting of the books. Scott Appleby of the University of Notre Dame served as consultant, advisor, presenter, and reader par excellence.

Many of the meeting participants took a keen interest in the project, even coming to more than one meeting: Tom Baker, Mary Segers, Mark Massa, John Coleman, Philip Murnion, Barbara Whitehead, Paul Moses, Richard Doerflinger, John McGreevy, and Ned Dolejsi were especially generous with their time and their knowledge. The joint meetings, which were an integral part of the project, were organized by Peter Steinfels on behalf of *Commonweal* and Robert Royal of The Faith and Reason Institute; they were an eye-opener to all of the participants. Luis Lugo of The Pew Charitable Trusts first proposed the project and with his colleague Kimon Sargent has maintained a steady interest in its progress.

Finally, the deepest gratitude goes to Regina Garvey, the project's administrator, whose intelligence, diligence, serenity, hospitality, and good humor kept us all on track and convinced that the project could be managed and brought to a successful end.

INTRODUCTION

HISTORICAL BACKGROUND

Catholics have been present in America since before the War for Independence. From Lord Baltimore's experiments in Maryland to the arrival of groups of immigrants in Pennsylvania, New York, and the New England states, Catholics faced a specific problem: how to maintain their religious identity in a nation that was overwhelmingly Protestant. By the 1840s, when many Americans took alarm at the new waves of Catholic immigrants, often impoverished and often Irish, the problem grew severe. In a certain Anglo-American understanding of the growth of free institutions, Catholicism was The Enemy. As a result, Catholics faced not only outright discrimination but even violence for both ethnic and religious reasons. In the nineteenth century, no other religious faith except Mormonism was treated as so fundamentally incompatible with the conception of the American nation entertained by many Christians. Catholics had to create their own institutions— churches, schools, hospitals, orphanages, relief services—with little help or encouragement from their fellow citizens. Yet Catholic leaders were grateful for the religious freedom that allowed them to do this, and they could not help but appreciate the open, enterprising society that had given immigrants refuge from famine, war, and persecution elsewhere. Still, for Catholic leaders, the first priority was understandably the survival and religious integrity of their own people. Catholic civic engagement was often vigorous but also turned inward. Catholic leadership in the landmark struggles for American freedom was accordingly minimal.

At the same time, Catholic leaders could not ignore the questions that separation of church and state and the American emphasis on participatory democracy and individual rights and responsibilities put to European

Catholic traditions of more centralized government and close collaboration between church and state. Thanks to the work of several American Catholic churchmen at the end of the nineteenth century, most notably James Cardinal Gibbons, John Ireland, John J. Keane, Denis J. O'Connell, and John Lancaster Spalding, as well as several later theorists and activists, Catholicism has not only found a secure place in America, but has itself been enriched by notions of human rights, pluralism, and religious liberty emanating from the United States.

The Difficult Balance

Yet the development of American Catholicism has been marked by serious tensions that continue to challenge people who wish to be both fully Catholic and unapologetically American—who wish, moreover, to be fully Catholic precisely when they are fully present in the American public square. Those tensions once centered on the fact that Catholics could not feel quite at home in the American polity: what might have been a particular Catholic contribution to American public life was frequently muted or marginal, and Catholics expended most of their energies within their own ethnic communities and religious subculture. Today the tensions may center on the fact that Catholics can feel almost too much at home in American society: what might be a distinctive Catholic note in American public life is in danger of being diluted and lost as a distinctive Catholic subculture dissolves.

Certainly, it took a long time for leaders in this country and in Rome to understand that the principles of the American Founders could be harmonized to a large extent with Catholic social principles. The great contributions of the Jesuit philosopher and theologian John Courtney Murray in this century inaugurated a way of reading the founding as embodying portions of natural law to which Catholics in America could give ready assent.

Murray gave a hopeful reading of the Declaration of Independence's assertion that "we hold these truths to be self-evident, that men have been endowed by their Creator with certain inalienable rights and that among these are Life, Liberty, and the Pursuit of Happiness." For Murray, this bold statement meant at least three main things: there are truths, we can know them, and we, as Americans, "hold" these truths as a basis for our common life together. Though Murray well knew that this highly condensed version of the natural law needed a great deal of unpacking, he was cautiously optimistic that Roman Catholics could find here common ground with their fellow citizens of other faiths in America. Murray's work not only helped shape developments at the Second Vatican Council on questions like religious liberty; he also stimulated a vigorous Catholic engagement with the foundations of American political philosophy.

The Tensions Remain

Along with these positive developments, however, another set of questions arose for American Catholics, especially in recent decades. Catholicism is one of the few world religions with a highly developed system of modern social teaching. That teaching goes a great deal further than the minimalist natural-law principles of the American Founding. If Catholic principles like "subsidiarity" may be rather easily harmonized with American notions like federalism or localism, other Catholic principles find little or no place in American thought. For instance, America's highly individualistic ethic clashes in various ways with ideas like the "common good," "solidarity," and Catholic personalism. In Catholic social thinking, the human person is neither an autonomous individual nor a mere fragment of a social mass as in several forms of twentieth-century collectivism. The person is constituted by links to the family, community, and political structure, and to independent sources of moral reflection and action. The person, then, exists in a matrix of relationships that is not given much attention in mainstream American thought. Catholic social teaching, with its highly technical and somewhat foreign terminology, has therefore found itself in some tension with mainstream American political discourse, and this tension has given rise to disputes, even among Catholics, about applicability of Catholic thought in the context of this nation.

Concrete historical developments in the United States have injected paradoxes and ironies into Catholic civic engagement. Besides the tensions long felt (but increasingly resolved) between the nation's founding principles and the Catholic tradition and the gap still remaining between America's individualistic ethics and political discourse on the one hand, and Catholicism's unfamiliar vocabulary and community focus on the other, at least three main developments have complicated the picture:

- The emergence of a current of political liberalism from the Progressive Era onwards that at many points converged with the Catholic tradition practically but diverged from it more and more culturally and philosophically.
- The nation's growing pluralism and the decline of mainline Protestant cultural and moral hegemony.
- The waning of the Catholic ethnic-religious subculture in the 1950s and 1960s followed by the dramatic reconfiguration of American Catholicism after the Second Vatican Council.

LIBERAL PROGRESSIVISM:
CONVERGENCE AND DIVERGENCE

Explicit Catholic social teaching, although rooted in an ancient theological and sacramental tradition, arose in the nineteenth century as a response to the industrial revolution, to the trauma of transition from a rural paternalism to an urban capitalism, and to the rival worldview of socialism. A parallel development took place in the United States. Appalled (and sometimes frightened) by hordes of immigrants, many of them Catholic, crowded into urban tenements and laboring in the harsh conditions of an expanding, unregulated economy, an unstable alliance of old-stock gentry, grassroots organizers and tribunes, evangelical and liberal proponents of the Social Gospel, and avant-garde cultural rebels sponsored a wide and sometimes contradictory agenda of reform, from economic regulation and trade-union organization to welfare provision and even Prohibition.

American Catholics, precariously exposed on the lower rungs of the American economy, stood to benefit from many, though not all, of these proposals and did not share the deep-seated antagonism to positive government intervention that marked the older Anglo-American liberalism. The Catholic Bishops' Program for Social Reconstruction of 1919 echoed many of these reform proposals and foreshadowed much of the New Deal. Of course, Catholics could not ignore some of the elements hostile to immigrants or immigrant culture in the reform alliances. But far more troubling was the fact that the new reformism, in its revolt against the complacencies of Victorian America, was suspicious of all tradition and religious authority, two hallmarks of the church. Indeed, the philosophical and cultural vanguards of the new progressivism appeared to reject the fixity of truth or morality altogether, even in the nation's founding documents. Many of the fault lines in the church's current efforts to project a distinctive Catholic presence in the public square can be traced to this history of practical convergence and philosophical divergence with a major twentieth-century current of American politics.

THE NAKED PUBLIC SQUARE

In recent decades, the decline of the old Protestant establishment has given rise to another set of questions for Catholics in the public square. Despite the conflicts and outright anti-Catholicism of the past, American Catholics and Protestants shared a common moral vision rooted in Scripture. If Catholics created their own school system to provide a kind of education that was missing or, sometimes, disparaged in the basically Protestant public school system, they still championed the American experiment and the largely sound social ethic they found all around them.

Explanations of the decline of Protestant Christian cultural hegemony are complex and much debated. Some factors are said to go back to the early nineteenth century. Others are tied to the liberal and progressive intellectual currents mentioned above. Others derive from the overreaching typical of any hegemony and from practices of exclusion that eventually discredited attempts to maintain the religious character of institutions that once upheld the Protestant culture. Still other factors are largely demographic, including the shifting profile of the American population, the lower birth rates of mainline Protestants, and the entry of Jews and Catholics into the ranks of the affluent and highly educated. By the 1920s and 1930s, certainly by the 1940s, Catholic bishops had already begun to replace leading Protestant clergymen as the ready spokesmen for traditional morality, but the Catholics were filling a role that had been defined by Protestant forebears. Then, in the past few decades, came the full-scale dismantling of the implicit Protestant establishment.

This dismantling, combined with a growing awareness of the multiplicity of worldviews in American society and the liberal argument that the public sphere should remain scrupulously neutral on ultimate questions, has led to what some observers call a naked public square in which not only Catholicism but all religious influence has been reduced to an extent possibly unprecedented in American history. In addition, it is not clear whether the foundational idea of an America based on "self-evident" truths derived from nature or nature's God retains more than a purely rhetorical place in contemporary American social discourse. By contrast, one recent Supreme Court decision warned against anything that would prevent individual Americans from defining for themselves their own idea of the mystery of the universe.

Exactly how naked is the naked public square, that is, how stripped of undisguised religious presence? The exact degree is a matter of debate, but the clear tendency, along with the decline of that "civil religion" that in the past held Americans together, has presented a whole set of new questions to religious Americans, Catholics not the least among them. The Catholic Church, for instance, runs the most extensive education system, health services, and relief efforts of any American faith group. It was inevitable, then, that it would be centrally involved at local, state, and national level in such issues as abortion, euthanasia, family stability, homosexuality, welfare reform, and economic policies. The church also has developed positions on war and peace, which were brought forward vigorously during the debates over nuclear deterrence during the Cold War and continue to be applied to conflict situations around the world where the United States often acts as the world's only remaining superpower. Under John Paul II, the church has been pressing for restrictions on use of the death penalty. All these issues and more inevitably flow from the church's social thought and practice.

THE POST-SUBCULTURE, POST-CONCILIAR SITUATION

Lying behind all these discrete problems, moreover, is a deeper question for American Catholics today. How are they to be present in an American public life that increasingly runs hot and cold about public religion, now welcoming, now allergic, now tolerant but only within strict limits? And how are they to achieve this presence while the cohesive Catholic subculture of at least a century's standing transforms itself into some as yet undetermined form?

The church, since Vatican II, has done three things of central importance to this challenge. First, it welcomed an understanding of the church's role that made striving for justice in the social arena an integral part of Christian witness and not, as had often been suggested, simply a preparation for a more spiritual or other worldly missionizing. Second, it argued that engagement with the public realm is primarily the responsibility of the laity. Third, by calling for a stance toward modern culture marked by dialogue at least as much as by combat or rejection, the church lowered the walls of the Catholic subculture and contributed, intentionally or not, to the assimilation of Catholics into mainstream American culture.

The first of these changes made distinctively Catholic civic engagement more religiously charged than before. What often remained on the periphery of a largely other worldly spirituality was now shifted toward the center. The positions of pastors, bishops, and pope on political or social questions could not as easily be set aside as idiosyncratic opinions irrelevant to the sacramental life or the work of salvation. A more conscious response was required, even if it was one ultimately of dismissing the authoritative character of church positions.

The second of these changes, emphasizing the role of the laity, harmonizes with what comes naturally to many Catholic lay people, acculturated as they are to America's remarkable tradition of popular initiatives and spontaneous organization for social purposes. But it appears that the lines of responsibility are not as clear in practice as the Council's principles would suggest. Some American lay people still have the habit of looking to their bishops, clerical organizations, and Rome itself to take the lead on social issues, even though many lay organizations have sprung up in the wake of the Council. Other Catholic laity take almost automatic offense at civic direction from church leaders.

The very energy of lay initiatives has, to some observers, led to a certain incoherence in the Catholic presence in American civic life. Bishops and clergy encourage lay participation but may look askance at some of the forms that this participation takes. In a church that has long been marked by its careful attention to doctrinal orthodoxy and unity with the Bishop of Rome, letting go of authority and trusting lay initiative has been difficult. In addition, it is the nature of the American context that groups may form calling themselves Catholic but who work at cross purposes to what the hierarchy may see as undeniable theological and moral teachings. Both clergy and laity find themselves in a delicate situation where the "Catholic" voice is diluted or obscured, where dramatic heterodoxy and mere differences in lay opinion cannot be distinguished. This long-standing tension has been heightened as a result of the revelations, beginning in Boston in 2002, of sexual abuse of minors by priests. Some bishops had already responded to an earlier wave of such charges by appointing lay-dominated review boards, and this became a national policy after the bishops met in Dallas in June 2002. Still, tensions persisted over the emergence of lay groups pressing for changes in church structures or procedures as a result of the scandals. In a few dioceses, bishops who saw these groups as threatening church teaching refused to meet with them or forbade them the use of church property for their gatherings. The news media and victims' advocates stood close watch over the work of the national review panel set up by the bishops themselves to assure implementation of their new national policy for handling allegations of abuse and instituting safeguards against future misconduct. Lay people frequently reacted with frustration at any sign that bishops were not cooperating fully with the panel's work, and some bishops grew similarly frustrated at what they felt were intemperate and unfair reactions from critics. The fact that many Catholics, lay and clerics alike, are vigorously pursuing issues of accountability and governance is likely, like the scandal itself, to have an impact on the Catholic presence in the public square.

The third change raises the question of how Catholics will blend their Catholicism with their assimilation to America. This was not a problem when Catholics mostly lived—by outside pressure and internal choice—in a kind of Catholic "ghetto." The success and acceptance in American society that Catholics have come to enjoy is a welcome development. So is the sense of responsibility and shared destiny that they feel with that society. But as with all other religious and ethnic groups who have come to these shores, integration into the American mainstream has costs as well as benefits. Can Catholic doctors, lawyers, politicians, educators, business executives—to say nothing of schools, colleges, universities, hospitals, relief services—remain both Catholic and American in a United States that, at least at a superficial level, seems to have moved far from the biblical and natural-law principles that provided a bridge between Catholicity and Americanness?

There is no question that one of the central challenges facing American Catholicism, clergy and laity, liberal and conservative alike, is how to maintain a specific identity in the face of forces, both national and global, both cultural and economic, that seem to be making for a much greater uniformity and far less vigorous and articulated religious participation in public affairs.

Peter Steinfels
Robert Royal

1

AGAINST THE GRAIN

The most apparent disagreement between Catholicism and American culture lay in the First Amendment prohibition of an established church and the guarantee of free exercise. That difference was ultimately reconciled by the Second Vatican Council's *Declaration on Religious Liberty* (1965), which enshrined the thinking and formulations of the American John Courtney Murray, S.J., in the teachings of the church. That formal resolution of the church–state question did not bring to an end, in matters political and cultural, the differences between Catholicism's communal and personalist view of the human person and the American preference for individualism and pluralism. John McGreevy traces this contested terrain from the abolitionist crusade of the nineteenth century to the reproductive rights crusade of the twentieth, weaving a story of dissensus and consensus over slavery, workers rights, social welfare, and abortion.

Today's continuing struggle was crystallized for Catholics in Cardinal Joseph Bernardin's plea for "a consistent ethic of life" from conception to death. The philosophical and practical differences between Catholicism and American culture on sexuality, marriage, divorce, women's rights, abortion, stem cell research, and physician-assisted suicide are laid out by Luke Timothy Johnson (with responses by Barbara Dafoe Whitehead and Susan Ross), Richard Doerflinger (response by Mary Segers), and Brian Doyle. Michele Dillon argues that the American bishops were astute and public-minded in casting their arguments against abortion in a discourse accessible to all. These essays demonstrate the impact of "neuralgic" issues within the Catholic community and on the American public square.

CATHOLICS IN AMERICA: ANTIPATHY AND ASSIMILATION

John T. McGreevy

S ince I am neither a philosopher nor a theologian I will not presume to say precisely what Catholic civil engagement should be. Since I am neither an expert in public policy nor a legislative strategist I will not play James Carville or Dick Morris to the United States Conference of Catholic Bishops (USCCB) administrative committee, hunkered down in the war room (or is it the chapel?) of the United States Catholic Conference in Washington.

What I am is a historian. And my modest contribution to this discussion lies in reflecting upon the Catholic experience in the United States, and how that experience might illuminate or obscure the choices faced by contemporary Catholic leaders.[1] I will draw from my book *Catholicism and American Freedom: A History* (W. W. Norton, 2003). Much of what follows draws from an immersion of several years in the particular problem of Catholicism and American liberalism.[2]

I'll briefly examine Catholic responses to three issues central to the relationship of Catholicism and American liberalism, the slavery debate of the 1850s and 1860s, the "social question" of the late nineteenth and early twentieth centuries, and the ongoing struggle over abortion.

SLAVERY

Like most Christians, Catholics in the early nineteenth century faced no restrictions on their ability to purchase, own, or sell slaves, and numerous lay Catholics, bishops, nuns, and priests took advantage of this opportunity. Masters must permit slave marriages, Catholic theologians agreed, and educate their slaves in the rudiments of the faith, but slavery itself, as suggested by Aristotle, Paul, and Thomas Aquinas, did not violate either the natural law or church teaching.[3]

The disjunction between Catholics and liberals on the slavery question, however, did not emerge in full force until the 1840s. A handful of European Catholic theologians attacked slavery in the early nineteenth century, and some Catholics were outraged, first by Jesuit slaveholding, and then by the decision of the Maryland Jesuits to sell the two hundred and seventy slaves owned by the order in 1838.[4] The great French Catholic liberal Charles Montalembert expressed his horror at American slavery as early as 1839, and led the Catholic component of the successful campaign to abolish slavery in French colonial possessions.[5] Daniel O'Connell attacked Irish-American acceptance of American slavery in 1842, emphasizing in one address that Africans served as priests in Rome.[6] One American abolitionist recalled that into the early 1850s that "it was still doubtful which side of the slavery question the Roman Church would take. O'Connell was in the zenith of his power and popularity, was decidedly anti-slavery, and members of Catholic churches chose sides according to personal feeling, as did those of other churches. It was not until 1852, that abolitionists began to feel the alliance between Romanism and slavery; but from that time, to be a member of the Roman Church was to be a friend of 'Southern interests.'"[7]

In fact, American Catholics, to the dismay of abolitionists, responded to Daniel O'Connell's appeals with alarm. Groups of Irish Americans wrote O'Connell asking him to stop urging slave emancipation, and the editor of the *New York Freeman's Journal*, the leading Catholic paper, first expressed disbelief that O'Connell could have uttered such words, and then chastised abolitionists, a "mischievous set of fanatics" for threatening to overturn the Constitution.[8]

Recent commentary on nineteenth-century Irish-Americans has emphasized the desire of working-class immigrants to deflect competition from African-American workers, and to capture the material and psychological benefits of identifying themselves as white. The Catholic Church, in this view, did little more than "reflect the racial attitude of its members."[9]

Such arguments appropriately highlight popular Irish-American racism, but the argument that Catholics opposed immediate emancipation solely out of psychological and economic self-interest neglects uneasiness about abolition found among German and French Catholics, as well as opposition to abolition among Catholics around the world. Studies of membership lists for American abolitionist organizations in the 1830s rarely find a Catholic name, and not one prominent American Catholic urged immediate abolition before the civil war.[10] Abolitionists in France and the French

Caribbean in the 1840s, Cuba in the 1860s and Brazil in the 1880s also bemoaned Catholic reluctance to join their cause.[11]

Catholic opposition to slave emancipation, in other words, cannot be reduced to the particular American racial dynamic. Instead, Catholic intellectuals accepted slavery as a legitimate, if tragic, institution. This acceptance rested upon the pervasive fear of liberal individualism and social disorder that so shaped Catholic thought during the nineteenth century Catholic revival, as well as the anti-Catholicism of many abolitionists. Indeed, even Pope Gregory XVI's cautious 1839 decision to condemn only the slave trade, not slavery itself, stemmed from abolitionism's association with a European liberalism that papal advisors considered anti-Catholic and revolutionary.[12]

In the United States, Catholic fears of disorder led to the calculation that societal stability outweighed any benefit to be gained from rapid emancipation. Orestes Brownson, for example, first questioned the sincerity of Daniel O'Connell's anti-slavery sentiments, but then emphasized the radicalism of American abolition, which he described as destructive "of the state, of government, of religious institutions, of all social organizations, and of all law but the law of every man unto himself."[13] "Only one religious body," complained another writer in a tribute to Catholicism, "has kept aloof from the political question which threatens to convulse the union."[14] Opponents of medieval slavery, Catholics explained, had moved incrementally, avoiding the chaos inevitable when abolition occurred in a society interwoven with slavery.[15]

Bishop Francis Kenrick of Philadelphia, author of the first American textbook in moral theology in 1843, solidified this acceptance. Kenrick's six years of study in Rome alerted him to new currents in Catholic philosophy, and his Latin text includes citations to various Italian Neo-Thomists. Jesuit Luigi d'Azeglio Taparelli, perhaps the most influential Italian Neo-Thomist, and a long-time editor at *Civilta Cattolicà*, insisted that slavery in the abstract might be permissible, although he speculated that in lands "where legal slavery has not been done away with" slaveholders rarely adhered to Catholic guidelines. But he also stressed that "certain philanthropic declarations against slavery in its general meaning" had led to a "false idea of an inalienable right to freedom."[16]

Kenrick made similar distinctions when analyzing American slavery: ownership of a slave's labor is permissible but not treatment of the slave as a thing, the slave trade is wrong, slaves must be allowed to partake of the sacraments and educated in the faith and lynching is abhorrent. Nonetheless, Kenrick concluded, slavery existed as part of the social order in the

American South, and those who "moved by humanity attempted to overturn the order of things, often made the condition of the slaves worse."[17]

Ultramontane Catholics like Kenrick, in contrast to a handful of liberal Catholics like O'Connell, Dupanloup, and Montalembert, tended to see slavery as only one among many hierarchical relationships. Brownson, early in his career, compared the "relation of master and man" to that of "father and son," concluding that "slavery as it exists in the southern states is an evil . . . but it is so accidentally not necessarily."[18] A writer for the *Boston Pilot* attacked the argument that "slavery is, in itself, intrinsically evil. This is nonsense, and it is so patent that we have never seen even a respectable attempt to prove it. In itself, slavery simply involves the right of one man to the proceeds of another. The principle of slavery is involved in apprenticeship, in imprisonment, in peonage, and in other forms of servitude."[19]

The same Catholics also found it difficult to distinguish the suffering endured by slaves from other forms of human agony. Elizabeth Clark demonstrates the importance of this conceptual leap, which in the United States typically occurred among Protestants who had abandoned Calvinist verities on the importance of Christ's atonement and the inevitability of human suffering. If human suffering is not foreordained or necessary, these Protestants asked, what about the suffering endured by innocent slaves?[20] By contrast, one Baltimore lecturer explained to a Catholic audience that "[slavery] may be an evil, so is sickness, and extreme poverty, and there are other ills in life which flesh is heir to, but as slavery now exists in this country, it is not a sin, and it has become a necessity."[21] Fr. John McMullen, educated in Rome and later bishop of Davenport, Iowa, conceded that the plight of a child born into slavery was tragic, and in 1865 he applauded slavery's abolition. But even at this late date McMullen compared slave children to those born of impoverished parents, noting that all children suffered in some fashion. In particular he denied that "it is man's free power to select a state of life more or less exempt from the grievances attending human existence."[22]

That Catholic tolerance of slavery included racism but did not wholly depend on it is suggested by a fascinating discussion of slavery in the *Propagateur Catholique* during the first year of the war. The New Orleans Catholic paper had already published Savannah bishop Augustin Verot's impassioned rejection of abolition. Verot exhorted slave owners to conform their practices to Catholic doctrine, but he also ridiculed the "allegation of agrarians and anarchists that 'all men are born free and equal.'"[23]

Another New Orleans newspaper criticized Verot for failing to mention that only Africans, not whites, should be enslaved. A writer for the *Propagateur Catholique* immediately defended Verot, and even as white Con-

federate soldiers battled Union foes, insisted that if Holy Scripture condoned slavery it surely condoned the "subjection of white to white." Taking a position held by only the most radical white Southern Protestants, the
Propagateur Catholique declared that the enslavement of whites is "approved
in the Bible and supported by the patriarchs [church fathers]." The "legitimacy of slavery [is not] uniquely in the color of the skin" because such
"fantastic theories" merely "flatter our pride."[24]

The Catholic acceptance of American slavery—because of racial prejudice, toleration of slavery by past Catholic authorities, fear of social disorder inevitable upon emancipation and an unwillingness to distinguish the
suffering of slaves from other human miseries—constituted one powerful set
of reasons for opposition to immediate emancipation. Daniel O'Connell's
specific appeal to his American brethren suggested another. O'Connell
urged Irish Americans not to support slavery, even if it was true "that there
are amongst the abolitionists many wicked and calumniating enemies of
Catholicity and the Irish."[25]

Unlike O'Connell, historians have neglected this point.[26] Even given
a broad animus toward institutions and orthodox church leaders; however,
the anti-Catholicism of American abolitionists deserves further emphasis.
Many abolitionists viewed slavery and Catholicism as parallel despotic systems, opposed to education, free speech and political liberty in predictable
synchronicity. Protestants who tolerated slavery betrayed their principles,
abolitionists believed, while Catholics who tolerated slavery applied them.
Catholic leaders forbade distribution of the Bible in Italy, abolitionists
claimed, just as slave holders stopped distribution of scripture in the
South. Slave holders exerted unlimited control over female slaves, just as
priests allegedly exercised sexual and emotional power over female penitents in the confessional. Slave quarters were likened to the "dungeons of
the Popish Inquisition."[27] Fugitive slave narratives bore a startling resem-
blance to tales of young women imprisoned in convents.[28] One Ohio
abolitionist, after comparing himself to Martin Luther, offered this com-
prehensive summary:

> In this country, popery finds its appropriate ally in the institution of slav-
> ery. They are both kindred systems. One enslaves the mind, the other
> both mind and body. Both deny the Bible to those under their control—
> both discourage free inquiry. . . . By its penances, masses for the dead, in-
> dulgences etc. popery extorts money without rendering an equivalent;
> slavery robs men of all their earnings, their wives and children.[29]

The list of anti-Catholic abolitionists is impressive. Elijah Lovejoy,
murdered in 1836 and the first martyr of the abolition movement, spent

much of 1835 warning of the Catholic menace.[30] George Bourne became, simultaneously, a leading anti-slavery and anti–Catholic agitator, writing attacks on Romanism and scurrilous convent narratives even as he became a vital influence on William Lloyd Garrison's *Liberator*.[31] In 1838, Bourne published both *Illustrations of Popery* and *Picture of Slavery in the United States of America*, and the metaphors used in each volume were interchangeable. "Like the Papists," Bourne claimed, southern preachers "will not permit the coloured citizen to learn to read or to possess the scriptures." Both slave masters and Catholic leaders tell their charges that the "desire to learn to read, that he may search the Scriptures, is rebellion against God."[32]

As anti-slavery sentiment expanded beyond its initial Garrisonian core, so too did anti–Catholicism, as suggested by the careers of a wide range of American abolitionists. The anti–Catholicism of the Beecher family began with father Lyman's warnings about papal advances in the West, but it included the Catholic slave owning St. Clare family in daughter Harriet's *Uncle Tom's Cabin*. (Uncle Tom conspicuously escorts Catholic Eva to Methodist meetings.)[33] Edward Beecher, also, attacked slavery even as he published an 1855 manifesto on papal conspiracy.[34] Frederick Douglass frequently displayed a casual anti-Catholicism, attacking the "cunning illusions" of Catholic leaders and tracing the origins of American liberty to Dutch Protestant victories over Spanish Catholic tyrants.[35]

Foreign abolitionists made similar remarks. Richard D. Webb, the Irish correspondent for the *National Anti-Slavery Standard*, compared "the rampant audacious, insolent Ultramontanism of the Romish clergy" with the "kindred system of chattel slavery."[36] The leading French abolitionist, Victor Schoelcher, combined sympathy for the slaves with a powerful anticlericalism and hostility to Catholicism.[37] The Mexican liberal, Matias Romero, pondered the "striking similarity which exists between the Church party of Mexico and the Slavery party in the United States."[38] In Canada, Toronto's George Brown helped found the Anti–Slavery Society of Canada, and serialized *Uncle Tom's Cabin* in his newspaper, the *Toronto Globe*. In 1855 a *Globe* editorial compared the Kansas–Nebraska act to laws passed aiding Canadian Catholic schools, concluding that "In Canada the Roman Catholic hierarchy is the slave power. It holds us subjects in bondage as slavish as the Southern taskmaster."[39]

Catholics responded to agitation over the slavery question with an entirely different vocabulary, a lexicon developed while observing the European revolutions of 1848. James McMaster compared "extreme abolitionists" to the "lawless Liberalism that has been making havoc of society in Europe" and the Boston *Pilot* explained that Catholics attacked European liberals such as Kossuth and Mazzini for the same reasons that they repudiated "Garrison abolitionism, or Free-Soilism, which is the same thing."[40] Fr. J. W. Cummings was perhaps the most explicit. "Those who talk about the 'rights of human nature and the inalienable rights of man,'" he argued, "ought to consider the evil done by the application of their principles. How far these men have gone in the late revolutions in Europe is now a matter of historical record. They have cut throats, overthrown altars, subverted thrones."[41]

The note of frustration evident in the few Catholic proponents of abolition suggests their isolation. Vermont's John Lambert explained to Pittsburgh Catholic readers that "as a Catholic Christian . . . I cannot but feel for the whole human race who are suffering in bondage and oppression." (The editor of the *Pittsburgh Catholic* chided Lambert, adding that "we did not believe in the existence of such a thing as a Catholic Free-Soiler.") At the 1855 meeting of the Massachusetts Anti-Slavery Society, Henry Kemp responded to an anti-Catholic aside. According to the minutes, Kemp announced that "various Popes" had "condemned slavery, and called upon the faithful everywhere in the name of Almighty God, to put it entirely away from them. Hence he [Kemp] considered Archbishop Hughes, and all the professed Catholics of America, who sympathize with, and aid the slave power, as excommunicated heretics. He thought himself about the only representative of the true Catholic Church in this country."[42]

THE SOCIAL QUESTION

The details of the composition of *Rerum novarum* are unusually well documented. In the late 1880s, nearing the age of eighty, Pope Leo XIII announced his desire to prepare an encyclical on the social question. In July 1890, another Italian octogenarian, Jesuit Matteo Liberatore, submitted a first draft. The pope himself monitored a series of subsequent versions before the release date of May 1891, dictating emendations and correcting the Latin.[43]

The assumptions shared by Vatican collaborators are illuminating. Liberatore had spearheaded the Neo-Thomist philosophical revival that so shaped Catholic thought in the late nineteenth century, using forty-two years of service as an editor at *Civiltà Cattolica* as a bully pulpit. His concern, and that of Leo XIII, with the conditions of workers was unsurprising. Catholic peasants flocked to the North Atlantic sites of industrial development in the nineteenth century, and large numbers inevitably labored in the most horrific conditions. In the heavily Catholic industrial towns of West-phalia and the Rhineland, the cities along the eastern coast of the United States, eastern France and a swath stretching from Belfast to Glasgow to Lancanshire, Catholics formed a significant percentage of the urban work-ing class. In much of France, and later, Italy and Spain, large numbers of Catholic workers rejected a church seen as irrelevant to this new industrial milieu or incapable of providing pastoral care. But in other areas an array of Catholic parishes and associations sustained the allegiance of workers more successfully than parallel efforts by their religious competitors. In Berlin, London, and New York, Protestant ministers marveled at Catholic loyalty. By 1890, Catholics numbered 75 percent of churchgoers in Boston, 68 per-cent of churchgoers in Chicago and New York, 58 percent in St. Louis, and 56 percent in Cleveland.[44]

The initial Catholic response to the plight of industrial laborers relied upon private charity, and an ingrained Catholic suspicion of the State always limited the extent to which Catholics would call for governmental assis-tance to the poor. Still, figures such as France's Frédérick Ozanam, organ-izer of the St. Vincent De Paul society in Paris in 1833, discovered a new clientele of bewildered families struggling to find work and shelter in the new economy. Ozanam mobilized thousands of middle- and upper-class Catholic men and women to visit and assist these families, and his example extended across the world.[45]

A second strand of Catholic interest in the "social question" came from Catholic nuns. In both Europe and America the number of women joining religious orders jumped dramatically in the last decades of the nine-teenth century, and by 1920, 90,000 women, many of them foreign-born, served in American religious orders.[46] The massive Catholic investment in parochial schools staffed by nuns exhausted much of their energy, but American nuns, like their European counterparts, also developed expertise in areas more closely connected to social welfare. Catholic laywomen and nuns also founded settlement houses and various welfare agencies, some prior to far better-known competitors such as Jane Addams's Hull House in Chicago.[47]

The language used by St. Vincent De Paul volunteers visiting poor families or nuns accepting children in their orphanages rarely moved be-yond that of traditional charity. Still, close contact with the urban poor dis-tinguished Catholic leaders from many contemporary policymakers, and fostered a jaundiced view of economics "laws." Catholic nuns, for example, knew that parents placed children in orphanages when out of work, and typically for a short period of time. They inevitably became dubious about the intentions of the foremost child welfare expert of the late nineteenth century, Charles Loring Brace, who warned of the "chilling formalism of the ignorant Roman Catholic" and urged New Yorkers not to let the public schools become "corrupted with priestcraft."[48]

The trajectory of Catholic intellectual life reinforced this tendency to view poverty as less an individual failing than as a social problem. The observation now seems unremarkable, but Thomas Haskell notes that one of the most momentous shifts of the nineteenth century was from a formalist understanding of the human self, in which self-denial, temperance, and education were the solutions to economic distress, toward an anti-formalist understanding that stressed social explanations for individual crisis.[49] The talismanic concept for mid-nineteenth-century liberals, freedom of contract, effectively served the cause of slave emancipation and laissez-faire. (Massachusetts senator Charles Sumner called slavery "labor without wages.") But freedom of contract seemed irrelevant to workers unable to procure wages above subsistence levels. A new formulation eagerly supported by Catholics, a "living wage," emerged in the late nineteenth and early twentieth centuries as part of an effort to ensure workers' dignity.[50]

Precisely because they rejected the tenets of political and theological liberalism, ultramontane Catholics found this more social understanding of political economy congenial. As early as the 1840s, Taparelli, Liberatore, and other Italian neo-Thomists attacked an economic liberalism that, in their view, allowed certain individuals to amass great wealth at the expense of the impoverished many. Invisible hands caused visible problems. Pius IX's 1864 Syllabus of Errors, deeply influenced by Jesuits working at *Civilta Cattolicà*, became notorious for its concluding attack on "progress, liberalism and civilization," but it also condemned the idea that "any system of morality, any honesty should consist of accumulating and increasing one's wealth in any fashion."[51] As archbishop of Perugia, the future Leo XIII denounced socialism, but he also attacked "modern economic schools" eager to consider man a "machine" and "suited to production."[52] Between 1887 and 1889, *Liberatore* published a series of essays in *Civiltà Cattolica* critical of Adam Smith and economic liberalism. "Free competition," he concluded, "is a terrible weapon, most effectual to crush the weak and reduce whole populations to economic slavery under a rod of iron wielded by the potent rulers of social wealth."[53]

In the United States, as early as 1844, New York's Bishop Hughes lamented the "mockery of freedom" evident in an economic system that pitted the "starving laborer" against the "bloated capitalist."[54] As a labor radical, prior to his conversion to Catholicism, Orestes Brownson authored the antebellum period's most powerful attack on inequality in an 1840 essay, "The Laboring Classes." "The evil," Brownson argued "is not merely individual in its character [but] . . . inherent in all our social arrangements." Following his conversion Brownson continued in the same vein, lamenting in 1857 "that the modern system of large industry . . . makes the great mass of operatives virtually slaves—slaves in all except the name—as much as are the Negroes on one of our southern plantations.[55] *The Catholic World* later added that "The theory of 'competition' as a solution of social and industrial disorder is as baseless as it is immoral." Political economy as elaborated by Adam Smith "makes the individual the unit of society. The true unit of society is the family."[56]

Again, the contrast with the debate over slavery is striking. The same Catholics disenchanted with economic liberalism only reluctantly advocated slave emancipation, if at all. Slaves deserved adequate food, clothing, and shelter, of course, and respect for their religious and human dignity, but Italian Jesuits such as Taparelli d'Azeglio kept open the possibility of a moral slave system.[57] Early in his career Brownson compared the situation of workers and slaves and decided that "as to actual freedom one has just as much as the other."[58] Philadelphia bishop Francis Patrick Kenrick defended slavery in his influential moral theology by quoting Matteo Liberatore on the importance of the common good, emphasizing that attempts to free large numbers of slaves might mean that the "condition of society would always remain uncertain, with very great danger to the people." At the same time, at a moment when this was unusual, Kenrick encouraged workers to unite in associations and advocated a minimum wage.[59]

By contrast, Catholic liberals such as Charles de Montalembert and Daniel O'Connell condemned Catholic complicity in slavery but expressed little interest in economic issues. Certainly O'Connell's devotion to political liberty and Catholic emancipation predisposed him to understand slavery as an unacceptable injustice. But like other nineteenth-century liberals, O'Connell feared that trade unions and minimum wage laws might restrict economic freedom. The aristocratic Montalembert also focused on political liberty and freedom within the church.[60]

Rerum novarum reflects its dependence upon the ultramontane social vision of Leo XIII and the Italian Jesuits, not the Catholic liberalism of Montalembert and O'Connell. Political liberty and democracy are absent from the text, and Leo XIII would soon emphasize his uneasiness with American definitions of religious freedom.[61] Leo XIII began with an attack on the "misery and wretchedness pressing so unjustly on the majority of the working class" before launching an extended polemic in defense of private property and against socialism. Unions received a papal blessing, as did, re-markably, government intervention in the economy when employers of-fered wages "insufficient to support a frugal and well-behaved wage earner."[62]

This Catholic focus on economic inequality and the regulatory state meshed with the views of non-Catholic reformers. That common ground existed at all is surprising, since Catholics and liberals now worked from starkly different philosophical premises. But these philosophical differences did not prevent political cooperation. Catholics and liberals might differ as to why the State must check the ability of employers to exploit workers, but they could unite on shared goals. And in fact, Catholics and American lib-erals often drew from the same wells. Daniel Rodgers has traced how the reaction against economic liberalism first entered American reform circles through cadres of graduate students studying at the German universities. In one 1906 survey of 116 leading economists and sociologists, 59 listed a year or more of study in Germany on their vita, often under the tutelage of Adolph Wagner and Gustav Schmoller, the leading economists at the Uni-versity of Berlin. When American students returned to the United States they carried with them a German-bred suspicion of laissez-faire, an admi-ration for the academic as policy expert, and a desire to prod the State into enhanced social insurance programs and regulatory measures.[63]

Catholics made similar journeys. Catholic University's William Kerby, Loyola sociologist Fr. Frederick Siedenberg, Fr. William Engelen, labor ac-tivist Fr. Peter Dietz, and others studied in Germany between 1890 and 1910 and Kerby and Siedenberg took courses from Schmoller and Wagner. ("It is clear," advised one of Kerby's professors at Catholic University, "that you will find the best facilities for your advancement in Berlin or Leipzig.")[64] The most important Catholic social theorist of the early twen-tieth century, and one with considerable influence among American Catholics, was German Jesuit Heinrich Pesch. Pesch also studied with Schmoller and Wagner, and became a fierce opponent of the "unrestrained nature of the free economic system based on economic individualism."[65]

The career of Fr. John A. Ryan best reflected this Catholic-liberal rap-prochement.[66] Ryan worked from a standard-issue scholastic template, and even his studies of wages and consumption contained excursions into Thomistic thickets. Ryan especially admired the work of Heinrich Pesch, terming Pesch's monumental *Lehrbuch der Nationalökonomie* "the most com-prehensive treatise ever put forth in the name of political economy" and a successful effort to define "solidarity" as a Catholic principle more com-pelling than "individualism and Socialism."[67]

Ryan's recommendations—that employers provide what he termed a "living wage" capable of supporting a (male) breadwinner and his family, that the State regulate the working hours of women and children, that progressives battle socialists through addressing the real demands of workers— placed him on the moderate left wing of American social reform. Like so many Progressive era reformers working inside the churches and the academy, Ryan self-consciously viewed economics and theology as a piece. (He taught both subjects at Catholic University in Washington, D.C.) Like John Dewey and *New Republic* founder Herbert Croly, Ryan viewed economic reform as the top priority, showing little interest in ameliorating racial segregation.[68] Catholics like Ryan held traditional ideas about men's and women's roles, but so did many non-Catholic reformers.[69]

Ryan published his first major study, *A Living Wage*, in 1906 with an introduction by Richard Ely, the country's most important reform economist. When Ryan sent a copy of one his pamphlets to Harvard law school professor and legal reformer Roscoe Pound, the eminent jurist congratulated him for not thinking solely in terms of the "individual."[70]

As a seminary professor in St. Paul, Minnesota, Ryan drafted what became one of the first state minimum wage laws. After moving to Washington in 1915, Ryan became an active member of the American Civil Liberties Union, a collaborator with Florence Kelley in her effort to establish minimum wage laws for women, and the inevitable Catholic name on a bewildering number of progressive mailing lists. He also taught a generation of priests and lay Catholics sent to Catholic University for graduate training, and these students filtered into the Catholic labor schools founded in the 1930s, parishes in industrial cities and local seminaries. One of Ryan's many protégés, Fr. Edwin O'Hara, led the successful Oregon campaign to pass the nation's most comprehensive minimum wage legislation for women.[71]

In 1919, Ryan drafted a plan for postwar Reconstruction issued under the name of the bishops on the Administrative Committee of the National Council of Catholic Welfare. Workers, the bishops recommended, should begin cooperative stores and thus learn "the folly of excessive selfishness and senseless individualism." Heavy taxation had the salutary effect of forcing a "small class of privileged capitalists . . . to return a part of their unearned gains to society."[72] The editors of liberal journals such as the *New Republic* responded to the bishops' proposals with delight, concluding, "if this sort of thing goes on unchecked, we shall soon arrive at a pass where the real stand-patter will be quite unable to find a spiritual fold."[73] A commentator for the *Nation* speculated that Catholics and reformers might establish a new "kinship."[74]

The release of *Quadragesimo anno* in 1931, and the election of Franklin D. Roosevelt a year later, seemed a culmination of this Catholic-liberal union. *Quadragesimo anno* stressed that "the right ordering of economic life cannot be left to a free competition of forces. For from this source, as from a poisoned spring, have originated and spread all the errors of individualist economic teaching."[75]

In ordinary times such an uncompromising, even utopian, document would have landed with an awkward thud on American shores. But the worldwide depression hammered the United States more severely than any other industrial nation, and by 1931 even Catholic bishops, such as Cincinnati's John T. McNicholas, were informing audiences that "one of the crimes of our country is the concentration of inconceivable wealth in the hands of a comparatively small group."[76]

And Catholics were hardly alone. Just before the election, Roosevelt sent a giddy tremor through Catholic circles by quoting *Quadragesimo anno* before a large Detroit crowd. The encyclical, Roosevelt explained, was "just as radical as I am" and "one of the greatest documents of modern times."[77] One New York reporter excitedly informed John Ryan that Roosevelt's victory would mean a "knowledgeful friend and intelligent champion of the social and economic doctrines recommended to us by authority and experience."[78]

The cornerstone program of Roosevelt's first one hundred days in office, the National Recovery Administration (NRA), seemed to confirm this optimistic view. The NRA established trade associations for the major industries that permitted companies to agree on common pricing and production strategies. Trade associations were required to negotiate with labor unions and accept an undefined level of government supervision.[79]

This focus on economic planning meshed with the vision outlined by Pius XI. The journal of the National Catholic Welfare Conference saw the NRA as a rebuttal to the idea that papal proposals were "difficult and vague." Instead, Roosevelt's program had "considerable similarity" to *Quadragesimo anno*. John Ryan described Pius XI and FDR as both rejecting "laissez-faire, economic liberalism and so-called rugged individualism." Another Catholic writer understood Roosevelt as moving toward "the Solidarism advocated by Father [Heinrich] Pesch in his *National Oeconomie* over forty years ago."[80]

ABORTION

The politics of abortion initially depended upon the politics of birth control. The 1873 federal law banning the distribution of contraceptive devices through the mail did not stem from Catholic lobbying, and neither did various state restrictions. And yet, from the 1920s into the 1960s, Catholics became the primary opponents of any loosening of restrictions on access to birth control in the United States. (Years later, one Boston Catholic, noting the absence of non-Catholic allies in the birth control fight, would wistfully note that "the old line non-Catholic population put these laws on the books.")[81]

As on economic matters, Fr. John Ryan spearheaded American activism. As early as 1906, in his *The Living Wage*, Ryan disparaged attempts to encourage low-paid workers to limit their offspring. Such recommendations, Ryan argued, pinned the blame for insufficient wages on the individual, and obscured the "responsibility of society and the necessity of social action." Men who obeyed such advice by not marrying would become "self-centered and unsympathetic" since "only in the family is it possible for the majority of men to develop those social feelings that are essential the welfare of a democratic society."[82]

A decade later Ryan urged fellow priests to overcome their inhibitions and address the problem of contraception more publicly. Already, Ryan warned, many Catholics find church teaching impracticable. Catholics needed "intelligent instruction" on the matter, and a reminder that use of birth control leads to "loss of reverence for the marital relation" as well as "softness, luxury and materialism."[83] In 1919, probably at Ryan's urging, the same bishops that surprised liberals by calling for a minimum wage and various social insurance programs attacked the "selfishness" and the "crime" of defeating the "obvious purpose" of marital relations.[84]

In the 1920s Catholics helped defeat laws that would allow public advertisements of birth control products and greater public access to information on contraception. In the 1930s and 1940s Catholics fought federal legislation and the remaining state laws that prohibited the opening of birth control clinics and limited the ability of doctors to prescribe birth control for even married patients. Birth control advocates such as Mary Ware Dennett and Margaret Sanger at once delighted that a church led by a celibate male clergy had become their primary opponent, but also feared its influence. As early as 1923 Dennett, when lobbying congressmen, would explain that "none but the Catholics" would provide "organized opposition."[85] Sanger specialized in goading Catholic opposition. "The R.C.'s are certainly taking their stand against this subject & me," Sanger wrote to a friend, "but it may serve to awaken the Protestant element, in time to save the country later on."[86] The last hurrah—to use a Boston phrase—of this Catholic activity occurred in Connecticut and Massachusetts in the 1940s and 1950s, as Catholics fiercely defended the remaining pair of state laws that prohibited doctors from distributing birth control devices to their patients. The Catholic argument still rested on the belief that since natural law logically condemned artificial birth control, "this issue is not a religious controversy."[87]

Such Catholic confidence quickly evaporated. As is well known, birth control became the central intra-Catholic debate of the 1950s and 1960s, and a rapidly increasing number of Catholic couples, priests, and bishops came to doubt the traditional teaching. Jesuit John Courtney Murray famously helped persuade the bishops assembled at the Second Vatican Council to stand for religious freedom.[88] At precisely the same time Murray was advising Boston's Cardinal Cushing to permit a relaxation of the Massachusetts birth control laws. Murray explained that "It is not the function of a civil law to prescribe everything that is morally right and to forbid everything that is morally wrong." Specifically on the matter of birth control, Murray emphasized that "It is difficult to see how the state can forbid, as contrary to public morality, a practice that numerous religious leaders approve as morally right."[89]

The most divisive moment in American Catholic history occurred in the aftermath of *Humanae vitae* (1968), and the teaching on contraception, and its all-male source, instantly made Catholic discussion of sexuality less credible for many believers and in the public mind. Finally, the long intra-Catholic discussion of birth control had also culminated in a widespread belief that no single religious group should impose its own moral vision in a diverse society. Advocates of abortion on demand immediately seized upon this point, and peppered the early state and congressional hearings on the subject with attacks on Catholic lobbying. Harvard's Lawrence Tribe saw Catholic opposition to abortion as potentially unconstitutional, since no "universal agreement in terms of values [existed] that do not divide the society religiously."[90]

In addition, the campaign for liberalized abortion laws also moved with astonishing speed. Advocates of birth control in the 1920s, 1930s, and 1940s tended to defend their position by attacking the horrific crime of abortion, and as late as the early 1960s only modest modifications in the law seemed imminent. In retrospect, however, a new kind of American liberalism emerged in the 1950s, setting the stage for a revolution through the courts, and a novel focus on the rights-bearing, autonomous individual. Equally important, a powerful women's movement found in a Catholic church opposed to birth control a convenient and appealing target on all matters of sexuality.[91]

Slowly, Catholics mustered a response. Most Catholic intellectuals and moralists, divided as they were on birth control, did oppose significant liberalization of abortion laws. A 1966 survey of theologians (both liberal and conservative) found unanimity on the matter of "Protection of the right of the unborn, the question of human dignity, the concern of the state for the health and welfare of its citizens."[92] Notre Dame (and then Berkeley) legal scholar John Noonan, fresh from agonizing defeat after advocating a change in church teaching on contraception in meetings of the papal birth control commission, organized scholarly opposition to abortion on demand.[93]

Even now, despite a recent infusion of energy from Protestant evangelicals, Catholics remain central to the anti-abortion struggle. Catholics, themselves, are only slightly less likely to approve of legalized abortion than non-Catholics, and some of this resistance can still be traced to the neuralgic problem of a church with few visible women leaders advocating positions on matters of particular concern to women. But again in contrast to the birth control debate, movement on this issue (among men and women) in the last generation has frequently been toward the pro-life side, and arguments that legalized abortion inevitably creates a welcoming climate for euthanasia, the death penalty and a less generous regime of social provision have garnered significant support.

What does it all mean? Broadly, the history of Catholic civic engagement is one of attempting to articulate a more social Catholic vision of society in a deeply individualist political culture. During the 1850s, the Catholic inability to see the importance of abolition reflected a fear of the political liberalism associated with slave emancipation; in the early twentieth century this same Catholic sensibility melded nicely with an American liberalism far more interested in economic questions than those of individual rights and appreciative of Catholic ability to talk about the communal whole. This planning, almost anti-capitalist strain in American liberalism disappeared with the Depression and World War II (in contrast to European nations with stronger socialist and Catholic political parties.) In its stead, American reformers began to focus on individual rights, and here Catholic opposition to, first, public access to birth control, and then abortion, made some forms of Catholic civic engagement more contentious.

I might suggest two morals:

1. Catholics eager to engage issues of the day must not reflexively dismiss reforms or programs that seem to spring from suspicious sources. The anti-Catholicism of many American abolitionists, precisely because they held views about individual autonomy antithetical to powerful Catholic traditions, was real. But those same abolitionists also understood the inhumanity of slavery more profoundly

than all but a few Catholics. Catholics might remember, along with philosopher Charles Taylor, that "modern culture, in breaking with the structures and beliefs of Christendom, also carried certain facets of Christian life further than they ever were taken or could have been taken within Christendom."[94]

2. The most effective Catholic witness to Christian values in the public sphere has come through placing single issues in a more systematic framework. In this regard I find Cardinal Bernardin's "consistent ethic of life" compelling, and not, as is frequently alleged, a way for liberal Catholics to dodge the wrenching issue of abortion. Instead, such a framework—and again the contrast with discussion about birth control is stark—may ultimately persuade a vast, skeptical and largely non-Catholic public that the Catholic social and sexual ethic does not rest upon opposition to women's equality.

NOTES

1. "On the dangers and opportunities of history for policymakers," Ernest May and Richard E. Neustadt, in *Thinking in Time: The Uses of History for Decision Makers*, (New York, 1986).

2. John T. McGreevy, *Catholicism and American Freedom: A History* (New York, 2003). For an early foray, John T. McGreevy, "Thinking on One's Own: Catholicism and the American Intellectual Imagination, 1928–1960," (*Journal of American History*, 84, June 1997, 97–131.

3. The basic source remains Madeline Hooke Rice, *American Catholic Opinion on the Slavery Controversy* (New York: Columbia University Press, 1944). The most useful and wide-ranging discussion is John Francis Maxwell, *Slavery and the Catholic Church: A History of Catholic Teaching Concerning the Moral Legitimacy of the Institution of Slavery*, (London: Barry Rose, 1975). A brief, but astute, treatment that recognizes the very high theological stakes is John T. Noonan Jr., "Development in Moral Doctrine," in *The Context of Casuistry*, James F. Keenan, S. J. and Thomas A. Shannon, eds. (Washington, D.C.: Georgetown University Press, 1995), 189–98. Also see Alasdair MacIntyre, *Are There Any Natural Rights?* (Brunswick, Me.: 1983), esp. pp. 3–8, 21. For a more extended examination, Joseph Capizzi, "A Development of Doctrine: The Challenge of Slavery to Moral Theology," (University of Notre Dame, Ph.D. diss., 1998). For the biblical debate in Protestant circles, Mark A. Noll, "The Bible and Slavery," in *Religion and the American Civil War*, Randall M. Miller, Harry S. Stout and Charles Reagan Wilson, eds. (New York: Oxford University Press, 1998), 43–73; François Renault, "Aux origines de la lettre a postolique de Grégoire XVI. *In Supreme* (1839). *ibid.* 2 (1995), 143–49.

4. Robert Emmett Curran, "Rome, the American Church and Slavery," in *Building the Church in America: Studies in Honor of Monsignor Robert F. Trisco on the Occasion*

of His Seventieth Birthday, Joseph C. Link, C.O. and Raymond Kupke, eds. (Washington, D.C.: Catholic University of America Press, 1999), 36–38; Robert Emmett Curran, S. J., "'Splendid Poverty': Jesuit Slaveholding in Maryland, 1805–1838," in Randall M. Miller and Jon L. Wakelyn, eds., *Catholics in the Old South* (Macon, Ga.: Mercer University Press, 1999), 142–46.

5. Charles de Montalembert to Fr. Jean Baptiste Henri Lacordaire, O.P. September 20, 1839, in *Lacordaire-Montalembert Correspondance Inédite*, Louis Le Guillou, ed. (Paris, Les Éditions Du Cerf, 1989), 449; Charles de Montalembert, "Emancipation des Esclaves," (April 7, 1845) and "Emancipation des Noirs dans les Colonies," (March 30, 1847), in *Montalembert Oeurves, Volume II* (Paris, 1860), 59–62, 461–72.

6. Daniel O'Connell, "Daniel O'Connell and the Committee of the Irish Repeal Association of Cincinnati," [1843] in *Union Pamphlets of the Civil War, 1861–1865: Volume II*, Frank Freidel, ed. (Cambridge, Mass.: Harvard University Press, 1967), 802–3. On this episode, Gilbert Osofsky, "Abolitionists, Irish Immigrants and the Dilemmas of Romantic Nationalism," *American Historical Review* 80 (October 1975), 889–912.

7. Jane Grey Swisshelm, *Half a Century*, (Chicago: J. G. Swisshelm [1880], 1970), 150.

8. "The Abolitionist," *New York Freeman's Journal* (March 5, 1842), 284. For abolitionist reaction, James Gillespie Birney to the Editor of the *Free Press*, April 29, 1842, in *Letters of James Gillespie Birney, 1831–1857 Volume II*, Dwight L. Dumond, ed. (New York: Appleton-Century, 1938), 681–84.

9. The growth of this literature is explosive. The most influential formulation is David R. Roediger, *The Wages of Whiteness: Race and the Making of the American Working Class*, (London: Verso, 1991), 133–86, quotation on 140. Also see Noel Ignatiev, *How the Irish Became White*, (New York: Routledge, 1995), 6–31; Eric Lott, *Love and Theft: Blackface Minstrelsy and the American Working Class*, (New York: Oxford, 1993).

10. John R. McKivigan, *The War against Proslavery Religion: Abolitionism and the Northern Churches, 1830–1865,* (Ithaca, N.Y.: Cornell University Press, 1984), 38; John W. Quist, "'The Great Majority of our Subscribers are Farmers': The Michigan Abolitionist Constituency of the 1840s," *Journal of the Early Republic* 14 (fall 1994), 357.

11. Philippe Delisle is sympathetic to French Catholic efforts to work among slaves in Martinque but acknowledges an absence of interest in abolition. See Philippe Delisle, *Renouveau Missionaire et Société La Martinique: 1815–1848*, (Paris: Centre National du Livre, 1997), 99–101; Arthur F. Corwin, *Spain and the Abolition of Slavery in Cuba, 1817–1886*, (Austin, Tex.: Institute for Latin American Studies, 1967), 166–68; Joaquim Nabuco, *Abolitionism: The Brazilian Antislavery Struggle*, Robert Conrad, tr. (Urbana: University of Illinois Press, 1977), 19.

12. Two recent essays are incisive on this point: Claude Prudhomme, "La papauté face à l'esclavage: quelle condamnation?" *Mémoire Spiritaine* 9 (First Semester, 1999), 135–60.

13. "Ireland, O'Connell, &c." *Brownson's Quarterly Review* 2 (July 1845), 400–404; "Loyal National Repeal Association," *New York Freeman's Journal* (September 20, 1845), 91.

14. "The Catholic Church and the Question of Slavery," *The Metropolitan* 3 (June 1855), 266, 268.

15. Rev. J. Balmes, *Protestantism and Catholicity Compared in Their Effects on the Civilization of Europe*, (Baltimore, Md.: John Murphy & Co., 1851), 90–115.

16. Luigi d'Azeglio Taparelli, *Saggio teoretica di dritto naturale appogiato sul fatto: Volume I*, (1855; Rome: Civiltà carrolica, 1949), 360–62.

17. Rev. Joseph D. Brokehage, Francis Patrick Kenrick's *Opinion on Slavery*, (Washington, D.C.: Catholic University of America Press, 1955), 123. Maxwell elucidates the dubious distinction between ownership as control of labor and ownership as personal property on pp. 86–87.

18. "The Higher Law," *Brownson's Quarterly Review* (January 1851), reprinted in *The Works of Orestes Brownson: Volume Seventeen* Henry F. Brownson, ed. (Detroit, Mich.: 1882–1887), 2.

19. "Free Soilism," reprinted in *Pittsburgh Catholic* (June 21, 1851), 113.

20. Elizabeth B. Clark, "'The Sacred Rights of the Weak': Pain Sympathy, and the Culture of Individual Rights in Antebellum America," *Journal of American History* 82 (September 1995), 463–93.

21. T. Parkin Scott, "An Inquiry into the Principles Involved in the late Presidential Election: A Lecture Delivered before the Catholic Institute of Baltimore," *New York Freeman's Journal* (February 7, 1856), 3.

22. Rev. John McMullen, "Bishop England on Domestic Slavery," [1865?] in Rev. James J. McGovern, *The Life and Writings of the Right Reverend John McMullen, D.D.*, (Chicago: Hoffmann Brothers, 1888), xcv.

23. Rev. A. Verot, "Slavery and Abolitionism: Being the Substance of a Sermon Preached in the Church of St. Augustine, Florida, on the 4th Day of January, 1861," *New York Freeman's Journal* (June 18, 1864), 1. The second part of the sermon was published in the *New York Freeman's Journal* (July 9, 1864), 1–2. Michael V. Gannon, *Rebel Bishop: The Life and Era of Augustin Verot*, (Milwaukee, Wis.: Bruce Publishing, 1964), 37.

24. "De la source légitime de l'Esclavage," *Propagateur Catholique* (January 18, 1862), 1; "De la source légitime de l'Esclavage," *Propagateur Catholique* (February 1, 1862), 1. The second quotation is from the second cited article. On white southerners and slavery, Eugene D. Genovese, *A Consuming Fire: The Fall of the Confederacy in the Mind of the White Christian South*, (Athens, Ga.: Mercer University Press, 1998).

25. Daniel O'Connell, "Daniel O'Connell and the Committee of the Irish Repeal Association of Cincinnati," in *Union Pamphlets of the Civil War, 1861–1865: Volume II*, Frank Freidel, ed. (Cambridge, Mass.: Harvard University Press, 1967), 809.

26. An exception to this generalization is Peter Walker, *Moral Choices: Memory Desire, and Imagination in Nineteenth-Century American Abolition*, (Baton Rouge: Louisiana State University Press, 1978), 161–166.

27. George Bourne, *Picture of Slavery in the United States of America* (Middletown, Conn.: E. Hunt, 1834), 151.

28. Franchot, 104–6, 171–81: Ronald G. Waters, "The Erotic South: Civilization and Sexuality in American Abolitionism," *American Quarterly* 25 (May 1973), 177–201.

29. *The Life and Writings of Rev. Joseph Gordon*, Written and Compiled by a Committee of the Free Presbyterian Synod (Cincinnati, Oh.: Free Presbyterian Synod, 1860), 302.

30. "Elijah P. Lovejoy as an Anti-Catholic," Records of the American Catholic Historical Society 62 (September 1951), 172–80.

31. John W. Christie and Dwight L. Dumont, *George Bourne and the Book and Slavery Irreconcilable*, (Wilmington, Del.: Historical Society of Delaware, 1969), 83–86, 99–101.

32. George Bourne, *Picture of Slavery in the United States of America*, (Boston, 1838), 167, 175.

33. Lyman Beecher, *Plea for the West*, (Cincinnati, Ohio: Truman & Smith, 1835); Harriet Beecher Stowe, "The Fete of St. Joseph in Rome," *National Anti-Slavery Standard* 20 (April 28, 1860), n.p.; Franchot, 103. Franchot identifies an undercurrent of attraction to Catholicism in Stowe's later work, 246–55.

34. Edward Beecher, *The Papal Conspiracy Exposed, and Protestantism Defended in the Light of Reason, History, and Scripture*, (1855; New York: Arno, 1977); Robert Merideth, *The Politics of the Universe: Edward Beecher, Abolition, and Orthodoxy*, (Nashville, Tenn.: Vanderbilt University Press, 1968), 120–24

35. Frederick Douglass, "Pictures and Progress: An Address Delivered in Boston, Massachusetts, on 3 December 1861," *The Frederick Douglass Papers: Series One: Speeches, Debates, and Interviews Volume 3: 1855–1863*, John W. Blassingame, ed. (New Haven, Conn.: Yale University Press, 1985), 461–62; "William The Silent: An Address Delivered in Cincinnati, Ohio, on 8 February 1869," in *The Frederick Douglass Papers: Series One: Speeches, Debates, and Interviews Volume 5: 1864–1880*, John W. Blassingame, ed. (New Haven, Conn.: Yale University Press, 1991), 186–91. Also see Richard Hardack, "The Slavery of Romanism: The Casting Out of the Irish in the Work of Frederick Douglass," in *Liberating Sojourn: Frederick Douglass & Transatlantic Reform*, Alan J. Rice and Martin Crawford, eds. (Athens: University of Georgia Press, 1999), 115–40.

36. Richard D. Webb, "Letter from Our Dublin Correspondent," *National Anti-slavery Standard*, 19 (January 22, 1859), n.p.

37. Nelly Schmidt, *Victor Schoelcher et l'abolition de l'esclavage* (Paris: Fayard, 1994), 197–200.

38. Matias Romero, "The Situation of Mexico: Speech Delivered by Senor Matias Romero, Envoy Extraordinary and Minister Plenipotentiary of the Republic of Mexico to the United States, at a Dinner in the City of New York, on the 16th of December, 1863" (New York, 1864), 11.

39. J. M. S. Careless, *Brown of The Globe. Volume One The Voice of Upper Canada 1818–1859*, (Toronto: Macmillan, 1959), 102–3; *Toronto Globe* quoted in *Provincial Freeman* (October 13, 1855), n.p.

40. "Catholicity and National Permanence" *New York Freeman's Journal* (January 5, 1850), 4; "Free Soilism," reprinted in *Pittsburg Catholic* (June 21, 1851), 113.

41. Dr. Cummings, "Slavery and the Union," *New York Freeman's Journal* (May 25, 1850), p.1.

42. "Free-Soilism," *Pittsburg Catholic* (June 7, 1851), 97–98; Annual Statement of the Massachusetts Anti-Slavery Society, at the Twenty-Third Annual Meeting, January 1855. (Boston, 1855), 41.

43. The manuscripts were first published in *L'Enciclica Rerum novarum e Il Suo Tempo*, Giovanni Antonazzi e Gabriele de Rose, eds. (Rome, [1957] 1991). I rely upon the informative summaries in John Moloney, "The Making of *Rerum novarum* April 1890–May 1891," in *The Church Faces the Modern World: Rerum Novarum and Its Impact*, Paul Furlong and David Curtis, eds. (Hull, Ont.: Earlsgate Press, 1994), 27–39; Paul Misner, "The Predecessors of *Rerum novarum* Within Catholicism," *Review of Social Economy* 49 (winter 1991), 444–64; Claude Prudhomme, "Leon XIII Et La Curei Romaine L' Epoque De *Rerum novarum*," in *Rerum novarum: Ecriture, Contentu et Reception D'Une Encyclique* (Rome: École Francaise De Rome, 1997), 29–48; Jean-Marie Mayeur, *Catholicisme Social et Démocratie Chrétienne: Principes romains, expériences francaises,* (Paris: Les Éditions Du Cerf, 1986), 47–65. For a more complete analysis, see John Molony, *The Worker Question*, (Melbourne: Gill & Macmillan, Ltd., 1991).

44. David Blackbourn, "The Catholic Church in Europe since the French Revolution," *Comparative Studies in Society in History* 33 (?1991), 785; Hugh McLeod, *Piety and Poverty: Working-Class Religion in Berlin, London and New York 1870–1914,* (New York: Holmes & Meier, 1996), 116–17; Kevin Christiano, *Religious Diversity and Social Change: American Cities 1890–1906,* (Cambridge, U.K.: Cambridge University Press, 1987), 172–75.

45. Rev. Daniel T. McColgan, *A Century of Charity: The First One Hundred Years of the Society of St. Vincent De Paul in the United States Volume I*, (Milwaukee, Wis.: Bruce Publishing, 1951), 45. On comparable events in Scotland, Bernard Aspinwall, "The Welfare State within the State: The St. Vincent de Paul Society in Glasgow, 1848–1920," *Voluntary Religion: Studies in Church History* 23 (1986) 445–59. Brown and McKeown, *On Politics: The Poor Belong to Us: Catholic Charities and American Welfare*, (Cambridge, Mass.: Harvard University Press, 1997), 26–27;

46. Carol K. Coburn and Martha Smith, *Spirited Lives: How Nuns Shaped Catholic Culture and American Life 1836–1920*, (Chapel Hill: University of North Carolina Press, 1999), 2.

47. Suellen Hoy, "Caring for Chicago's Women and Girls: The Sisters of the Good Shepherd, 1859–1911," *Journal of Urban History* 23 (March 1997), 260–94. For France, see Sylbie Fayet-Scribe, *Associations Féminines et Catholicisme: De la chariteé à l'action sociale XIX–XX siécle*, (Paris: Editions ouvriéres, 1990).

48. Charles Loring Brace, *The Dangerous Classes of New York, and Twenty Years' Work Among Them*, (New York: [1872] 1880), 154, 426.

49. Thomas L. Haskell, *Objectivity Is Not Neutrality: Explanatory Schemes in History*, (Baltimore, Md.: Johns Hopkins University Press, 1998), 307–317. The classic American study remains Morton G. White, *Social Thought in America: The Revolt*

Against Formalism, (New York: Viking Press, 1949). Superb on both the United States and Europe is James T. Kloppenberg, *Uncertain Victory: Social Democracy and Progressivism in European and American Thought, 1870–1920*, (New York: Oxford University Press, 1986).

50. Amy Dru Stanley, *From Bondage to Contract: Wage Labor, Marriage and the Market in the Age of Slave Emancipation*, (Cambridge, U.K.: Cambridge University Press, 1998), esp. 168; Sumner quoted in John Ashworth, "Free Labor, Wage Labor, Slavery Power," in *The Market Revolution in America: Social, Political, and Religious Expressions, 1800–1880*, Melvyn Stokes and Stephen Conway eds., (Charlottesville: University Press of Virginia, 1996), 138; *Lawrence B. Glickman, A Living Wage: American Workers and the Making of Consumer Society*, (Ithaca, N.Y.: Cornell University Press, 1997).

51. Paul Droulers, S. J., " Question sociale, Etat, Eglise dans la Civiltà Cattolica À ses Débuts," in *Droulers, Cattolicesimo Sociale Nei Secoli XIX e XX*, (Rome, [1962], 1982), 97–147.

52. Phillipe Boutry, "*Rerum novarum* et Le Climat Des Années 40 du XIX Siécle," in *Rerum novarum: Ecriture, Contenu et Réception d'une Encyclique*, (Rome: École Francaise de Rome, 1997), 71; Fr. Matteo Liberatore, S. J., *Principles of Political Economy*, Edward Heneage Dering, tr. (London, 1891), 194.

53. Fabrice Bouthillon, "Les LumiÉres Dans *Rerum novarum*," in *Rerum novarum: Ecriture, Contentu Et Réception D'une Encyclique* (École Francaise de Rome, 1997), 65.

54. Bishop John Hughes, "A Lecture on the Importance of a Christian Basis for the Science of Political Economy, and Its Application to the Affairs of Life," [1844] in *Complete Works of the Most Rev. John Hughes, D.D., Archbishop of New York. Comprising His Sermons, Letters, Lectures, Speeches, Etc.: Volume I*, (New York: 1865), 521.

55. Orestes A. Brownson, *The Laboring Classes* (1840) with Brownson's *Defence of the Article on the Laboring Classes*, (New York: Scholar's Facsims, 1978), 14; Orestes Brownson, in *Brownson Works*, vol. v, p. 63

56. "The Material Mission of the Church," *Catholic World* 28 (February 1878), 662.

57. Luigi d'Azeglio Taparelli, *Saggio teoretica di dritto naturale appoggiato sul fatto: Volume I*, (1855; Rome: Civiltà carrolica, 1949), 360–62; David C. R. Heisser, "Bishop Lynch's Civil War Pamphlet on Slavery," *Catholic Historical Review* 134 (October 1998), 685, 695.

58. Orestes A. Brownson, *The Laboring Classes* (1840) with Brownson's *Defence of the Article on the Laboring Classes*, (New York: Scholar's Facsims, 1978), 10.

59. Rev. Joseph D. Brakhage, S.T.L., *Francis Patrick Kenrick's Opinion on Slavery* (Washington, D.C.: Catholic University of America, 1955), 156, 160, 162; James Healy, S. J., *The Just Wage: A Study of Moralists from Saint Alphonsus to Leo XIII,* (The Hague: Martinus Nijhoff, 1966), 337–38.

60. Joseph Lee, "The Social and Economic Ideas of O'Connell," in *Daniel O'Connell: Portrait of a Radical*, Kevin B. Nowlan and Maurice R. O'Connell, eds. (New York: Fordham University Press, 1985), 75–78; James C. Finlay, *The Liberal Who Failed*, (Washington, D.C.: Corpus Books, 1968), 149–51.

61. The papal encylicals *Longinqua oceani* (1895) and *Testem benevolentiae* (1899).

62. *Rerum novarum* (1891) in *The Papal Encyclicals 1878–1903*, Claudia Carlen, IHM, ed. (Raleigh, N.C.: McGrath, 1981), 3, 19, 20, 46, 45. On *Rerum novarum* and Locke, Sullivan, esp. 196–206; José María Díez-Alegría, "Ownership and Labour: The Development of Papal Teaching," in John Coleman and Gregory Baum, eds. *Rerum Novarum: One Hundred Years of Catholic Social Teaching*, (Philadelphia: Trinity Press International, 1991), 18–19.

63. Daniel T. Rodgers, *Atlantic Crossings: Social Politics in a Progressive Age*, (Cambridge, Mass.: Harvard University Press, 1998), 76–119.

64. Mary Thomas Bouquillon to William J. Kerby, May 26, 1895, Box 1, Kerby papers, Archives of the Catholic University of America. Also see Kerby's course notebook, Ammedebuch, Box 1, ACUA. On Seidenburg, see the entry in *The New Catholic Encyclopedia*, p. 198

65. Pesch quoted in *Church and Society: Catholic Social and Political Thought and Movements, 1789–1950*, (New York: Arts, Inc., 1953), 547; Pesch second quote in Ederer, tr. p. 29; Richard E. Mulcahy, S. J., *The Economics of Heinrich Pesch*, (New York: Henry Holt, 1952), 3, 162; Gustav Gundlach, S. J. "Solidarist Economics," *Social Order* 1 (April 1951), 181.

66. Francis L. Broderick, *Right Reverend New Dealer John A. Ryan*, (New York: The Macmillan Co., 1963).

67. John A. Ryan, "A Great Catholic Work on Political Economy," *Fortnightly Review* 17 (May 1910), 289.

68. Gary Gerstle, "The Protean Character of American Liberalism," *American Historical Review* 99 (October 1994), 1044–46, 1061.

69. Robyn Muncy, *Creating a Female Dominion in American Reform 1890–1935*, (New York: Oxford University Press, 1991), 162.

70. Roscoe Pound to John A. Ryan, July 5, 1923, Reel 43, Roscoe Pound papers, Harvard Law School; John A. Ryan to Roscoe Pound, October 18, 1923, reel 43, Roscoe Pound papers, Harvard Law School.

71. Timothy Michael Dolan, "Some Seed Fell on Good Ground": *The Life of Edwin V. O'Hara*, (Washington, D.C.: Catholic University of America Press, 1992), 29–40. Quote on 34.

72. Program of Social Reconstruction, February 12, 1919, in *Pastoral Letters of the United States Catholic Bishops: Volume I, 1792–1940*, (Washington, D.C.: National Conference of Catholic Bishops, 1984), 255–71; On the plan, Joseph M. McShane, S. J., *Sufficiently Radical: Catholicism, Progressivism and the Bishops' Program of 1919*, (Washington, D.C.: Catholic University of America Press, 1986).

73. Editorial, *New Republic* (February 22, 1919), 99.

74. Raymond Swing, "The Catholic View of Reconstruction," *Nation* 108 (March 29, 1919), 467, 468.

75. *Quadragesimo anno* in *The Papal Encyclicals: Volume 3*, Claudia Carlen, ed. (Wilmington, N.C.: McGrath Publishing Company, 1981), 49, 88, 93; Geza B. Grosschmid, "Pesch's Concept of the Living Wage in *Quadregisimo anno*," *Review of Social Economy* 12 (September 1954), 146–55.

76. John T. McNicholas, O. P., "Justice and the Present Crisis," *Catholic Mind* 29 (October 22, 1931), 475.

77. *The Public Papers and Addresses of Franklin D. Roosevelt, Volume One: The Genesis of the New Deal 1928–1932*, (New York: Random House, 1938), 778.

78. John McHugh Stuart to Ryan October 29, 1932, Ryan papers.

79. Alan Brinkley, *The End of Reform: New Deal Liberalism and the Social Order* (New York, 1995), 36–39.

80. R. A. McGowan, "Reconstructing the Social Order," in Proceedings of the Ninth Annual Meeting of the American Catholic Philosophical Association (1933), 188; Catholic Action (July 1933), 6; John A. Ryan, "New Deal and Social Justice," *Catholic Mind* 19 (April 13, 1934), 658; Joseph Thorning, S. J., "Principles and Practice of the NRA," *Catholic Mind* 19 (October 8, 1934) 363

81. Joseph Doyle to Eugene Butler, December 13, 1954, Birth Control file, Box 19, Dept. of Education, NCWC.

82. Ryan, *Living Wage*, 287. Leslie Tentler's ongoing work on priests and birth control will shed vital, much needed light on this entire issue. My account here is in part indebted to preliminary papers Professor Tentler has generously let me read.

83. John A. Ryan, "Family Limitation," *Ecclesiastical Review* 54 (June 1916), 684–85, 690.

84. Pastoral Letter of the Archbishops and Bishops of the United States, September 25, 1919.

85. Congressional Diary of Mary Ware Dennett, January 26, 1923, Reel 12 Dennett papers, Schlesinger Library, Harvard University.

86. Chesler biography of Sanger, 213.

87. Continued Public Hearing Upon House #1748 before Joint Committee on Public Health, Boston April 8, 1948, in House Bills/Briefs file, Box 21 Chanc. Archives of the Archdiocese of Boston.

88. John Noonan, *The Lustre of Our Country: The American Experience of Religious Freedom* (Berkeley, Calif.: University of California Press, 1998), 321–53.

89. Murray Memo to Cardinal Cushing (1965), Archives of the Archdiocese of Boston.

90. Abortion Part III Hearings before the Subcommittee on Constitutional Amendments of the Committee on the Judiciary United States Senate Ninety-Third Congress Second Session on S.J. Res 119 and S.J. Res. 130 (Washington, D.C.: U.S. Government Printing Office, 1974), September 12, 1974, 391.

91. On Noonan, John T. McGreevy, "A Case for Doctrinal Development," *Commonweal* (November 17, 2000), 12–17.

92. McHugh to Tanner August 25, 1966, in File 7, Box 87 SAD NCWC.

93. *The Morality of Abortion: Legal and Historical Perspectives*, John T. Noonan Jr., ed. (Cambridge, Mass.: Harvard University Press, 1970)

94. Charles Taylor, *A Catholic Modernity?* (New York, 1999), 16.

ABORTION, SEXUALITY, AND CATHOLICISM'S PUBLIC PRESENCE

Luke Timothy Johnson

The Roman Catholic Church in the United States, it can safely be said, is facing a crisis of considerable proportions in the glare of massive and negative publicity. On the surface, the crisis is about sex. Beneath the surface, the crisis is about the Church's teaching authority. My topic is how these two have become intertwined over the past several decades, and how together they threaten the integrity of the Catholic Church.

Over the span of my lifetime, official church teaching on sex has remained both severe and consistent. When I was a child, the church forbade masturbation, divorce, adultery, fornication—see premarital sexual relations—abortion, and artificial birth control. Male and female members of religious orders took a vow of chastity and ordained priests were obligated to celibacy. As I near the age of sixty, none of these positions has been substantially modified. This official Catholic sexual ethics is, moreover, countercultural within an American society that, over the same sixty-year period, became ever more profoundly individualistic and pervasively sexualized. To use biblical language, the church's teaching on sexuality can be regarded, in important ways, as prophetic. It stands for a vision of the world defined by God over and against practices that distort creation.

Demanding fidelity in marriage challenges an ethos in which easy divorce testifies to the erosion of a sense of covenant. Insisting that religious and clergy be celibate is a witness to the power of the Resurrection against a culture whose lust for pleasure and acquisition proclaims that this mortal existence is the only life to be had. Restricting licit sexual activity to marriage declares that sexuality is meant to be covenantal and mutually responsible, against impulses that define sexuality simply in terms of pleasure or personal gratification. Most striking, the church's unwavering stance against abortion stands in the classic prophetic tradition of the protection of the powerless against the powerful. The church's sexual teaching can, in short, be regarded as a prophetic voice within American culture.

The teaching of any religion on any moral subject, however, must always involve more than words from a pulpit or statements in the press. Teaching is real and convincing only to the extent that it is actually embraced by believers, embodied in their practices, coherently and consistently expressed by the community of faith. The "reception" of Catholic sexual teaching by Catholics themselves—both clergy and lay—is an essential ingredient of that teaching. Only to the degree that moral teaching is expressed by the attitudes and actions of Catholics themselves can it challenge anyone. Only if a prophet's message is clear, consistent, internally coherent, and corresponds to the prophet's own manner of life can or should a prophet be heard.

It is precisely here that a profound change has occurred over the fifty-some years of my life, a change that has compromised and perhaps even discredited the prophetic voice of the church in matters of sexual morality.

Before taking up the argument, I should make two disclosures. First, I am myself a lifelong Roman Catholic. My five older siblings have a total of twenty-four children. I was a seminarian at thirteen, a Benedictine monk for nine years, a priest for three years, and a married layman for twenty-eight years. Joy and I have seven children, ten grandchildren, and three great-grandchildren. I am therefore not a detached analyst but rather speak as a participant in the changes I am about to describe. Second, as a participant-observer my report is based more anecdotally than statistically. There are certainly exceptions and countertendencies to the ones I describe, but I think my overall perception is nevertheless accurate. Many young Catholics today, for example, are seeking a return to the ethos of the preconciliar church, but even that reaction is defined by the dramatic social changes I am about to describe.

THAT WAS THEN

From 1940 through mid-1960, Catholic teaching about sexuality was remarkably consistent. More impressive, in the United States of America it was embodied by a clergy and a laity who wore their rigorous sexual code as a badge of honor, distinguishing Catholics from their less impressive Protestant rivals. The prohibition of artificial birth control, of divorce, of premarital sex, and of mixed marriages marked Catholics, they fondly thought, as the serious Christians in this country, in distinction to the Protestants who had capitulated to Freud and Kinsey and Americanism in general. Catholics acknowledged, to be sure, a difference between nominal and practicing Catholics. But when they said Catholics they meant only the practitioners.

Practicing Catholics not only obeyed the strict sexual teaching of the church. They extended that teaching through sets of attitudes and actions that comprehended the minutest aspects of everyday life. Humorous and bitter memoirs of Growing Up Catholic recall how the prohibition of fornication, for example, led logically to a complete semiotics of modesty in dress that was spelled out by highly specific norms, from loose blouses to non-reflecting shoes. Modesty was so internalized that the possibility of becoming an occasion of someone else's sexual arousal—called "impure thoughts"—was taken as seriously as actually having such impulses oneself. The Legion of Decency's ranking of films was more than a list tacked to the bulletin board. It provided a guide to moral discernment in the home. I vividly remember an argument between my mother and my teenaged sisters when I was about eight years old about viewing *Joan of Arc*. My sisters argued that it was about a saint. My mother countered that it starred Ingrid Bergman, who had abandoned her husband; attending this film would countenance adultery and divorce.

Catholics of my age well remember the totalizing character of the Catholic ethos of the fifties. Devotion to Pius XII and to the Blessed Mother; fasting on Friday; keeping the Eucharistic fast; avoiding blasphemy (any use of "Jesus" without bowing the head), masturbation, and impure thoughts were all pretty much at the same level of obligation, woven together in a single, unquestioning and unquestionable fabric of belief and practice, of fear and love, of resentment and pride.

Weekly confession on Saturday afternoons marked the practicing Catholic. Yes, it was terrifying to acknowledge every impure thought and act. In adolescence, who can keep count? But it all made sense, not least because the confessional line each Saturday afternoon included family and friends and neighbors. Catholics, we told each other, were unlike Protestants also in this respect: Protestants had—and needed—psychotherapy. But we had the confessional.

Catholic sexual mores during those years marked the church as an immigrant religion out of step with an America whose postwar affluence and freedom saw Hugh Hefner and Marilyn Monroe give way to more spectacular and more sinister entrepreneurs of sex. But Americans also paid a certain respect to the Catholic insistence on remaining aloof from the sexual mainstream, a respect suggested by Hollywood's cautious and usually positive portrayal of Catholic priests and nuns. Catholic sexual mores may have been alien but they were impressive. The priests portrayed by Bing Crosby and Spencer Tracy in the 1940s were virile, musical, and unequivocally committed to the good of humanity. The depiction of nuns by Deborah Kerr (in *Heaven Knows, Mr. Allison*) and Audrey Hepburn (in *The Nun's Story*) were notable for the seriousness with which they took religious vows and the desire of religious women to seek God's will. Hollywood producers were neither Catholic nor particularly moral. But they knew that Catholics voted at the ticket office.

THIS IS NOW

One way of indicating the seismic shift in the practice and perception of Catholic sexual teaching is viewing more recent Hollywood portrayals of Catholics. When not simply silly (Whoopi Goldberg in *Sister Act* and *Sister Act II*) or horrifying (Meg Tilley in *Agnes of God*), the depictions of Catholics tend toward the puerile (*Keeping the Faith, Dogma*). It's not just films. In live and televised drama, characters are presented positively when they struggle against Catholic teaching and are presented negatively when they straightforwardly act according to it.

Stand-up comics, a disproportionate number of whom seem to be, in the current phrase, "recovering Catholics," treat traditional sexual teaching as self-evidently ludicrous. Religious women are, in comedic routines, systematically held up for ridicule. In a world of pervasive political correctness, practicing Catholics are among the very few remaining safe targets for easy mockery.

Attacking Catholic sexual mores, however, seems increasingly arbitrary and even irrelevant, since the formerly monolithic Catholic sexual ethos has all but disappeared. Most of the young people in a comedy club laughing at jokes about sexually neurotic nuns have never met an actual nun, much less had one for a teacher. American Catholics now divorce about as often as non-Catholics do. Catholics are not notably better at avoiding adultery and fornication than non-Catholics. Young Catholics sleep together before marriage with little sense of "living in sin." Masturbation is of course practiced as often as it ever was, except that now few confess it as a mortal sin. With clear conscience or not, married Catholics practice artificial birth control. Enough Catholic women have abortions to make post-abortion counseling and reconciliation a substantial ministry. Vocations to religious orders demanding chastity are scarce. As for a celibate priesthood, the lack of vocations has once again made the United States a missionary country.

If Catholic sexual teaching includes the willing reception, glad enact-
ment, and unquestioning proclamation of that teaching by Catholics themselves, then that teaching is, in the year 2002, far less coherent, consistent,
and clear than it was in 1950, simply because many Catholics today themselves either don't believe it or don't consistently practice it.

A TIME OF TURNING

How did American Catholicism reach its present state? I suggest that the
shift is due both to factors external to Catholicism in American culture, and
to factors internal to Catholicism, and that the link between the two—
indeed perhaps the best explanation—is the way the external became internal, or the way in which American Catholics truly became American at a
moment when America itself was undergoing a cultural revolution.

It has become a cliché to "blame it on the 1960s," but the cultural
change in the United States affected from the middle of that decade to the
present is not trite. Doubtless, a more adequate analysis would show complexities and ambiguities before and after the transition, but would also
show that the transition itself was real and profound.

At least six elements pertinent to my subject were part of the cultural
upheaval in the United States during the 1960s. The first was a sustained
material prosperity unparalleled in human history. The same technological
expertise brought forth both the microchip and a reliable birth control pill,
appeared to make possible a simultaneous war against foreign communism
and domestic poverty, and enabled—and then demanded—the full participation of both men and women in the economic sphere.

The second was the sexual revolution that swept first across college
campuses and then into homes and elementary schools. Masters and Johnson brought the orgasm into polite company. Alex Comfort brought *The Joy
of Sex* to the local bookstore, with drawings that a decade earlier would have
required a brown paper wrapper. Post-pill and pre-AIDS, sexual activity was
preached and practiced as a matter of fun and freedom, with sex and procreation increasingly regarded as quite separate concerns.

The third element was the marriage of the sexual revolution to commerce in the media, above all in advertising. As movies and rock and roll
tested the boundaries of sexual expression, each risky extension was do-
mesticated with breathtaking speed by television. By the beginning of the
twenty-first century, no form of sexual exploitation, including soft-core
child pornography, has gone unexploited by glossy-magazine advertisers. As

for hard-core pornography, it has become the most lucrative branch of film-making, and parents must make a special request in motel rooms to keep such films from being offered to their children. Pornography and prostitution are available for sale on the Internet to every child. The distinction between sex selling and selling sex has virtually disappeared.

The fourth element was the impact of the political scandals of the 1960s on the American consciousness, especially on the Boomer generation, whose outsized path through life has had such a disproportionate cultural effect. The late 1950s and early 1960s encouraged a sense of political optimism among the young. Involvement in the civil rights struggle, the Peace Corps, and the war against poverty could make a difference. But the assassination of the Kennedys and King, the secret war in Asia uncovered by the Pentagon papers, the Watergate coverup—all these had two profound effects. One was the emergence of the hermeneutics of suspicion. America finally emerged from its cocoon of political naiveté, as more and more Americans saw that politics was about power, that power was most often self-interested, and that politicians lied out of both habit and choice. The other was a shift in the sense of what was morally more important, from the private to the public. The Eisenhower generation had cultivated sexual propriety but winked at racial, class, and gender inequities. The Boomers (before AIDS) saw nothing wrong with sexual promiscuity, so long as the right social issues were engaged. These are genuine shifts in moral consciousness.

The fifth element was the women's movement, which drew upon and extended each of the other elements. An economic prosperity based on labor-saving technology freed women from biological determinism and domestic servitude. The pill liberated them from the constant threat of pregnancy and childrearing and enabled them to pursue careers. The sexual revolution saw women as well as men seeking sexual adventure apart from commitment. The media's marriage of sex and commerce, in turn, revealed how commodification simultaneously glorified and degraded women's bodies. It was women who concluded that if all politics is personal, so everything personal is also political. Women above all seized on the hermeneutics of suspicion: the validation of their own voices required the demystification of patriarchal structures constructed for the benefit of men and the suppression of women. Women translated the equation of private and public morality into an advocacy of the legality of abortion, so that the killing of a fetus was interpreted in terms of "women's rights over their own bodies." In short, the women's movement, the most controversial and threatening element in the cultural revolution, forced all Americans to recognize that sex is also always about gender, and that gender always involves social construction, and that social construction always involves somebody's interest.

Finally, the 1960s saw the birth of the Gay and Lesbian Rights movements in the cities of America. That relatively small portion of humanity whose identity had always been defined by others in terms of deviance also discovered through solidarity its name and its right to speak for itself and to define itself. As a result, more and more Americans discovered that they or their children or their spouses were homosexual. And what should they think or do about that?

In moral terms, these six elements of cultural revolution are a mixed bag. America's material prosperity brought obvious blessings but also shaped an entitled population. The pill gave women freedom but its long-term health effects remain uncertain. The sexual revolution, however inevitable, had disastrous consequences on a number of fronts. The sexualization of identity in the media has coarsened the American soul. The hermeneutics of suspicion has disabled many from civic participation. Yet it was past time for Americans to mature politically, past time for moral consciousness to embrace the social as well as the domestic sphere, past time for women and homosexuals to receive full recognition of their humanity and place in the world. However, we might evaluate the morality of each element separately; the more important point is that they all occurred simultaneously over a very short period of time. And in combination, they profoundly altered American culture.

Now the pertinence of all this to my theme of sex and American Catholics is twofold. First, this cultural upheaval was happening at the very moment when American Catholics finally became fully American. Second, it coincided with the greatest cultural upheaval within the Catholic Church since the sixteenth century, generated and symbolized by the Second Vatican Council (1963–1965).

INCONSISTENCY AND CONFUSION

John F. Kennedy's election as president signaled American Catholicism's turn from an immigrant and second-class status to full participation in American culture. It may be difficult now to appreciate how, in the early 1960s, the American church was prosperous, was growing together with the suburbs, was becoming American in its hierarchy, was increasingly assertive intellectually, and was attracting so many young men and women to religious vocations that huge new seminaries and convents were being built across the country to accommodate them all. Few noticed that American Catholics were also entering more fully into the cultural maelstrom that was the 1960s.

As much as the Kennedy presidency, the Council seemed to symbolize the coming of age of American Catholicism. The American Jesuit theologian, John Courtney Murray, spearheaded the passage of the Council's *Decree on Religious Freedom*. Imagine: the church of the Inquisition recognizing the supremacy of the individual conscience before God! The Council appeared to be reforming the church in the direction of distinctively American values. It advocated strong lay leadership, consultation, and decentralized decision-making by national organizations of bishops.

The Council notably did not address the sexual revolution. It said nothing about the role of women. It did not acknowledge homosexuals. It emphatically changed nothing in the rule of priestly celibacy. But it raised expectations, especially concerning the issue that was existentially most pressing for married Catholics, artificial birth control. Among these expectations was that the promised decision on this difficult issue would be reached on the basis of the values inculcated by the Council itself. Change was possible, because the authority structure of the church was changing.

By the late 1960s, while awaiting a decision that many thought could reasonably go only toward approval of birth control, American Catholics found themselves caught up in a cultural revolution with little moral guidance. The Council had explicitly called for the church to engage modernity. But in moral matters, the Council offered little to help Americans through an overwhelming flood of change.

Catholics did not suddenly become sexual adventurers. But they were—many of them—sexually confused in a way they had not been before. Some priests and nuns went through a delayed adolescence of sexual experimentation. Some lay Catholics—confused by the news that eating meat on Friday no longer assured a place in hell—understandably began to reassess other items on the code of forbidden behaviors. Catholics were not prepared to sort through issues that few people then were in a position to assess accurately.

In the 1960s, moreover, the most respected Catholic moral theologians had begun to shift from a language of rules and law, to a language of relationship and discernment, especially in sexual matters. They spoke of sex in marriage as serving relational values as well as procreation. At the same time, the most powerful new theological movement within the church, liberation theology, emphasized that Scripture is more concerned with social oppression through economic and political systems than with how people arrange themselves sexually.

These were not, however, the only voices Catholics heard. The Vatican Council, after all, was a disputed territory, especially for those who had fought its liberalizing tendencies. Among them were powerful bishops and moral theologians who vigorously opposed the new vision of morality, and continued to emphasize a rule-based sexual ethics.

In hindsight, it is scarcely surprising that American Catholics—now themselves more than ever American in their individualism and consumerism—began to choose teachers and tenets for themselves. Small wonder, also, that priests in the pulpit and in the confessional exhibited a considerable variety of opinions on issues like birth control. It was at this moment that American Catholicism began to become, in effect, the largest mainline Protestant denomination in the country, precisely in its loss of a single vision and a single voice. Within the span of a decade, American Catholicism went from a clear and confident sense of sexual morality to a state of confusion and loss of self-confidence. Everything seemed to hinge on Paul VI's clarification on the matter of birth control. Married Catholics, in particular, had high expectations, for the media had already made widely known that the process of consultation had pointed to the need to change the rules on contraception.

INCOHERENCE AND CORRUPTION

At the beginning of the twenty-first century, American Catholics are not simply confused and conflicted concerning sexual morality. They are increasingly suspicious of, and hostile towards, a hierarchy that appears, in the harsh light of publicity, to be no longer credible because of incoherence and even corruption.

The decisive moment was Pope Paul VI's 1968 publication of the encyclical *Humanae vitae*. Not only did the papal letter reaffirm the prohibition of all forms of artificial birth control on the basis of patently poor logic. It was above all an act of papal authoritarianism in the face of a process of discernment that the Pope himself had initiated. Contrary to the Pope's expectations, the encyclical's equation of artificial birth control and abortion did not serve to strengthen the moral argument against birth control, but served instead to weaken the church's prophetic stand against abortion. The subsequent strenuous efforts by John Paul II to shore up *Humanae vitae* through a "theology of the body" have only sharpened the perception that, lacking a convincing theological basis, the magisterium's intractability on this point is really about keeping women in their place and maintaining the aura of papal authority.

The birth control issue finally initiated many American Catholics into the hermeneutics of suspicion, enabling them, at last, to see and name many other forms of inconsistency and corruption that they had formerly allowed to pass in the name of loyalty and obedience.

The church's way of dealing with divorce and remarriage, for example, lacks any moral coherence. The prohibition of divorce is not really absolute. Everyone knows that some Catholics are allowed to divorce and remarry with the approval of the church, so long as they (or their ecclesiastical lawyer) can make a case for annulment even after years of cohabitation, and if they are rich or prominent enough to demand such special attention. The poor and the legally unrepresented, in contrast, can find themselves in disastrous or abusive marriages without hope of divorce and remarriage in the church. The moral incoherence is revealed particularly by the exception. If a first marriage was not really "in the church," then it can be dissolved without consequence. People with serial non-sacramental marriages in the past are free to marry in the church and enjoy the benefits of full communion. Only if a sacramental marriage fails are faithful Catholics unable to seek another sanctified partnership.

Equally inconsistent and incoherent is the fiction of a totally celibate priesthood. I leave aside the anecdotal evidence that reminds us that theoretical celibacy is not always translated into actual chastity. What challenges logic is Rome's insistence on a male celibate clergy in the face of the contrary evidence from Scripture and tradition and the experience of Protestant and Orthodox communions; and Rome accepts into the Roman priesthood men who are married, but who have converted from Anglicanism. The Roman Church's willingness to lose an ordained priesthood altogether—and with it the sacramental heart of Catholicism—rather than ordain married men or (horrors) women may appear noble to some, but to more and more American Catholics, it appears as suicidal self-delusion. The willingness to ordain older men who are widowers to the priesthood, and married men to the diaconate, appear as desperate avoidance mechanisms, an expression of fear and loathing toward normal sexual behavior and above all toward women's bodies.

It is now no longer even permissible for theologians under the recently crafted *mandatum* to speak in favor of women's ordination, despite the fact that every theological argument advanced for an all-male clergy is laughable (at best) and blasphemous (at worst). No wonder the suspicion grows—and has been given explicit voice by at least one brave moral theologian—that the obsessive protection of this male privilege owes something to its capacity to provide cover for homosexual men using their priesthood (and perhaps their episcopacy) as an extremely effective closet. I mean nothing slanderous by making this statement. Indeed, I think an argument can be made for homosexual as well as heterosexual priests. My point, rather, is that if homosexuality among its clergy were to be honestly faced by the hierarchy, then other things would need honestly to be addressed as well.

The magisterium might then need to take account of the archbishops who have had long-term affairs with female staff members, or short-term affairs with male friends, or bishops who decide they want to get married and stay bishops, or African priests who carry out a campaign of rape against African nuns.

The magisterium might need to ask whether the cumulative effect of such behaviors might indicate something more than human weakness; might, in fact, point to a deeply distorted understanding of sexuality; might, in fact, indict an ecclesiastical practice that virtually guarantees a sexually immature clergy, or at the very least, one that encourages a caste mentality that is removed from and insensitive to the cares and concerns of those who are married and are raising children.

Publicly, most scandalous to Catholic laity, and deeply injurious to their already diminished sense of confidence in the hierarchy's moral guidance in matters of sexuality, is the decades-long practice of enabling and covering up crimes of child abuse by pedophile priests, who continued to be moved from one parish to another to perpetuate their infantile and predatory sexual practices at the expense of innocent children. The sheer numbers of priests involved and the numbers of their victims is shocking enough, but even more disgusting are the self-serving gestures of a hierarchy that has had to pay possibly hundreds of millions of dollars in lawsuits (presumably drawn from the collection plate) and has, to this day, only reluctantly supported laws to forestall such crimes against the helpless.

Finally, the all-male magisterium has not grasped that its profound, deliberate, and systemic sexism compromises the capacity of the church to speak prophetically. Everyone knows that most Catholic parishes in this country would have to close up tomorrow if it weren't for women. I don't mean this in the sense that women have always been more loyal and religious than men, attending Mass while their husbands waited outside smoking cigarettes. I mean this in the very specific sense that women carry out most of the work of ministry in many, if not most parishes in this country. But the same abuse of power, by which the male clergy exploited but never fully honored the ministerial labors of religious women in parishes, hospitals, and schools, is now being perpetuated in the exploitation of single and married women in local parishes. And this exploitation takes place even while such women are denied ordination with the argument that only males can really represent Christ!

Not all parishioners in the United States have yet awakened to this pattern of sexism. They worry over the fact that their parish now has one priest when it formerly had three. But they know they are better off than the parishes that can celebrate the Eucharist only when a priest visits. They are so pleased to see (and to be) women acolytes and lectors and Eucharistic ministers and catechists that they do not yet appreciate how such accommodation simply continues with slight variations the traditional exploitation of women by male leadership.

But an increasing number of American Catholic women do see the pattern, and they are angry. They correctly see that the rejection of women lies at the heart of a great deal of the church's twisted and confusing sexual practice. And while many of them fervently support the church's opposition to abortion, even they find it increasingly difficult, in the shadow of this pattern, to respond cogently to the non-Catholic feminists' charge that the church's objection to abortion is only the most radical form of its desire for women above all to be controlled. And if Catholic women finally get angry enough to walk out, then the game is close to over.

My argument has been that although the words have stayed the same, the actual content of Catholic sexual morality in America has not. The combination of cultural upheaval, inconsistent teaching and practice, and the corruption and abuse of authority, has led to the present situation. If my analysis is even partially correct, the improvement of this situation will demand both a more coherent and clearly expressed sexual morality, and a reform of the Catholic Church's authority structure. Unless the leaders of the church begin a serious examination of conscience with regard to their practice and a serious process of discernment with regard to their teaching, little better can be expected. And unless that process of discernment involves women and those who are married, then neither the teaching on sex and marriage nor the integrity and credibility of the clergy can hope for much improvement. At a time when a seriously disordered world most needs a prophetic word concerning humans as sexual creatures before God, the church's ability to speak and embody that prophetic word will be hopelessly compromised.

CONNECTING SEXUALITY, MARRIAGE, FAMILY, AND CHILDREN: A RESPONSE

Barbara Dafoe Whitehead

One of the things that I've learned over the years is that our ideas and attitudes about sex are not only shaped by religious teachings, but also by our personal and generational experience. I like the way that Luke Johnson put his autobiographical cards on the table, and told us something about his own life experience and "where he's coming from," as we used to say in the 1960s, before he put on his professional hat as a theologian and scholar to take a critical look at the church's teachings on sexuality. In fact, all the papers for this symposium interweave personal experience and professional perspectives in a similar way.

In my brief response to Luke Johnson's paper, I want to attempt the same approach. First, I want to offer some observations based on my personal experience as a Catholic—and a very new one, at that. And then I will turn to a perspective that has been shaped by my professional engagement in the decade-long public square debate about sex, marriage, and family.

Luke Johnson tells a story that sees Catholic teachings as deeply problematic, incoherent and corrupt. I hope to tell a different story from a decidedly different vantage point.

On the personal side of things, I bring a perspective to this topic that is probably unique in this room: it is the perspective of a convert, who has become a Catholic much closer to the grave than to the cradle.

I spent most of my adult life as a fallen-away Congregationalist. But I grew up in a town with a large Catholic population, and my first job at age sixteen was as a nurse's aide at St. Elizabeth's Hospital in Appleton, Wisconsin. I stood in the same awe of the nuns as any Catholic schoolgirl, and my father, who was a doctor at the hospital, deeply respected the dedication and expertise of the sisters who ran the hospital. Then in high school, I met a smart Catholic boy from Chicago, eventually dated him, and have been married to him for thirty-four years. A couple of years ago, I started going to Mass with my husband and son, and this Easter, at the age of fifty-six, I was received into the church. I tell you all of this so that you will understand that I am not equipped to comment on church teachings on sexuality with the kind of deep knowledge and long life experience that Luke Johnson can bring to bear on the subject.

Nevertheless, the experience of becoming a Catholic at such an advanced stage of life has brought some interesting discoveries and illuminations. One such discovery has to do with how others view the church teachings on sexuality. It's one thing to encounter the church's teachings respectfully as an outsider, as I have done for most of my life, and another thing altogether to become a Catholic and to be held responsible by non-Catholics for defending, or at least explaining, these teachings.

I have also been shaped by my time and place. I live in Amherst, Massachusetts, home to three colleges—Amherst College, Hampshire College, the University of Massachusetts, and a neighbor to Smith and Mt. Holyoke.

Like most college towns, Amherst is suffused with what you might call the spirit of the faculty club. It's secular, liberal, feminist, and pro-choice. So when I told some close friends, great believers in tolerance and a respect for diversity, that I was going to become Catholic, their response was shock and horror. How could someone they thought was intelligent get involved in a religion that's so sexist, repressive, and unenlightened on matters of sexuality? After all, it's one thing to be born into the faith and stick with it, but why would anyone want to choose it?

No one said to me, you know, I admire the social teachings of the church, or I agree with the church's work to help the poor, and its stand against the death penalty, and its leadership on Third World debt relief. None of that came to the surface. Instead, the view was, why does the Catholic Church cover up these horrific acts of pedophilia by priests, and what about trafficking in annulments? Their portrait of the Catholic Church was based almost entirely on what people understood as the church's teachings on sexuality, and even more so on their revulsion at sexual crimes committed by priests.

At the time, I tried to make the best defense I could. I said of course I wasn't going to defend pedophilia or rape, by priests or anyone else. I agreed that the commerce in annulments was troubling. As for the church teachings on birth control, I admitted that I, too, had difficulty with the ban on artificial birth control for married couples. But then, I added, you really couldn't reduce the Catholic Church to its teachings on sexuality, and you certainly couldn't confuse the church's teachings on sexuality with the terrible abuses and crimes committed in violation of its teachings.

Still, I felt vulnerable and lame in this defense, because my friends' portrait of the church—and the faculty club view it represents—is not just blind prejudice. It is based on some of the specific crimes and corruptions that Luke Johnson cites. It has to be taken seriously. It has standing in the public square; it shapes both public and media opinion.

Indeed, one of the implications of Johnson's paper is that such crimes and abuses undermine the church's influence and obscure the positive impact of its teachings in the public square. Yet, at the same time, I think that his portrait is too harsh and one-sided. He leaves out some of the positive contributions of the church to the public debate on sex, marriage and family, at least as I have experienced it.

For more than a decade, I've been involved in a public square debate on the problems of unwed teenage pregnancy, divorce, family structure change, and child well-being. Most of these initiatives have been bipartisan, and one effort—The National Campaign to Prevent Teen Pregnancy—is led by a former official in the Clinton White House, Bill Galston, and by economist Isabel Sawhill of the Urban Institute.

In the corner of the public square where family and child well-being are the focus of concern, there is a growing body of empirical evidence that supports Catholic teachings on sex, marriage, and the family.

Let me say a bit more about the National Campaign. Its goal has been to forge a broad coalition across a spectrum of opinion in order to prevent unwed teen pregnancy without increasing abortion. As a member of the Campaign's Task Force on Religion and Public Values, I can say that this group does not consider Catholic teachings on sexuality as bankrupt or obsolete. Indeed, social science evidence suggests that Catholic teenaged girls are more likely to delay their sexual debut than girls who from other denominations or girls who have no religious affiliation. (Girls from fundamentalist Protestant backgrounds are also more likely to avoid having sex.)

I've also discovered that many of the professionals who work in the area of teen pregnancy prevention see sexual abstinence as a pro-feminist approach, a pro-girl approach that protects young girls against the sexually libertine adolescent peer and media culture.

In the debate on the relationship between family structure and child well-being, Catholic teachings have found support in a growing body of empirical evidence as well, though that has not been the intention of the social scientists. Catholic teaching connects sexuality to marriage, the family, and children. In my opinion, this is one of its great strengths. When you talk about human sexuality, you have to consider the whole spectrum of family life, and that obviously includes more than just adult sexuality. It also includes marriage and children. However, for several decades, opinion among the experts ran contrary to the Catholic perspective. Social scientists minimized the impact of high divorce rates, absent fathers and rising numbers of single-parent households on children's well-being. Their focus was much more on the adults, and adult sexual freedoms and satisfactions, than on the children.

However, there has been a notable shift in expert opinion on these issues in recent times.

To give you an appreciation for how expert opinion has shifted over this period of time, a recently published article states the following: "From a child's point of view, according to a growing body of social research, the most supportive household is one with two biological parents in a low-conflict marriage." Now where does that statement come from? The answer is not the Catholic bishops or Bill Bennett, but the *New York Times* ("Two Parent Families Rise after Change in Welfare Laws," August 12, 2001). Indeed, the *Times* goes on to state that a powerful consensus has emerged among scholars and policymakers that the rise in single-parent families with its associated problems is one of the most important indicators of child pathology.

So in the secular public debate, there is an effort to try to bring the discussion about adult sexuality and what's beneficial for adults into some kind of balance with what's best for children.

Finally, there is a growing movement in the civil society to strengthen marriage. Here the Catholic Church has a body of experience in marriage preparation and enrichment that serves as an inspiration for other religious groups and faith-based efforts. The generation of young adults who are crossing the threshold into marriage and family life do not see the world through the same spectacles as the baby boom generation. They aren't nearly as worried about their sexual freedoms or even about gender equity. They take these things for granted. What worries them is how to avoid divorce and family disintegration. The National Marriage Project at Rutgers University commissioned a Gallup survey of twenty-something young adults on sex, marriage, family formation, single parenthood and so on, and the most salient issue for these young adults was how to have a marriage that lasts. When I interview young adults or talk to them in focus groups, many say that their prime goal in life is to recover from the emotional damages caused by parental divorce.

So I'd like to conclude my remarks with this observation: The public square is a big place. In it, Luke Johnson's story occupies a highly visible place. I've tried to tell a story about another corner of the public square where Catholic teachings have not lost their prophetic influence.

THE COMPLEXITIES AND AMBIGUITIES OF THE "PROPHETIC DIMENSION": A RESPONSE

Susan A. Ross

First, of all, let me thank Luke Timothy Johnson for his provocative paper on Roman Catholic sexual teaching in America. As I read the paper, I found myself nodding in agreement with many of his observations. The countercultural dimension of the church's teachings, not only in sexual matters, but in its teachings on social justice, should—and does—give us pause. My students are sometimes surprised that I, a feminist and former director of a women's studies program, urge (and often require) them to read church documents on sexuality. Most often they have decided in advance that the church has nothing to teach them, that its understanding of sexuality is both uninformed and irrelevant. Professor Johnson's paper suggests that the church's position has been compromised by a number of factors over the last forty years or so. I agree with this, but I would also want to argue that the kind of uncompromising approach that he so admires as prophetic has itself something to do with the problems the church faces. I would label this a striking lack of tolerance of any ambiguity, particularly when it comes to sexuality. And I find this as well in Professor Johnson's setting up the picture as one of polar opposites: the church's uncompromising stance, and the culture of hedonism and personal fulfillment that we see now. I would like to suggest that the picture is somewhat more complex and, yes, even more ambiguous, than this stark one of blacks and whites.

Let me outline a few places where I see this lack of sensitivity to the complexities and ambiguities of life, particularly when it comes to sexuality. First, the church's teaching on divorce and remarriage: This is a system in which there is no ambiguity whatsoever. I recall a famous article by the noted moral theologian John C. Ford, who wrote that even in a completely loveless marriage, where there is no affection, there is still a sacramental marriage because the conditions were met (for consent and consummation). My own parents, now dead, were divorced when I was in college. A few years later, my mother remarried (my father was still living at the time) and she was advised by her pastor to apply for an annulment, so she could receive the sacraments. My parents had been married for twenty-six years. She was horrified at the idea that her children would be then illegitimate, and I assured her that this would not be the case. But she was still not convinced by the reasoning. How could she say in good conscience that there really was no marriage, when indeed there was? It had been good, but then things had not gone well, and over the years, the marriage died. But in the church's teaching there is no room, at least theologically, for such recognition. And I am convinced that some of the scandal over church teaching on annulments (which Johnson mentions) is because of the criterion that an annulment means that there was no marriage—ever. I am well aware that there are "pastoral" solutions to this issue, but the utter lack of recognition on the part of theology to the ambiguities of marital life and death is also what causes scandal—not just the behavior of some of the church authorities or rich people who can pay for annulments.

Another example: the requirement for celibacy for religious and clergy. Here again, the complete bifurcation of sexual activity and ministry means than there can be no reconciliation of the two (except when married Episcopal priests or Lutheran pastors, often unhappy with the ordination of women, want to be ordained Catholic priests). As someone married to a resigned and laicized priest, I can speak of the enormous loss of gifts that the church could well use. And I would also want to point out the punitive nature of the church's position on resigned priests: a resigned priest is forbidden to do anything related to ministry, supposedly for fear of scandalizing the faithful. In the rules, the resigned priest is even advised to move away from where he formerly lived, again so as not to cause scandal. This makes me wonder where the real scandal is.

Third, the limiting of licit sexual activity to marriage, Professor Johnson argues, means that sexuality is covenantal and mutually responsible, as opposed to the drive for pleasure and individual fulfillment that our culture glorifies. But here again, I would argue (and I think Johnson would agree with at least some of what I have to say) that the church's lack of a theology of sexuality that includes pleasure (not hedonism) and a recognition of women's sexuality, not only of men's, contributes to this bifurcation. A friend and colleague of mine at Northwestern has written about how the church's theology of sexuality in marriage is in fact so unrealistic that if she had actually applied it to her own marriage, it would have resulted in disaster. What I mean is that the understanding of sexuality that is characteristic of the Vatican assumes, basically, that each and every act of sexual intercourse should be on the level of the Fourth of July and the millennium combined, as well as being open to children, no matter what the circumstances! Anyone with an active sex life knows that it too has its ups and downs, and that is a part of what living in sexual intimacy with another person is all about.

Finally, the neuralgic issue of abortion. Yes, the church has advocated for the protection of these powerless and innocent ones. But when the church proclaims a theology of womanhood that identifies all women as mothers, whether physical or spiritual, that allows for moral ambiguity in decision making that leads to death, as does the church's teaching on just war, but does not see any ambiguity at all in women's decisions over their future—since there is no ambiguity: all women are mothers!—and when the church offers few resources for women at crisis points in their lives, it is no surprise to me that it lacks credibility in its teaching. Here again, I would say that the church's failure to see any moral ambiguity whatsoever in a woman's decision whether or not to continue a pregnancy is not only theologically but pastorally problematic.

When it comes to sexuality, the church's default mode has been to resort to legalism. So while I would agree that there is a prophetic dimension to this situation, it is a picture in black and white, almost in silhouette, and it does not allow for complexity here, where it does in other areas. I would argue that the church's prophetic stance when it comes to social justice does have greater credibility, precisely because it is informed by those most affected by these decisions, and it is cognizant of the many complexities involved. A friend of mine who lives in another archdiocese reported a conversation he had with his bishop shortly before the implementation of the requirement for a *mandatum*. My friend was telling the bishop about how he approaches issues like capital punishment in his courses on ethics, and how he tries to place these issues in their historical and social context. The bishop responded to him: "When it comes to life issues, there is no context." I was told by a member of the church's hierarchy that my own approach to theology was really not theological, to my great surprise; what I taught, I was told, was in reality the history of ideas! So what are we to say when we are told that context and history are meaningless, when it comes to the church's theology? Why is it that life issues have no context and why is it that theology and the history of ideas are seen as two entirely separate endeavors?

Now when it comes to how the church is perceived publicly, while it is difficult to convey a sense of ambiguity in theology, how much more so when we come to the media! I don't mean to put the blame on anyone here, but merely to observe that having a tolerance and an appreciation for ambiguity takes time, and a willingness to think in something more than sound bytes. I know from my own twenty-one years of teaching experience how difficult it is to get students to think any other way than in sound bytes. What I am suggesting is that this tradition's failure to reach the present generation is due not just to the revolutions that Professor Johnson has described, but also because of the church's and the faithfuls' lack of willingness to think long and hard, and with patience, about these things.

Let me respond to some of the diagnoses that Johnson has offered. The issue of postwar prosperity raises some profound questions about material reality and the way in which the church has failed to do a good job of communicating its very good ideas, due yet again to its own dichotomizing tendencies. The church tells us that women should be equals in the economic sphere, but says that women should not "act like men" and should somehow preserve their sacred femininity. The present pope has spoken out in the strongest ways on the downside of our materialist culture, but with very little understanding of the practical dynamics of human relationships.

When it comes to the sexual revolution, I would connect this (as does Professor Johnson) with prosperity and technology, as well as with his fifth issue: the women's movement. One of the issues that I encounter with my students is their sense (and I speak of women as well as men) of sex as a recreational right. In large part, because the church's teaching has lacked credibility, students simply do not see the church as having anything meaningful to say to them. When it comes to models of commitment and a theology of marriage that takes commitment seriously, this has not been well provided by the tradition either. Karl Barth, the great Protestant Swiss theologian of the last century, commented once that the Roman Catholic theology of marriage began and ended on the wedding night. Pre-Cana conferences are wonderful contributions, but they also go against cultural trends. One of my graduate students is a native of Nigeria, and he laughingly commented to me recently that he could not really tell the difference between African polygamy and the serial monogamy that seems to be the norm in American culture. I find the comments on advertising and our late capitalist situation very astute; many of us wonder now what is to become of our system. The events of September 11 gave us pause to ask, as so many headlines have put it: "Why do they hate us?" Does it have something to do with the cavalier way that some of us regard our relationships?

Let me say something in defense of the women's movement here and quibble a bit with Professor Johnson's characterization of the movement as having "made women full partners of men in seeking sexual adventure separated from commitment." There is no question that this is the case for many women today, including some of my students. And there is no question that the issue of abortion as the right to kill a fetus can be grossly and simply understood as "power over one's body." But part of what makes me uneasy with the church's wholesale condemnation of abortion is its failure to take women's experiences seriously into account in the doing of theology. Recall Archbishop Rembert Weakland's experience of having an honorary degree withdrawn, after protests were made to Rome that he actually wanted to listen to women on the issue of abortion. Similarly Bishop Joseph Imesch of Joliet, on the committee for the women's pastoral in the late 1980s and early 1990s, was admonished by Rome that he as a bishop was there to teach, not to learn. A very good case can be made (and I will make it here if anyone wants to hear it) that the theology of sexuality that is our inheritance from Augustine is based on an almost entirely male experience of sexuality. It's on this basis that any form of "artificial" birth control is prohibited; but from the experiences of women, this does not make the same kind of sense. Women's seeking after sexual pleasure can well be demonized as women being just as reckless and selfish as men can be. But when has women's sexual pleasure even been given any attention in theology? Not until very recently, and by women theologians who are by definition out of the decision-making loop.

The issue of women and abortion is a complex one, and so I want to add my plea for its complexity and ambiguity here as well. Theologians who are pro-choice are not pro-abortion, but argue that women need to be seen as competent moral agents, and that these decisions are not simple ones. Now I know that Sidney Callahan has done a wonderful job of responding to the feminist pro-choice position, and I want you to know that I require my students to read both sides of the issue. But the disproportionality given to this issue touches women's personal lives, and is not reflected in other dimensions of the church's teachings. Let me be more specific. Asking women to sacrifice nine months or twenty years of their lives to bear and raise a child that they did not want or plan for is to ask women to be self-sacrificing. Sidney Callahan points this out very well in her article on feminism and the pro-life agenda. I suggest to you that this concern for self-sacrifice has almost no other counterparts in our tradition that touch people at the same personal level. Where else are we asked to make these kinds of sacrifices? I am not arguing that we ought not to make them, but there is little or no support for this in the church's praxis. Yes, there are places that will support women, but they are the exception.

I would argue that this issue is a tragic one that includes the kind of extreme individuality that Johnson so rightly criticizes, but there is also a moral imbalance here. It is also worth saying that many women do not have full control over their sexuality, and current birth control teaching makes this even worse. Women are not seen as fully competent moral agents, but as objects, as mothers. True, many women do have a lot of control over their sexuality, and many women are engrossed in self-serving lives. But I would argue with the assertion that the focus on gender automatically connotes narrow self-interest.

If as much energy were spent on a consistent ethic that went across so-cial and personal issues, then I think the church would have more credibil-ity. But because issues of sexuality are the place where the church speaks un-ambiguously and (to quote a bishop) "without context," many people see that the church is insensitive to their own personal lives. We need, on the part of the church's public voices, both more sensitivity to the complexity of moral decision making and a clearer and more consistent voice.

So what are the consequences for public debate? First, I see a real sense of social responsibility in many of my students—if the "best-kept secret" is being let out, I can see some positive consequences. Students are giving years to volunteer services, living simply and in community, and, I think, making a difference.

Second, I'm not as concerned as some are about Roman Catholics looking "different" from Protestants and no longer being so distinctively a separate group. I think too much energy is expended on what makes us "Catholic" rather than on what makes us moral. Still, even though I have spent years on and off being a long-time guest in Lutheran and Episcopalian churches, I am still Catholic in that sense which is hard to describe, but which I know when I see it.

Third, I am concerned about the women students I teach who are in-creasingly dissatisfied with the church's position on women. It's only through a deep appreciation for ambiguity that I can stay, and if the leadership of the church does not recognize and acknowledge these difficulties honestly, I fear that our young women will vote with their feet. In fact, many already have.

One of the many things that I find attractive about my Catholic tradi-tion is its willingness to take life as we get it, in all its messiness and ambi-guity. While I admire the Protestant tradition's dialectical stress on the en-counter of each of us with the Word, I also want (as Peter Steinfels has put it) to "smell some smoke." I want to smell it and dwell with it and appreci-ate its many dimensions.

Our tradition does this well in many ways, but not nearly enough with sex and especially not nearly enough with women's experiences of sexual-ity. I don't think this means that we sell the farm if we open the door a crack (pardon my mixed metaphors!) to a more thoughtful and considered ap-proach to sexuality.

Can we do this? Can this be communicated, by the church and by the media, with sensitivity and complexity? If we have to resort to simplistic sound bytes, we won't progress. The church will speak into the wind and I fear that it will not be heard.

THE PRO-LIFE MESSAGE AND CATHOLIC SOCIAL TEACHING: PROBLEMS OF RECEPTION

Richard M. Doerflinger

THE IDEAL

In the logic of the church's teaching, the inviolability of human life should be a linchpin of Catholic social witness: "The first right of the human person is his life. He has other goods and some are more precious, but this one is fundamental—the condition of all the others. Hence it must be protected above all others. ("Declaration on Abortion" [1974], para. 11).

This is not a matter of turf battles or one-upmanship but of logical priority: To enjoy any rights one must first be allowed to exist; anyone who can take away your life has the power to take away all other rights along with it; and attempts to deny any class of human beings their right to life—based, for example, on age or level of development or physical and mental abilities—undermine the human rights of all, by treating our inherent rights as mere privileges, enjoyed just so long as we continue to possess the important characteristics.

Moreover, within the sphere of life issues, negative norms ("Thou shalt not kill") are in a sense more basic or more absolute than positive norms ("Thou shalt feed the poor"). That is because negative norms establish a basic floor for human responsibility that must never be allowed to crumble—first of all, we can at least do no harm. The Gospel's positive injunctions to feed the hungry, clothe the naked, and so on, are also absolute in their own way—their call upon us never ceases—but there is no ceiling to this positive call, no point at which we could say we have fulfilled the norm and can move on to other things. (*Veritatis splendor* [1993], para. 52).

In short, the pro-life message against killing and the pro-justice call to serve people's needs and enhance the quality of their life are very much in need of each other. Without a firm foundation in the radical value of each

49

and every human life, efforts for justice are blind; without compassionate service to help those struggling to lead lives of dignity, the defense of life will be empty.

THE AMERICAN REALITY

This is not the way these issues are seen in most of American society. They are subjected to cultural and political distortions that have become endemic even among Catholics in the United States. Culturally, abortion is perceived by many on both sides of the issue as part and parcel of a culture war over sexuality and the role of women. Conservative Protestants, for example, link abortion with homosexuality and easy divorce as threats to the family. Secular feminist groups see abortion as integrally linked to the advancement of women and their liberation from traditional roles. In *Abortion and the Politics of Motherhood*, Kristin Luker documented how abortion has become a battleground for culture wars over sexuality and the traditional family.

This view does have some validity. In Catholic teaching, defending the integrity of the family is a vitally important way to defend human rights: The unconditional love of husband and wife for each other and their children is the first and most important training those children receive in having unconditional respect for all human persons. And distorted views of sexuality and personal freedom have indeed led to a demand for abortion. In its 1992 *Casey* decision the Supreme Court announced in effect that the reason *Roe v. Wade* cannot be reversed is that the availability of abortion has now been taken for granted by so many people in planning their careers and sexual lifestyles.

However, abortion is not only a sex issue, and placing it solely in that compartment is a barrier to giving it its proper place in the social justice agenda. Within that agenda it needs to be seen as maintaining the equal dignity and freedom of all members of the human family, male and female, by defending their lives—not as restricting people's personal choices.

The relegation of abortion to the supposedly private arena of choices about sexuality was even exacerbated for Catholics by disputes over the 1968 encyclical *Humanae vitae*. The teaching on birth control was not well argued; it confounded expectations of change that many had done their best to promote, and it seemed to impose great burdens on married couples struggling to live as Catholics in an increasingly secularized society. The merits of the teaching itself were all but forgotten in the ensuing battle over church authority. When the social and political debate on abortion followed almost immediately in the United States, many Catholics were prevented from assessing that teaching on its merits as well—there was a temptation to dismiss it as another rigid pronouncement by church authorities that would prevent them from living personally liberated lifestyles, as well as from fitting in with the "progressive" forces in their own society. That image was monumentally unfair: The church's efforts on abortion were (and are) driven in no small part by the dedication and persistence of the laity, who have often found themselves prodding priests and bishops to give this matter more attention. But the image persists for many nonetheless. It remains true even for many Catholics that a church leader is one of the less credible spokespersons on the abortion issue. They are more likely to see a physician or nurse, or a woman who has experienced abortion, as a credible spokesperson.

As for the role of abortion in women's liberation, it is remarkable that, after thirty years of propaganda claiming the benefits of abortion for women, so few women have bought this claim. Most opinion polls on abortion show somewhat higher pro-life support among women than men. In the *Los Angeles Times* poll of June 2000, for example, 60 percent of women (as opposed to only 45 percent of men) said that life begins at conception, 61 percent of women (as opposed to 52 percent of men) agreed with the statement that abortion is murder, and 72 percent of women (as opposed to 58 percent of men) said that abortion should not be legal in the second trimester of pregnancy. Fifteen percent of women (as opposed to only 8 percent of men) said they had tried to convince someone not to have an abortion; and 68 percent of women said they would not consider an abortion in the event of an unplanned pregnancy (while somewhat fewer men, 63 percent, said they would not consider it as an option in the event of their partner's unplanned pregnancy.) At the same time, 48 percent of women (as opposed to only 33 percent of men) agreed with the statement: "If men had babies, it would be a lot easier to get an abortion."

The way the abortion issue has been envisioned and compartmentalized helps to ensure that there are very different problems of reception for the teaching on protecting unborn life and the teaching on other aspects of social justice. One of the most serious problems in communicating the church's social teaching to Catholics is showing their personal relevance. To many middle-class Catholics (and others), the problems of the homeless or of families without health insurance or of starving African children simply seem far away and all too easy to ignore. The teaching on abortion sometimes runs into the opposite problem—it is seen as being all too relevant to people's personal lives, in a way that restricts choices that they may want available (or that their loved ones may want, or may already have made). In a state like Oregon, which has legalized physician-assisted suicide, the same may soon be true of the teaching on euthanasia.

The Supreme Court's 1973 decision to legalize abortion, and the way this has been positioned as part of a broader agenda for civil liberties, has created a similar political distortion. The Democratic Party's leadership has seized on legalized abortion as an aspect of personal liberty; Catholics opposed to abortion were driven into the waiting arms of the Republican Party, where abortion was combined with other "social conservative" issues. While there is some validity in seeing the pro-life stance as one that seeks to conserve traditional moral values, one could also envision it as a progressive demand for always expanding the circle of those members of the human family whose fate concerns us—an insistence that the weakest and most vulnerable members of the species must not be left behind in our drive for individual or social progress. But it is not easy to articulate and build upon that progressive vision of the pro-life message if most secular progressives choose to view the unborn as inconvenient obstacles to the advancement of rights for others.

This partisan imprisonment of the abortion issue has not only reduced the appeal of the message to those who support other key goals of the Democratic Party. It has also fueled an influx of churchgoers generally, including churchgoing Catholics, into the Republican Party. Once there, Catholics are likely to be persuaded that other Republican positions not so fully in accord with Catholic social teaching are plausible as well. Meanwhile, those who remain in the Democratic Party have a choice of becoming dissidents from their church or from their party on the fundamental issue of life.

THE CONSISTENT ETHIC OF LIFE

The "consistent ethic" or "seamless garment" theme articulated by Cardinal Joseph Bernardin in the 1980s may be seen as a way to counter these distortions and give the inviolability of human life its proper place within a consistent social teaching framework. The value of each human life was to be seen as a principle for individual and social ethics that cut across the usual political lines and grounded a consistent agenda for defending and enhancing life. This theme helped many Catholics to maintain their religious identity and their sense of self-respect. The church's witness on life, peace, and justice was not beholden to either secular political party; more positively, it was a distinctive way of relating issues that had a specifically theological source in the church's understanding of the dignity of each and every human person.

Many forget, or never knew, that when Archbishop Bernardin of Cincinnati first used the phrase "seamless garment" in this context in 1976, it was in a pro-life homily designed to show the fundamental importance of the teaching on abortion and euthanasia: "Life before and after birth," he said, "is like a seamless garment. . . . If we become insensitive to the beginning of life and condone abortion or if we become careless about the end of life and justify euthanasia, we have no reason to believe that there will be much respect for life in between" (J. Shea, "Bernardin: Church Supports Life," *Mirror* [Diocesan newspaper of Des Moines], Feb. 5, 1976).

Efforts in the 1980s to link the "life" and "justice" teachings through this rubric ran into difficulties, however. The consistent ethic approach seemed to many to mix a variety of distinct issues into a homogeneous mass, where the value of life could be promoted in any number of ways but without important distinctions or the ability to set priorities. (This potential for misunderstanding soon led Cardinal Bernardin himself to stop using the phrase "seamless garment," though it remained the most memorable way of summing up the theme for many others.) Pro-life activists felt they were being called narrow "single issue" people, called to divide their time among a wide array of other issues to retain their credibility. Pro-choice politicians seized on the theme to insist that, after all, they supported 90 percent of the "seamless garment" and should not be faulted for the minor lapse of supporting destruction of unborn life.

Cardinal Bernardin tried to counter these distortions. But the consistency theme could not itself do all the work necessary to restore balance to this approach. Consistency is one important value; but by itself it does not draw distinctions or set priorities.

More recent documents issued by the U.S. bishops have tried to correct misuses of the consistency theme, by reasserting a hierarchy of values and emphasizing the fundamental importance of human life in the church's social teaching. This was dramatized in a 1998 document of the bishops that shifted images, from a seamless garment to a house with walls and foundations. After reviewing several important issues that are part of the Church's social witness within a "consistent ethic of life," this document declared:

> Catholic public officials are obliged to address each of these issues as they seek to build consistent policies which promote respect for the human person at all stages of life. But being "right" in such matters can never excuse a wrong choice regarding direct attacks on innocent human life.

Indeed, the failure to protect and defend life in its most vulnerable stages renders suspect any claims to the "rightness" of positions in other matters affecting the poorest and least powerful of the human community. If we understand the human person as the "temple of the Holy Spirit"—the living house of God—then these latter issues fall logically into place as the crossbeams and walls of that house. All direct attacks on innocent human life, such as abortion and euthanasia, strike at the house's foundation. These directly and immediately violate the human person's most fundamental right—the right to life. Neglect of these issues is the equivalent of building our house on sand. Such attacks cannot help but lull the social conscience in ways ultimately destructive of other human rights. (*Living the Gospel of Life: A Challenge to American Catholics* [1998], para. 23)

Such efforts to clarify the logic of the church's social teaching have, of course, also been misunderstood and misused by others—primarily by those who (in an attempt to praise or to blame the bishops) now see the church as encouraging Catholics (or at least regular churchgoing Catholics) to vote Republican.

NEW OPPORTUNITIES

The emergence of new issues involving the sanctity of human life offers new opportunities to transcend the old stereotypes and provoke new reflection among Catholics and others.

Partial-Birth Abortion / Infanticide

Late-term abortion, partial-birth abortion, and the lethal neglect of live-born children who have survived abortion have garnered new interest in the public debate. They have probably played a role in shifting public opinion on abortion generally, with an increasing number of Americans willing to support restrictions on abortion and even to identify themselves as pro-life. This latter phenomenon is especially significant, because Catholics and others who might otherwise be sympathetic on the abortion issue have been completely turned off by negative stereotypes of pro-life people as judgmental, obnoxious, and even violent. Now it is the pro-choice side that seems extreme and willing to defend violence—even violence that is partly or completely outside the womb. Abortion advocacy groups have made a similar strategic error by opposing laws to protect the unborn from violence in non-abortion contexts—even in cases where the children were wanted and loved by their mothers and were helpless victims, alone with them, of violent attacks by uncaring men.

These issues offer an opportunity to raise important questions. Is the abortion debate about women's right to control their bodies, or about a general right to destroy the bodies of others? Which side is defending the rights and bodily integrity of women? Is the consistent ethic of life proving true, as support for abortion sets the stage for demeaning views of life after birth?

Euthanasia/Assisted Suicide

Whatever can be said of abortion, euthanasia cannot be dismissed as a "sex issue" or as an issue that involves the distinctive rights of women. If anything, the case has been made that feminist concerns cut in the other direction: Jack Kevorkian was seen as preferentially exploiting widowed or otherwise isolated women with chronic ailments, and one of the most notorious cases emerging from Oregon's first two years of assisted suicide involved an older women with dementia who seemed to be railroaded into premature death by her adult daughter and her profit-conscious HMO.

Public opinion on this issue tends to run along the same lines as opinion on abortion: Women are somewhat more against it, as are the poor and marginalized and racial minorities. Perhaps most interesting of all is the fact that even polls by the Hemlock Society show older Americans as much more opposed than the young. (One thing the abortion debate does not have is a poll showing the views of the unborn!)

In states where the church, under the pressure of pending public referenda, has focused on educating Catholics in the pews on what is at stake in physician-assisted suicide, polls have shown an impressive consensus of churchgoing Catholics on election day (with 80 percent or more voting against legalization). These crises have allowed the church not only to take a strong and reasoned stand on a public policy issue, but also to teach the theological roots of that issue and to highlight the church's own role in providing and promoting compassionate care as an alternative. Reception among Catholics has been much more positive than with similar efforts on abortion, perhaps because the issue does not carry the mental or psychological baggage described earlier as tainting the reception of the message on abortion.

Here the issue of the equal dignity of all human life comes forward in sharp relief. Moreover, the opportunity has arisen for new ad hoc alliances with medical groups, disability rights advocates, and others not bound to the "religious right" stereotype who are seen as part of the progressive forces in society (including many who disagree with the church's stance on abortion).

Embryo Research/Human Cloning

Though it focuses on human life at its very earliest stage, when personal sympathies for the unborn may be most difficult to evoke, human embryo research has also emerged as an issue that places the inherent sanctity of human life front and center. To a great extent, the issues of women's rights, sexuality, and pregnancy are beside the point in this debate. Those competing with the interests of the unborn are results-oriented scientists who want complete freedom of inquiry—even if it means destroying some human lives for the sake of others. (One interesting point that has emerged from this debate is that even the strongest supporters of embryo research acknowledge the early embryo as an individual "human life," while denying that human life has any necessary claim on the rights of "personhood.")

The real competition here, of course, is the claim of many patient groups that they need human embryo research to cure many devastating diseases—a claim that has perdured and even intensified as the evidence against it mounts. Here, as with abortion and euthanasia, the church's active support for effective and compassionate alternatives has become essential to its witness on behalf of life.

However, new alliances have also arisen on such issues. The issues of human embryo research and human cloning tie in with traditional liberal concerns about human dignity, the commercialization of human life, and the protection of human subjects in medical research (e.g., selling human organs, the Tuskegee syphilis experiments, irresponsible use of genetic technology). Cloning, especially, evokes fears of a new eugenics that rightly motivate activists with Green Party, civil rights, and environmentalist backgrounds.

One recent congressional briefing on human cloning featured a former political director of the Sierra Club, a former director of the American Humane Association, a prestigious cell biologist, and a women's rights activist who coauthored the latest edition of *Our Bodies, Ourselves*. All the speakers spoke favorably of the legislation against human cloning that the U.S. Conference of Catholic Bishops had endorsed some weeks before.

To consider an issue that transcends all the old "pro-life vs. pro-choice" stereotypes and that could reshape our political and human future, one could do worse than study the debate that is emerging on human cloning. The church and its pro-life witness are active at the center of that debate.

Capital Punishment

There has always been an unfair stereotype about conservative pro-lifers strongly supporting the death penalty. Research has shown that those who oppose all abortions (a heavily Catholic population) are more against capital punishment than other Americans. The pro-life movement has become linked with conservative public figures who support the death penalty because of the increasingly visible role of the "religious right" and the marriage of convenience with Republicans prompted by the Democratic Party's tragic wrong turn on abortion.

Pope John Paul II's encyclical *Evangelium vitae* has significantly shifted debate on this issue—not only because he expressed a stronger presumption against capital punishment than has previously appeared in an official teaching document, but also because he expressed it as a corollary of the need to increase respect for all human life in our society, in a document that also raised the stakes in our discussions of abortion and euthanasia.

As a result, many politically conservative Catholics have had to rethink their support for the death penalty—even if they had previously dismissed the link between abortion and capital punishment as one of the more obvious excesses of the "seamless garment" theme. Oddly, at the same time, many secular Democrats seem to have lost any fire in their belly for opposing capital punishment—perhaps moved by public opinion supporting it and the perceived need to look "tough on crime," and perhaps moved by the appeals of consistency on the "pro-death" side. If even innocent life can be trumped by personal choice, why can't guilty life be trumped by social need?

If, as now seems possible, public opinion shifts significantly against the death penalty, there will be new opportunities to reopen a broader debate about the sanctity of the individual over against the state—and the fundamental danger of any power to take another's life. Organizationally, while public policy efforts against capital punishment at the Catholic bishops' conference are directed by the office of Domestic Social Development, the Pro-Life Secretariat's Respect Life educational program has published articles against capital punishment for the last three or four consecutive years. Here also, highlighting the logical linkages between issues can help to dispel stereotypes about "right" and "left" and get Catholics to think about the church's vision of right and wrong.

If these and other issues provoke people to go back and rethink their stereotypes about the "pro-life agenda," new opportunities may arise for articulating a consistent, principled, and compelling vision for Catholic social justice. In this renewed vision, the sanctity of human life can assume the fundamental role it deserves, to enrich the articulation and promotion of the full social justice agenda.

THE STRENGTHS AND WEAKNESSES
OF THE PRO-LIFE AGENDA:
A RESPONSE

Mary C. Segers

What has been the impact of the Catholic pro-life agenda on the reception and perception of Catholic social teaching in the United States? What have been the strengths and weaknesses in the transmission of this teaching? Has the emphasis on the pro-life agenda hurt or enhanced other Catholic social justice efforts? How has this affected American Catholics and non-Catholic Americans?" These were the questions put to me in framing this discussion.

Let me set the stage for my response with this observation made in 1968 by Robert Drinan, S.J.:

> It is painfully clear that Catholics confront in the abortion issue an agonizing question of public policy which could divide Catholics, weaken ecumenical relations, and place Catholics and the Church in the years and decades ahead either in the position of having sinned by the use of its prestige and power against the sincerely held convictions of non-Catholics and non-believers or as a group which failed by silence to speak up when misguided men and women changed the law to permit the extermination of undesirable and unwanted human beings. It seems self-evident that this challenge is unique in American Catholic experience, that it is awesome, and that it is inescapable. Hopefully, it is a challenge which, unlike any previous challenge, will arouse the minds and consciences of American Catholics to original, creative thought on a legal, moral problem of incalculable significance.

Father Drinan's prophetic remarks were made thirty-three years ago at the annual convention of the Catholic Theological Society of America. As he predicted, the abortion issue has been fateful for the Catholic Church in the United States. Over the years, many U.S. bishops and conservative

Catholics have made it a litmus test of Catholic orthodoxy and a criterion of electability for public officials and candidates, Catholic and non-Catholic. The Catholic Church, of course, has addressed many public policy issues over the last thirty years. The bishops have issued major statements on war and peace, economic justice, child welfare, AIDS, and racism (to name a few). However, nothing has had quite the saliency of the abortion issue. Arguably, no other political issue has gotten the emphasis, the funding, the attention, the energy, which the United States Conference of Catholic Bishops (USCCB) has given to public policy on abortion.

I am a political scientist by training, so the crucial question from my perspective is: what is appropriate public policy on abortion? And what are appropriate political strategies and tactics to achieve such a policy? The context of policymaking is crucial, of course. The United States is a liberal democracy in a religiously pluralistic and ethnically diverse society having a constitutional commitment to religious freedom and church–state separation. This context is the framework in which the American church seeks to translate its position on the immorality of abortion into law and public policy. It frames or sets limits on what the church can do and what it may hope to achieve.

Of course, there is the perennial question of how one defines the church. By "church," I mean the USCCB, although, obviously, the larger Catholic community is involved in this issue, sometimes through pro-life organizations such as the National Right to Life Committee and, on the other side of the spectrum, groups like Catholics for a Free Choice.

So the questions are: what are the strengths and weaknesses in the transmission of this teaching and how has it affected other aspects of the Catholic social justice agenda in the United States? Has the emphasis on the pro-life agenda undermined or enhanced other Catholic social justice efforts? Has the church's focus on abortion had positive, beneficial effects on American Catholics' political participation and on a Catholic presence in the public square? What are the positives and negatives, the pros and cons of the church's emphasis on abortion in the last thirty years? Let's look at the positive aspects first. I think I can identify three positive things here.

STRENGTHS OF THE PRO-LIFE AGENDA

First, perhaps pro-life activism has made the church more vigorous as a social and political participant. While clergy and laity had been involved in the civil rights and antiwar movements of the 1950s and 1960s, several studies suggest that *Roe* was really a wake-up call for Catholic pro-lifers. (See Kristin Luker, *Abortion and the Politics of Motherhood*). Michael Cuneo ("Life Battles:

The Rise of Catholic Militancy within the American Pro-Life Movement," in *Being Right*, eds. Mary Jo Weaver and R. Scott Appleby), and James Kelly ("Learning and Teaching Consistency: Catholics and the Right-to-Life Movement" in *The Catholic Church and the Politics of Abortion*, eds. Timothy A. Byrnes and Mary C. Segers), have chronicled the strong Catholic participation in the anti-abortion movement from the very beginning—from the National Right to Life Committee (organized in 1967 by Father James McHugh of the Catholic Family Life Bureau) to the many direct action groups which sprang up in the late 1970s and 1980s. Even before *Roe* and indeed throughout the 1960s, whenever there were state referenda or state initiatives to reform state abortion laws, it was usually Catholics who were prominent in opposing those. *Roe* was also a wake-up call for the bishops, who immediately went into action denouncing the Supreme Court's ruling, pushing for conscience clauses, and having four cardinals testifying before the House Judiciary Committee in 1976. In terms of political participation, I think the American Catholic community will probably be remembered most for its strong participation in the anti-abortion movement of the last quarter of the twentieth century.

I don't know of any empirical studies of the effect of Catholic pro-life activism on Catholics themselves, in terms of their willingness to be more politically active on other social justice issues. However, David Leege (*American Catholics and Civic Engagement: A Distinctive Voice*, volume 1 of the American Catholics in the Public Square Series), in discussing the attitudes of Catholics toward political information and direction by the clergy, notes that for Catholics, only abortion cues from clergy (usually through sermons) seemed to affect political activities, whereas for groups like African-American Evangelicals, political activity was stimulated by a wide range of social justice and social welfare concerns. There is also the study by Verba, Schlozman, and Brady (*Voice and Equality*) that reported that the only issue area stimulating increased political activity by Catholics was abortion. That's quite a finding, actually. Why is this so? We might think about that.

Second, as Richard Doerflinger notes, Cardinal Joseph Bernardin's "consistent life ethic," provided a formula by which the Catholic Church could broaden its concern for human life and include issues like euthanasia, physician assisted suicide, and capital punishment. I think the consistent ethic was an intellectual contribution that directed attention away from single-issue politics, and helped Catholics who were politically involved in other issues to make sense of their activity. It may even have been an effort to counter polarization by suggesting that "liberal Catholics" and "conservative Catholics" could indeed live under the same umbrella, and be involved in politics for the common good.

However, as Doerflinger points out, there were problems and distortions and misapplications of the "seamless garment." As he states, "Consistency is one important value; but by itself it does not draw distinctions or set priorities. More recent documents by the U.S. bishops have tried to correct misuses of the consistency theme by reasserting a hierarchy of values and emphasizing the fundamental importance of human life in the Church's social teaching." Doerflinger's way of resolving misapplications of the consistent ethic is to talk about the fundamental and foundational right to life, and to assume that this inheres in the fetus from the moment of conception. However, assuming that the consistent ethic needs prioritization, another way to prioritize might be to say that our first obligation might be to those who are born, to the living. We must not harm them, and we must help our less fortunate brothers and sisters.

Just a little personal vignette about the "consistent ethic of life." My local parish in Summit, New Jersey, is a self-described pro-life parish. However, about six weeks ago, I heard, for the first time ever, mention of another issue; it was in the weeks immediately before the execution of Timothy McVeigh. In our parish bulletin, the clergy reprinted a statement against the death penalty that the Summit Ministerium, the group of all ministers and clergy in our town, had prepared. One of our curates called attention to this from the pulpit, but surrounded it with caveats and qualifications such as, "We don't want to make up your mind for you or anything, but there is this statement and there is this concern." It was the first time I ever heard this, and it sort of tickled me.

Third, the focus on a pro-life agenda has forced all of us to deal with some really wrenching political questions. Here are a few of them.

- What does it mean for an American Catholic to live in a constitutional democracy in a religiously diverse society?
- What is the relationship between religion, public morality, and public policy?
- How are lawmakers to reconcile conflicting obligations to conscience, constituents, the Constitution, and the common good?
- What do I, as an ordinary Catholic in the pew, think when my local pastor urges me to vote for pro-life candidates? How do I, as citizen in a democratic republic, reconcile my respect for Church authority with my obligation to make up my own mind and decide how to vote?
- How is it that the tradition of Catholic Christianity opposes abortion morally and legally while other Christians support legal abortion? (Do we not read the same Gospels? Doesn't error have rights?)

WEAKNESSES OF THE PRO-LIFE AGENDA

The forty-year controversy over appropriate abortion policy has forced us all to grapple with these issues. Perhaps the quality of debate, which has been rude and crude in the streets, has improved in intellectual circles to the point where, at least among Catholics, we recognize that people can respectfully disagree on these issues. So these three points, I suggest, are positive, especially regarding the increase in Catholic political participation.

But I think there are negatives here, weaknesses in the transmission of this teaching. I want to say that the high priority given by the church to its campaign to restrict, if not completely recriminalize, abortion has come at some considerable cost. These costs include:

- Failure to fully or even minimally support a major social justice issue of our time, justice and equality for women.
- Appearing, and I stress *appearing*, to condone illegal and dangerous activities of the radical militant Catholics involved in some of the violence at abortion clinics. This of course, has the effect of tarnishing all in the pro-life movement, and it is unfortunate.
- Failure to appreciate the complex policy dilemmas faced by lawmakers who must reconcile conflicting obligations to conscience, constituency, the Constitution, and the common good.
- Moving away from the American Catholic tradition of political realism regarding jurisprudence and the relationship between law and morals.
- Uneven treatment of public policy on issues such as abortion, economic justice, and nuclear war.

I want to take time to explain several of these.

Failure to Fully Support Justice and Equality for Women

The first kind of weakness in the transmission of this teaching to Catholics and to non-Catholics is, I think, the Church's failure to fully support a major social justice issue of our time, equality and justice for women. The Church's uncompromising opposition to abortion and to artificial contraception has left it in the position of appearing to oppose progress and the advancement of half of the human race. More importantly, abortion became the chief criterion determining whether the Church would support policies for gender justice. As a political scientist, I am interested in both politics and public policy here, so let me just give you some examples of this. Recall the nomination of Geraldine Ferraro in 1984, the first woman ever to be nominated by a major party for vice president. Instead of rejoicing at this historic event, prominent Catholic bishops treated her as a pariah because of her position on abortion policy—as if this were the only issue on the political spectrum—despite the fact that Catholic male politicians with precisely the same views had never been so criticized. I'm not sure that Catholic feminists have ever gotten over the treatment of Ferraro in 1984.

Recall also the failure of the bishops to endorse the Equal Rights Amendment because they feared it would somehow legitimate abortion and would renew pressure on them to revisit the issue of women's ordination. The bishops remained neutral in the end. I have had conversations with Maureen Fielder, who headed a group called Catholics for the ERA from 1977 to about 1982, and who was involved in a thirty-seven-day fast at the state legislature in Illinois. She and other people in her small group actively contacted bishops, talking to them one-on-one. She succeeded in getting twenty-three of them to declare support the Equal Rights Amendment in 1982; this effectively prevented the full body of the USCCB from formally opposing the ERA (since the USCCB likes to be unanimous).

Another example was the failure of the church to support the Pregnancy Discrimination Act of 1978, a piece of legislation which prohibited discrimination against pregnant women in all areas of employment, and required employers who offered health insurance and temporary disability plans to provide coverage to women for pregnancy, child birth, and related medical conditions. The Bishops' Conference supported the legislation, but insisted upon the addition of an abortion-neutral amendment allowing employers to exclude elective abortions from medical coverage. The USCCB's action delayed the approval of the law for more than two years.

Still another example: The 1988 Civil Rights Restoration Act, supported by a broad coalition of groups—racial minorities, women, the disabled, and the elderly—barred discrimination in education by entire universities, not just specific departments or programs. In making an antiabortion amendment part of its price for support of this bill, the bishops managed to alienate the civil rights community and to block the passage of the Civil Rights Restoration Act for three years.

Given this kind of record, David Leege's finding of a sharp cleavage between young Catholic men (who tend to be Republican) and young Catholic women (who stand in the ranks of the Democratic Party) does not seem surprising. According to Leege, "The steady decline in the number of Catholic women as homemakers, the remarkable increase in those completing higher education, and the equally large growth of young women in business and professional occupations has created a sea change in political behavior."

The cumulative effect of all these examples—where the USCCB put opposition to abortion ahead of laws promoting justice for women—suggests that the U.S. Catholic Church did not take seriously the justice and equality claims of half the human race. It failed to understand and support the long struggle for the emancipation of women.

Catholic Right to Lifers and the Lunatic Fringe

A second cost of the Catholic campaign to restrict and/or recriminalize abortion was that the church appeared to condone the kind of violence that started at abortion clinics in the mid-1980s and escalated to killings of clinic personnel in the 1990s. In the 1980s, militant or radical pro-lifers (mostly Catholic, according to Michael Cuneo) began to move away from the pragmatic approach of the National Right to Life Committee and to advocate direct action and civil disobedience at clinics (lock-and-block protests, sit-ins, etc.). In the mid-1980s, clinic bombings began. And in the 1990s, seven doctors and clinic workers were killed. The anti-abortion movement has also been linked to fourteen attempted murders as well as hundreds of incidents of trespass, assault, acid and anthrax attacks, and fires. John Salvi, a Catholic, killed two clinic workers in Brookline, Massachusetts, in 1994. James Kopp, a Catholic convert, allegedly killed Dr. Barney Slepian in his home in upstate New York in 1998; the FBI thinks Kopp shot four other doctors in the period between 1994 and 1998. Kopp worked with another group, the Lambs of Christ, founded by Father Norman Weslin, which served as the shock troops of the rescue movement in the 1990s.

Civil disobedience, direct action, and illegal activities may be one thing, but the really worrisome thing in the 1990s was that rescue and militant elements of the anti-abortion movement began to justify the idea of killing doctors to defend the sanctity of life. Such advocates included a few evangelicals and even one Catholic priest, the Rev. David Troesch of the diocese of Mobile, Alabama.

Of course, the Church tried to take steps to correct such statements, and the fact is that it would be illogical and far-fetched to blame the Church for such excesses of individual freelancers. At the same time, the fact that two killers were Catholic caught the media's attention, and a public difference between Cardinals Law and O'Connor (Law called a halt to clinic protests, O'Connor did not) gave the media an opportunity to write front-page stories about this. Perhaps the Church should have anticipated that the media would focus on this kind of story about the lunatic fringe, and the Church's communication departments could have planned press releases in anticipation.

Uneven Treatment of Public Policy on Issues Such as Abortion, Nuclear War and Deterrence, and Economic Justice

A third negative aspect of the Church's focus on the pro-life part of its social teaching was the uneven treatment of public policy on issues such as abortion, nuclear war, and economic justice. There were procedural as well as substantive inconsistencies in the way the Church worked to transmit its views to Catholics and to non-Catholics. I'm thinking, of course, of the two Pastoral Letters in the 1980s, the *Pastoral on War and Peace*, and the *Pastoral Letter on the Economy*. Some significant differences between the bishops' development of public policy recommendations on nuclear war and the economy, on one hand, and on abortion, on the other, is that the peace and economic pastorals were written only after consultation with specialists who, in many cases, opposed church views. By contrast, the development of policy recommendations on abortion has not, for the most part, involved formal consultation with demographers, family planners, feminists, and legal and medical experts who do not accept the church's moral teaching on abortion. There is something odd about this uneven treatment of these public policy issues.

Perhaps this is related to a second difference in the Church's policy approach, namely, the absolutism of the Church's position on abortion. Catholic moral teaching holds that the direct killing of innocent unborn human life is never permissible. The bishops argue that Catholic citizens and lawmakers must make vigorous efforts to translate this moral conviction into public policy. However, on other "life" issues such as nuclear warfare, the Church's policy position was more subtle and nuanced, and little pressure was applied to Catholic politicians to adopt the Church's policy views.

Recall this paragraph in the *Pastoral on War and Peace*. "The Church's teaching authority does not carry the same force when it deals with technical solutions involving particular means as it does when it speaks of principles or ends. People may agree in repairing an injustice, for instance, yet sincerely disagree as to what practical approach will achieve justice. Religious groups are entitled as others to their opinion in such cases, but they should not claim that their opinions are the only ones that people of good will may hold." Well, this distinction between means and ends was made with respect to the pastorals on economic justice and war and peace, but it seemed to have been overlooked in the Bishops' efforts to oppose abortion.

In complex matters of war and peace, the bishops clearly recognize the contextual nature and prudential character of practical judgments about the relation between morality and public policy. They acknowledge that people of good will can disagree about which public policies will best realize desired moral goals or objectives. Now if loyal Catholics can differ about appropriate nuclear policy, they can also reach different conclusions about sound abortion policy. I am puzzled as to why the Church does not recognize that issues of fertility control and reproductive decision making are similarly complex and require the same kind of subtle, balanced, contextual approach as do questions of economic or defense policy.

Failure to Appreciate the Dilemmas Faced by Lawmakers and Policymakers

Catholic politicians favoring legal abortion have been threatened with excommunication, denied Communion, banned from speaking at church-sponsored events, told to resign from parish councils, and forbidden to serve in minor liturgical roles as lectors or Eucharistic ministers. The sanctioning of politicians has not been one of the Church's finer moments. The bishops have demonstrated a baffling failure to understand the dilemma of living in a pluralistic society, an inability to appreciate the complex demands of being a lawmaker with duties to conscience, the Constitution, their constituents, and the common good.

The criticism of former Health, Education, and Welfare Secretary Joseph Califano is a case in point. The Hyde Amendment regulating public funding of poor women's abortions presented Califano with a major dilemma: reconciling his religious beliefs as a Roman Catholic with his public duties as HEW Secretary under President Jimmy Carter. In his confirmation hearings in the Senate, Califano stated clearly his opposition to abortion. However, once the Congress enacted the Hyde Amendment, Califano was charged with drawing up regulations to apply the new policy for Medicaid abortions. How did Califano resolve this dilemma?

Reflecting on his experience as a Catholic and as a cabinet executive, Califano noted that the abortion issue was complex and that he "found no automatic answers in Christian theology and the teachings of my church to the vexing questions of public policy it raised." Moreover, he discovered that religious belief could not be decisive, that there were a variety of factors to be weighed and values to be balanced in making public policy. He summarized the competing values and obligations every public servant must consider in exercising political judgment and executing constitutional responsibilities:

> Throughout the abortion debate, I did—as I believe I should have—espouse a position I deeply held. I tried to recognize that to have and be guided by convictions of conscience is not a license to impose them indiscriminately on others by one-dimensionally translating them into public policy. Public policy, if it is to serve the common good of a fundamentally just and free pluralistic society, must balance competing values, such as freedom, order, equity, and justice. If I failed to weigh those competing values—or to fulfill my public obligations to be firm without being provocative, or to recognize my duty once Congress had acted—I would have served neither my private conscience nor the public morality. I tried to do credit to both.

Califano's case illustrates how Catholic public officials have a duty to represent Catholics and non-Catholics alike. In a religiously diverse democracy, they must make public policy for believers and nonbelievers. If the church's moral teaching against abortion is not persuasive to a majority of the citizenry, there is little warrant for using the coercive sanctions of public law to ban or restrict abortion.

A Departure from Catholic Political Realism

Yet another cost of the church's intense campaign to restrict abortion is a departure from the tradition of Catholic political realism that has guided thinking about jurisprudence and the relation between law and morality. Catholic political thought has always acknowledged that the translation of religious values into public policy is a matter not of doctrine but of prudential judgment. The church's traditional thinking about the state, law, and politics recognizes that not every sin need be made a crime and that prudence and calculation of the consequences of public policies are essential in a well-ordered society, particularly one of divided religious allegiance.

However, in the matter of public policy on abortion, the church has conflated morality and legality. Take, for example, Cardinal O'Connor's challenge during the 1984 presidential campaign: "I don't see how in conscience a Catholic can vote for someone who explicitly supports abortion." In failing to distinguish law and morals, this statement obscures the possibility that someone could be against abortion on moral grounds but still think it should be legal.

Experts in jurisprudence and sociology know that there are limits to the law as a method of social control. Similarly, Catholic political realism recognizes that not all moral prohibitions can be enacted into coercive law, and that attention must be paid to the effects, the efficacy, and the enforceability of law. Of necessity, sound policymaking is consequentialist and prudent. Sadly, however, on the issue of abortion policy, the bishops seem to have lost sight of their own rich tradition of political realism.

Politicization of Church Services and Mobilization of Catholic Voters

An additional cost of the Church's intense campaign to ban abortion has been the politicization of the liturgy. In some dioceses, pastors have used religious services as a means of mobilizing Catholics to vote for pro-life candidates or as a means of organizing a "life roll" of Catholic voters to be contacted whenever anti-abortion legislation is before the state legislature.

However, politicizing the liturgy in this manner is questionable. The Catholic Mass is an inappropriate forum for conducting political mobilization campaigns. It could be argued that using sermon time to exhort a captive audience of congregants to sign pledge cards is coercive of conscience and disrespectful to Catholic citizens, who have a right and a duty to make their own judgments about sound public policy. Within the church bishops are moral teachers, but in a pluralistic democracy, members of the hierarchy do not necessarily have either the competence or the right to tell citizens how to vote or what policies to support.

To conclude: In my view, the church's placing high priority on the abortion issue has had serious consequences for the rest of the church's social justice agenda in the United States. The focus on abortion has moved church leaders away from the tradition of Catholic political realism, and has associated Catholic pro-lifers with the militant extremists of what might be called "the lunatic fringe." Clergy and some bishops have risked politicizing the sacred liturgy. They have also failed to understand the complex policy dilemmas faced by lawmakers and public officials. Finally, because of their focus on the abortion issue, church leaders were not fully supportive of gender justice and equality of the sexes. Perhaps the church could have convinced women that it was genuinely serious about Paragraph 29 of *Gaudium et spes*: "Every type of discrimination based on sex is to be overcome and eradicated as contrary to God's intent," by endorsing the ERA and supporting other policies designed to realize equal opportunity in education and employment—at the same time that it took serious exception to legalized abortion.

THE ABORTION DEBATE: GOOD FOR THE CHURCH AND GOOD FOR AMERICAN SOCIETY

Michele Dillon

It is common in some circles today to hear middle-aged Catholics talk about the fact that they preferred the church when, before Vatican II, it had certain restrictions that made being a Catholic more distinctive. Some recall with great pride being at a friend's house as children or as young teenagers and boldly announcing that since it was Friday, they had to eat fish, and not the meat that was being served.

While I appreciate the valued symbolic distinctiveness being alluded to in such comments, it is also perhaps a bit outlandish that religious identity in everyday life would be reduced to such acts. It would be a sad commentary on the state of Catholicism at the beginning of the twenty-first century if one of the most visible signs of the public distinctiveness of Catholicism was that Catholics still had to eat fish rather than meat on Fridays.

It seems to me that if we're to look for ways to enhance the Catholic public presence in American life, we need—and when I say "we," I mean ordinary Catholics, as well as the elites within the church—to discover ways to recreate and rediscover the Catholic doctrinal tradition, broadly defined, and to look at the motifs and cultural symbols it offers for forging a public conversation about what it means to be a moral community in contemporary times.

In recent decades, the abortion debate has provided Americans with a publicly complex and multifaceted issue with which to grapple. I would suggest that the abortion debate, has, on the whole, been good for the church and, by extension, for American society. Many reasonable people may shudder at the unequivocal nature of some of the conclusions reached by church officials with regard to abortion in general and with regard to specific abortion policy proposals. Irrespective of one's own views on abortion, however, I would like to suggest that there is a lot to be learned about

the possibility for Catholicism's public presence from how the church hierarchy has handled its public statements on abortion.

From the outset of the legalization of abortion in 1973, the hierarchy
has presented what I can be seen as a relatively sophisticated cultural discourse. I say "relatively sophisticated" because I think they could go further,
but that's not my topic now.

What I want to highlight is the culturally engaged way in which the
hierarchy has framed its opposition to abortion as a public rather than a private issue. On the day the *Roe v. Wade* opinion was announced, the National
Conference of Catholic Bishops stated that "abortion is not an issue of sec-
tarian morality," but one that concerns "the basis of civilized society." Emphasizing that abortion "is entirely contrary to the fundamental principles
of morality," the bishops' public statements have repeatedly affirmed that
abortion is not simply a Catholic concern, but because it violated the moral
order of civil society, a question of public virtue. Catholic teaching on abortion is grounded in natural-law, and there is the clear echo of natural-law
thinking in the quotes I've cited.

What is sociologically exciting, however, is the fact that the bishops
have not just been content to invoke the relatively abstract language of natural law in making the case against abortion. Rather, they have explicitly re-
worked that language to fit the symbols and themes at the core of American
political culture. There are many examples of this, but if you look at all of
the statements issued by the bishops, whether in public forums, in testimony
to congressional committees, in some of the briefs filed before the Supreme
Court, or in their general public statements, you find a consistent pattern: the
bishops have framed Catholic opposition to abortion as being consistent
with the values enshrined in the U.S. Constitution and Declaration of Independence. The language the bishops use in addressing these audiences varies
somewhat, depending on the particular forum, but they repeatedly emphasize "our fellow citizens" and invoke "our history"—our history as a nation,
over two hundred years of our history, and the ways in which the American
Declaration of Independence and the Constitution have given respect to life.

The bishops, in using these arguments, have been able to transpose opposition to abortion from Catholic dogma to core American moral and legal principles of respect for life. The bishops' argument that abortion is contrary to the basis of civilized society has echoed notions of public virtue
articulated by America's founding fathers. Many will recognize that their famous biblical exhortation, first mentioned in response to *Roe*—"Choose
life, that you and your descendants may live"—is part of a pattern of public
consciousness-raising that has a long tradition in American political culture,
dating back to John Winthrop and the first Pilgrims.

The bishops forward an anti-abortion discourse, therefore, that challenges their fellow citizens to enact America's founding ideals, presenting abortion as a deviation from the nation's guiding values. What greater claim to cultural legitimacy could the bishops articulate than to construct a discourse that is consistent with some of the ethics first articulated by the Puritan settlers in American society?

As the bishops echo those prophetic statements of the Pilgrims, there is a thoroughly American discourse, as opposed to what some might also see purely as a natural-law discourse, one that is very much reframed in terms of American culture and the values and motifs at the core of the culture.

Of course, the bishops also use other arguments, drawing on Scripture as well as social scientific and biological evidence. But today it might be interesting to comment on how the bishops' cultural engagement advances the case for the Catholic public presence in American society, and moves it away from an ethnic model of Catholicism, toward a way of thinking of Catholicism as a public church, able to articulate its perspective in terms of a public theology that is indeed relevant for the whole of American society.

The bishops' apprehension of American bedrock cultural values is significant on many fronts. First of all, it allows the church to establish itself as an insider in American society, invoking our nation's traditions, our fellow citizens. The bishops, too, are American citizens, just like the citizens they address. I applaud this strategy because it helps to eradicate the image of the immigrant outsider, the poor church, the church that doesn't eat meat on Friday, and simultaneously moves the church to a central position in the vanguard of a larger cultural vision of an American society.

As cultural insiders, as citizens, the bishops and all Catholics have a right, therefore, to speak in the public domain, and to challenge the individualization and privatization of morality, not just on abortion, but—as we have seen with the expanding evolution of Catholic thinking—the broader life issues emphasized in church teaching on the consistent ethic of life at all stages and in all contexts.

The rights conferred by American citizenship are complemented by the obligations imposed on all Catholics, as Catholics, by Vatican II's exhortation to create just institutions and communities. So while taking seriously their Americanness and taking seriously Vatican II—or you can go further back—this approach sets the larger frame in which Catholics in general can participate in the public domain.

The challenge, of course, is that once cultural argumentation is embraced, the authority to speak in the public domain rests on the reasonableness of the arguments that are advanced, and not on the authority of sacred office or of tradition, or appeals to political partisanship. Catholic teaching has to be seen as *teaching*, as opposed to *ideology*, because it doesn't fit within one political view. That is precisely its strength. So the fact that one has to advance cultural arguments should be welcomed, because it opens up the conversation. I'd like to suggest that the authority of reason—not disembodied reason, but reason as it is lived in community life—if taken seriously, opens up and enhances the public conversation and the practical consensus that can be negotiated and renegotiated as politics and other aspects of the society change.

We can clearly see this in the bishops' own public participation on abortion. They present more nuanced arguments when they're talking to congressional audiences, as opposed to explicitly Catholic audiences. This is not actually a dumbing-down of Catholic theology; rather, it's giving respect to the pluralism represented in your audience when you present your case for a particular viewpoint.

Recourse to cultural argumentation has enabled bishops and other religious leaders to become legitimate figures in public debates, notwithstanding the criticisms of those who think the separation of church and state means that religious figures should be silent on legislative matters.

But the very fact that the American bishops have so publicly and so vigorously engaged abortion in public has also, I think, been significant in opening up the larger conversations within the church, and in particular, engaging some of the Catholic groups who take a contrary view. Again, regardless of one's own views on an issue, one could argue that, as we see more spokespersons entering the public domain, it becomes clear that there isn't in fact a monolithic Catholic position on abortion or on the death penalty or on many other various issues. The diversity of voices is to be welcomed, because alternative perspectives allow you the best possible chance to evaluate them all reasonably, within the constraints we face as a society. Although more is not always better, the best way to counter bad arguments is to articulate better (more reasonable) arguments in the defense of one's own position.

What is significant here is the opening up of the conversation; in a sense, it democratizes the conversation. And as a result of this, educated citizens—and Catholics are educated citizens even if they are not as literate about Catholicism as one might wish them to be—should be able to develop an informed view on how the various motifs of life, liberty, and equality apply in practice to various contested issues.

In so doing, there is nothing to prevent Catholics drawing on the Catholic tradition—or on some other tradition, for that matter—to develop and articulate their view. The Catholic imagination is particularly well-suited for this, given its emphasis on the communal relationality of individuals, and the Catholics trust in the ultimate goodness of people and of institutions. Robert Bellah, himself a Protestant, has recently argued that American society can profit from greater attentiveness to the Catholic imagination, and to what it can offer in counterbalancing the excessive individualism in American political culture.

And thankfully, the bishops' participation in the abortion debate has emboldened them to actively engage other issues, such as economic justice, nuclear disarmament, and the death penalty.

Public opinion, as we know, is often fickle. On most issues, however, most Americans are quite sensible and are able to make good decisions, even if they sometimes have difficulty in explaining the rationale behind the particular decisions that they make. My hope is that a greater number of ordinary Catholics will take the time to get to know the doctrinal resources within the Catholic tradition, and use those resources, particularly its emphasis on relational communality, to articulate viewpoints that can show how distinctively Catholic ideas and distinctively Catholic ways of thinking can offer new but not necessarily culturally alien ways of thinking about and remedying some of the inequalities in American society.

KILLING YOURSELF:
PHYSICIAN-ASSISTED
SUICIDE IN OREGON

Brian Doyle

Sometime between November 4, 1997, and March 24, 1998, an Oregon citizen (described only as "an adult suffering from cancer" in newspaper stories) committed suicide with the assistance or his or her doctor—the first legal assisted suicide in the history of the United States.

She or he "died very peacefully with the family present," said a close relative who was present and who declined to convey specific details of the event. "It went very nicely . . . and was certainly satisfactory as far as helping someone who wanted to go." This relative also said, in an *Oregonian* newspaper story on March 26, that when the possibility of scheduling the person's death was confirmed, and arrangements made, "it was like the sun had come out when the person finally realized that there was a way to do it."

Death occurred within five minutes of the lethal dose of "medication." "There was a little sigh as the last breath," said the relative.

The *Oregonian* of March 26 also reported that a second assisted suicide had occurred two days before, on March 24, somewhere in the state: a woman in her mid-eighties with breast cancer, deteriorating body functions, and severe shortness of breath. She took a lethal dose of barbiturates, mixed with syrup, chased with a glass of brandy. She made an audiotape two days before her death: "I'm looking forward to it being because I was always active. . . . I will be relieved of all the stress I have. . . . I can't even walk. . . . I have trouble breathing. . . . I'm just looking at the four walls. . . . I cannot comfortably see myself living out two more months like this." Within five minutes of the dose she was in a deep sleep, and she died twenty-five minutes later. The "assurance [of a way to die] has been a load lifted from my spouse," said her husband before her death.

These two people—anonymous, the stories of their lives unknown to the public and very probably never to be known, despite the furor over their deaths—were the Adam and Eve of lawful assisted suicide in this nation. They were the first two of approximately one hundred people to date to have killed themselves in Oregon with the conscious acquiescence and assistance of their doctors, and they are, despite their anonymity, the harrowed human faces of an issue that began in Oregon and is a now a very serious national debate. Physician-assisted suicide is also a very serious matter indeed for the American Catholic Church, and a close look at the issue in Oregon—especially the Church's role in it—is instructive as the debate over suicide swirls in legal, religious, judicial, and legislative circles.

A little background on Catholicism in Oregon will help clarify matters.

Organized religion preceded civil organization here: settlers sent a letter to the bishop of Red River, Canada, in 1834, asking for a mission to be established, Pope Gregory XVI promptly agreed, and the Archdiocese of Portland (then called the Archdiocese of Oregon City) was founded in 1846—thirteen years before Oregon was admitted to the Union in 1859. Portland is the second-oldest archdiocese in the country, after Baltimore, and there is a great apocryphal story that the pope spread out a map of the United States, noted that Oregon was at the other end of the universe from Baltimore, and instantly approved the archdiocese, telling his subordinates to work now to fill in the middle of this new country.

The great church and state controversy in Oregon came in the 1920s, when the state's voters approved a ballot measure forbidding private education. (Oregon maintains a lively ballot measure system to this day, which looms large in the assisted suicide issue, as we shall see.) This measure, sponsored by the Ku Klux Klan during its heyday in Oregon, passed in 1922 and was instantly fought by a novel coalition of independent schools in Oregon, among them religious schools of every stripe. Leading the battle were four attorneys with connections to the state's only Catholic university, the University of Portland. Court appeals went all the way to the Supreme Court of the United States, which overturned the law in 1925.

The 1922 ballot measure may seem obscure history, but it catches something still true about Oregon: the state's citizens are not especially religious, and they are suspicious of organized religion. Oregon is among the three "least-churched" states in America, with Washington and Alaska, and Oregon ranks behind only Nevada among states with the lowest percentages of residents attending church regularly: 32.2 to 32.1 percent. Oregonians are also still, as perhaps they have always been, remarkably suspicious of outsiders—from the Californians (called Californicators) who buy up formerly cheap real estate, to the many outsiders who were told "please visit but please don't stay" in a much-ballyhooed 1972 ad campaign featuring then Governor Tom McCall.

So in some ways not much has changed in Oregon since 1922. The state today has two Catholic universities, both with fewer than 3,000 students, and while there are 159 parishes, there are merely 334,000 Catholics, all told, in a state with a population of 3.5 million. And although Catholics are less than 10 percent of the population, they are by far the largest organized religionists in the state.

Some cold numbers will give you a sense of the limited scope of Catholicism in Oregon: there is one archbishop, three bishops (one retired), one seminary, fourteen Catholic high schools (in 100,000 square miles, an area the size of all of New York state and New England together), and about two hundred active priests of various orders. The total number of men from Oregon studying for the priesthood around the world, in various orders, is sixty-four

And a look at Oregonians themselves is educational.

Oregon was a determinedly independent territory, fending off the national claims of Britain, Russia, and Spain, before it ever became one of the American states. The initiative process itself, a deliberate effort at "direct democracy," as the Oregon historian Kimbark MacColl says, is now a century old in Oregon, and largely as a result of it Oregon is either out of step with its peer states or ahead of them, depending on your vantage point: Oregon was the first state in the Union to guarantee public access to all beaches, and among the first to ban no-deposit bottles, to clean its rivers, and to install land-use laws deliberately designed to protect farmland from urban sprawl— these latter laws are still the most ferocious urban-restraint laws in the land. Oregon is one of only five states to hold out against a sales tax, one of two to offer comprehensive health insurance to every citizen, and one of two to insist legally that you cannot pump your own gas at gas stations, for reasons that elude me no matter how hard I try to understand them.

Into this milieu, in 1988, came Derek Humphry, the controversial English-born founder and director of the National Hemlock Society, a group founded in 1980 and devoted to, as its literature had it, "death with dignity"—or, as its opponents had it, legal suicide. (Suicide was no stranger to Humphry himself; he publicly claimed to have helped his first wife, Jean, kill herself in England, and his second wife, Wickett, killed herself in the Oregon woods, leaving behind a note accusing Humphry of suffocating Jean to death.) Humphry's group had been headquartered in California, where it had tried and failed to place a proposed "Humane and Dignified Death Act" on the state ballot. He then moved the Hemlock Society to the most liberal city in Oregon, Eugene, and stated publicly that his aim was to put assisted suicide on the ballots of Oregon and Washington by 1990.

The society's first act in Oregon was to release the results of a national poll it had commissioned about attitudes on euthanasia. Pollsters from the Roper organization asked 1,900 adults around the country if physicians should be allowed to end the lives of terminally ill patients at the patient's request: 58 percent said yes, 27 percent said no, and 10 percent were undecided.

The Hemlock Society's arrival in Oregon served as the firestarter for assisted suicide here, but the issues of end-of-life care and the ethics of terminal illness were already in the public square. The growth of the hospice movement had begun to publicize what had always before been a private matter between families and healthcare facilities, laws on "advance-care directives" were being debated in the Oregon legislature, and it was the unusual hospital that did not have at least a consulting ethicist on staff. Nor were these professional ethicists at Catholic hospitals alone; Barbara Coombs Lee, who would be a key pro-suicide spokesperson in the Oregon debate, was a nurse and staff ethicist at Oregon Health Sciences University, the large, sprawling, and well-funded state hospital and medical school in Portland (on "Pill Hill").

In 1989, the Oregon legislature concluded a four-year debate by passing laws on advance healthcare directives and powers-of-attorney—laws that gave patients the option of refusing life-sustaining treatments. In April of that year, the Archbishop of Portland, William Levada (now archbishop of San Francisco) was sufficiently moved by events to write an op-ed, "Suicide Does Not Lend Dignity to Death," about end-of-life issues for the *Oregonian*, the region's major newspaper.

Levada then worked diligently with Washington's three bishops (among them Francis George, O.M.I., now a cardinal and archbishop of Chicago), to craft the Northwest bishops' first pastoral letter ever, *Living and Dying Well: A Pastoral Letter about the End of Life*, which was published in 1991, and subsequently adapted for use by California's bishops. "The thrust of the op-ed and the pastoral letter was to educate Catholics about the many issues around end-of-life care—pain treatment, death with dignity, advance directives to the family and physicians by the patient, living wills, Church teachings, ethical concerns, social concerns," says the archdiocesan chancellor then and now, Mary Jo Tully.

In June of 1990 an Oregon woman named Janet Adkins killed herself with the assistance of "Doctor Death," Jack Kevorkian. She was fifty-four years old and suffered from Alzheimer's Disease. She was physically healthy—she had recently climbed to the top of Oregon's 11,000-foot Mount Hood, had climbed in the Himalayan Mountains of Nepal, and a week before her death defeated one of her sons in a tennis match. But the former English teacher and accomplished musician could no longer play the piano or read, and after seeing a show about Kevorkian on *Donahue,* she traveled to Michigan, where laws on assisted suicide were murky, and a man who helped find a gun for a drunken friend to kill himself had been found not guilty in 1983. (Oregon law in 1990 held that assisting a suicide was a felony punishable by up to ten years in prison.) Kevorkian helped her kill herself with a lethal injection of potassium chloride in his Volkswagen van, parked in a campground in suburban Detroit. Adkins's was the first of more than 130 suicides Kevorkian would oversee in the next few years, in one of the most controversial and macabre medical careers in American history.

Kevorkian was then tried for first-degree murder in Michigan ("For me not to charge Dr. Kevorkian would have turned Oakland County into the suicide mecca of our nation," said the county prosecutor, Richard Thompson), but the suit was dismissed by a judge who ruled that Michigan, having no law against physician-assisted suicide, could not charge Kevorkian with a crime.

His trial, Adkins's death, and the publication in the summer of 1991 of Derek Humphry's suicide primer, *Final Exit* (which spent eighteen weeks on the *New York Times* bestseller list and sold more than half a million copies) caused a national uproar, a surge in organized pro- and anti-suicide activity in Oregon, and a roaring blizzard of public statements and appearances in the Northwest from folks representing most of the known universe: Oregon Right to Die, Compassion in Dying, the American Civil Liberties Union, the Gray Panthers, the Northwest AIDS Foundation, the National Right to Life Committee, the National Conference of Catholic Bishops' Domestic Policy Committee and Secretariat for Pro-Life Activities, the Oregon Catholic Conference, the Catholic Supportive Care of the Dying Coalition, Washington Citizens for Death with Dignity, the World Federation of Right to Die Societies (headquartered in Oxford, England), the Oregon Medical Association (which steadfastly refused to take a stand on assisted suicide), the Washington Medical Association and American Medical Association (both of which vociferously opposed assisted suicide), the Washington Catholic Conference, the National Association for Retarded Citizens, the Washington Hospice Organization, Pat Robertson's Christian Coalition (which opposed assisted suicide), the Traditional Values Coalition, the Oregon Citizens Alliance (a far-right conservative group obsessed with sponsoring anti-gay measures), the Death with Dignity Task Force, Last Acts (a coalition of 72 groups, among them the American Cancer Society and Catholic lay societies, chaired by Rosalynn Carter and armed with $12 million from the Robert Wood Johnson Foundation to "develop new models for end-of-life care"), Physicians for Compassionate Care, the Oregon Health Division, the Oregon Legislature's Health Care and Bioethics Committee, the International Anti-Euthanasia

Task Force, and the former Surgeon General of the United States, C. Everett Koop, who called assisted suicide "dangerous to society's health."

Matters came to a head in the Pacific Northwest, legislatively, in 1991, when organizers of the right-to-die movement filed a "death with dignity" initiative in Washington (Initiative 119) and euthanasia legislation in Oregon (State Bill 1141). For the first time, Oregon legislators were asked to formally consider, as a matter of state law, whether or not they should vote to allow themselves and their fellow citizens to kill themselves.

Let us pause to take a brief look at the history of assisted suicide itself, beginning with 350 B.C. or so, when what would eventually be called the Hippocratic Oath emerged among Greek physicians. "I will not give poison to anyone though asked to do so, nor will I suggest such a plan," says part of that oath today.

Saint Augustine, in the fifth century: "It is never licit to kill another; even if he should wish it, indeed if he request it, because, hanging between life and death, he begs for help in freeing the soul struggling against the bonds of the body and longing to be released; nor is it licit even when a sick person is no longer able to live."

That was essentially the stance of both common law and law that hailed from Jewish and Christian belief: suicide was either wrong completely or, if condoned individually (as in Rome) was a blow against the state if assisted. In the United States, where laws were based on English common law, suicide was forbidden. The first American Western region to deal with suicide directly was the Dakota Territory, which adopted the Field Penal Code in 1877, forbidding suicide and assisted suicide.

In 1920 a Michigan court ruled that a man who aided in a suicide was to be charged with murder. In 1936 the Voluntary Euthanasia Society of England introduced a bill in the House of Lords to legalize voluntary euthanasia, which failed, but it prompted similar (and unsuccessful) proposals in New York and Nebraska.

In 1957 Pope Pius XII wrote that doctors can administer pain relief, even if it would shorten life. In 1965 the Second Vatican Council condemned euthanasia as a crime on par with murder, genocide, and abortion. It is up to God alone to decide when life ends, the Council writes.

In 1973 Dutch courts refused to penalize doctors who participate in assisted suicide and euthanasia—a stance maintained by the Dutch ever since, although suicide and euthanasia remained technically illegal until the year 2000. In 1980, alarmed by euthanasia in the Netherlands, the Vatican released a thirteen-page document saying that a suicide attempt is really a plea for help and love. Taking an innocent life opposes God's love, says the Vatican, which adds that suffering at the end of life is a sharing in Christ's passion.

In 1984 the Dutch Supreme Court accepted assisted suicide and euthanasia not only for terminally ill patients, but for ill or elderly patients whose deaths are not imminent.

In 1986 the family of a comatose New Jersey woman named Karen Ann Quinlan went to court to assert their right to have her removed from life-support systems—essentially beginning the right to die movement in the United States.

And in 1988 Derek Humphry, having failed to get a suicide proposition on the California ballot, carefully chose a state with a free-form ballot measure system, a substantial liberal voting bloc, and a relatively small number of voters affiliated with organized religion: Oregon.

Both Washington's Initiative 119 and Oregon's State Bill 1141 failed (the Oregon bill died in committee and the Washington initiative was defeated 54–46), but the Oregon "right-to-die" movement doubled its energies, and over the next two years prepared a measure for the 1994 statewide ballot. Oregon Right to Die, the lead organization in the effort, needed to collect 67,771 signatures, by law; its 500 collectors, working daily until July 8, 1994, collected almost 100,000 (and were paid a dollar per signature). Thus Measure 16 entered Oregon's vocabulary.

Measure 16, if passed, would allow patients who had been diagnosed as terminally ill (less than six months to live) by two physicians (attending and consulting) to request "life-ending medication." Such a request had to be made in writing, witnessed by two people not related to the patient. The patient's soundness of mind had to be affirmed by both the attending and consulting physicians. If all these requirements were met, the attending physician could write a prescription for a lethal dose of medication, which would then be taken at the patient's discretion, by the patient's hand. No one would be allowed to assist the patient in taking the medication, and doctors were forbidden to inject lethal doses of medication into the patient.

The Catholic Church in the West fought this initiative every step of the way. In 1991 the Northwest bishops released their pastoral letter. In 1992 the Catholic bishops of California, using a pastoral letter based on the Northwest's and raising $1.6 million through the California Catholic Conference (CCC), helped defeat that state's Proposition 161 (54-46), though according to polls more than 70 percent of Californians supported assisted suicide. (One telling remark: "While we raised a lot of money," said David Pollard of the CCC, "the greatest impact was through education.")

In 1993 Oregon's two bishops, Archbishop William Levada and Bishop Thomas Connolly (of Baker City, seat of the church in rural and thinly populated eastern Oregon) sent letters to every registered Catholic in the state, asking for $50 each to fight assisted suicide. "We make this exceptional request because of the seriousness of this proposed initiative," they wrote. "A euthanasia initiative permitting physician-assisted suicide would cross the moral boundary line by legalizing intentional acts to end life." A second collection, "in pew," was held September 18, 1994, on the same Sunday that all priests in Oregon were instructed to preach against the measure. (It raised $276,748 from 13,000 donors; all told the Oregon Catholic community would spend $1.3 million on the campaign, most of it from out-of-state Catholics.) "Measure 16 is about selling murder in the name of mercy," said the archbishop in a written statement that day.

But also uttered that day was the sort of remark that would become increasingly common in Oregon between 1994 and 1997: "This politicking from the pulpit clearly shows our opponents' intention to promote Catholic religious doctrine by influencing Oregon voters," said Geoff Sugerman, spokesman for Oregon Right to Die. "Spending money to push their religious doctrine on the rest of Oregonians is nothing new for the Oregon Catholic Conference."

This early salvo heralded a stance that would, I believe, be crucially effective in the debate: placing the Catholic Church in opposition to the rest of the voters in Oregon. "Are we going to let one church make the rules for all of us?" as a sobbing woman said in the first right-to-die television ad in October of 1994. "This is a decision that shouldn't be made by a foreign power," said Barbara Coombs Lee, the former ethicist and nurse who had become the pro-suicide movement's leading speaker. "Don't buy the garbage the Catholic Church is putting out," said a radio advertisement.

Where were the other religious denominations in Oregon during the Measure 16 debate?

The Mormons, the second largest denomination at 100,000 strong (about 4 percent of the population), were against assisted suicide, though even their leaders—among them the ethicist Courtney Campbell at Oregon State University—conceded that their stance was "more symbolic than substantive," as Campbell noted.

The Unitarians supported assisted suicide, stating that it gives "dying people more choices and dignity." The Jewish community was split on the issue and spoke individually for both sides. The tiny Buddhist and Muslim communities spoke individually against it.

The other seventeen organized Christian faiths in Oregon—Baptist, Greek Orthodox, Lutheran, Congregationalist, Presbyterian, etc.—collectively so small that they are represented in matters of public policy by an umbrella group called Ecumenical Ministries of Oregon, took no stance on the issue until three weeks before the election, and even then, according to one informed observer, only opposed the measure because it was literally begged to do so by representatives of the archdiocese.

Where was the medical community?

The short answer: split. The Oregon Medical Association (OMA) took no stand on the issue before the 1994 election, a crucial silence, especially given the undeniably important role of the publicly anti-suicide stance of the Washington and California state medical associations, and the adamant opposition offered by the American Medical Association and the American Nurses Association. While there was a group of Oregon doctors and medical professionals against suicide, the Physicians for Compassionate Care, Oregon's Catholic medical community—a significant player, as there are fourteen Catholic hospitals in the state—was not active. Oregon Catholic Conference director Robert Castagna remembers Archbishop Levada convening a meeting of Catholic physicians in 1994, and drawing only six doctors, and Archbishop (now Cardinal) Francis George challenging the Catholic Physicians Guild in 1996, asking them where they were during the 1994 campaign.

The official silence of the state's doctors echoed. Dr. Leigh Dolin, president of the Oregon Medical Association, said that his members viewed Measure 16 as a "patient's decision" initiative, and that the OMA would have fought it if it entailed lethal injections. "But merely prescribing lethal pills," as he said, was not something Oregon's medical association could oppose. Nor did the Oregon Medical Association cotton to advice from the national association of doctors: when the American Medical Association board of directors publicly advised the OMA that Measure 16 was "unethical" and "a mistake," Dolin replied, "We'll see how Oregonians feel about outsiders trying to tell them how to vote."

After the election, when the assisted suicide measure had passed by a mere 32,000 votes of the 1.2 million cast, Robert Castagna, director of the Oregon Catholic Conference, was unabashedly bitter. "Castagna called the Oregon Medical Association's refusal to take a stand the most devastating blow," reported the *Oregonian*. "'What other profession would not stand up for its own ethics?' asked Castagna, calling the OMA's neutrality irresponsible."

Karen Bell, a hospice nurse who campaigned against Measure 16 and volunteered to be in anti-Measure 16 television commercials, said, "It was amazing how many people I talked to who said, 'The doctors aren't opposed to this. It must be okay.'"

On November 8, 1994, Measure 16 passed by a hair, 51 percent to 49 percent. The difference was 31,962 votes.

The characteristics of the vote are fascinating. Exit polls showed that men had voted for assisted suicide, 59 to 41 percent. Women voted against it by a hair, 51 to 49 percent. Young people (ages 18 to 29) had voted overwhelmingly for it, 65 to 35 percent. People older than 60 had voted against it, 54 to 46 percent. People ages 45 to 59—middle-aged people caring for their aging parents?—had voted heavily for it, 59 to 41 percent. Democrats and independent voters had voted for it, 60 to 40 percent—the same ratio by which Republicans had voted against it.

Why did it pass?

Jim Moore, political science professor at the University of Portland and political analyst for KPDX TV, the Fox affiliate in Portland:

> First, Measure 16 wasn't the central issue on the ballot, wasn't the most controversial—Measure 13 was. This was the second anti-gay measure in two years, it had been enormously controversial in the 1992 vote, and here it was again. Interestingly the Church was vehement against it in 1992 and neutral in 1994, choosing instead to concentrate its efforts against assisted suicide. But its very public wishy-washy stance on the anti-gay initiative hurt its efforts against Measure 16, I think. Plus there were seventeen other measures on the ballot—school funding, pension reform, mining restrictions, campaign reform, cougar and bear hunting, all sorts of things. Assisted suicide was one of many issues before Oregonians at the polls in 1994.
>
> Second, the lack of support until the very last minute from the other organized Christian religions in the state hurt—that allowed the pro-suicide forces to paint the argument as the *Church vs. Oregon.*
>
> Third, the Oregon Catholic Conference, and particularly its strident and sharp-tongued director Robert Castagna, conducted a scare-tactic ad campaign, linking assisted suicide to abortion and murder. This was an understandable approach, given the moral beliefs of Catholics that all life is sacred, but it had little effect on Oregon voters, who clearly didn't think of assisted suicide as a moral issue so much as a matter of independent choice and end-of-life autonomy.

Father David Tyson, C.S.C., president of the University of Portland (the state's larger Catholic university, which later hosted a public anti-suicide symposium in the summer of 1997):

> The strategy crafted by the Oregon Catholic community, with the approval of then Archbishop William Levada, seemed to me to set this issue in a strictly moral context. Catholicism is correctly unequivocal about the value of life. But in this state, with this issue, it was misguided. It made the

Church the flashpoint, it made voters' opinion of organized Catholicism crucial, when really the matter at hand was what happens to the very ill.

I think a strategy that focused more on education of voters would have been far more effective. The Church is an excellent teacher on matters of life, and the Catholic hospitals in the state were filled with articulate and expert spokesmen and spokeswomen about advance directives for care, end-of-life issues, quality of life. Throwing down the moral gauntlet made the church the issue in the election—not life.

The Catholic campaign political action committee, Coalition for Compassionate Care, did sponsor a "pastoral education program" in the spring of 1994, at the direct request of the archbishop. This program was conducted "at parishes throughout the state," as Castagna noted, but to no avail.

Measure 16 was slated to go into effect on December 8—the Feast of the Immaculate Conception. On November 13 the Vatican newspaper *L'Osservatore Romano,* in an article by theologian Gian Concetti, denounced Oregon's new assisted-suicide law as "aberrant" and de facto euthanasia, "an abominable crime that can never be justified." On November 19 the National Conference of Catholic Bishops called the assisted-suicide movement a "cancer," intimated that legal challenges were forthcoming, and expressly forbade the nation's 1,200 Catholic hospitals, clinics, nursing homes, and healthcare facilities to participate in assisted suicide. (The bishops also said, memorably and forcefully, "A society which destroys its children, abandons its old, and relies on vengeance fails fundamental moral tests. Violence is not the solution; it is the most clear sign of our failures.")

On November 25 a request for a permanent injunction stopping the measure was filed in U.S. District Court in Eugene—headquarters of the Hemlock Society. Leading the legal fight was James Bopp of Indiana, chief attorney for National Right to Life, the nation's largest anti-abortion group. Oregon Right to Life led the funding agencies for the suit.

Bopp articulated the law's flaws, as he saw them, and for each of the enumerated flaws he found an Oregonian to stand as plaintiff. The law, said Bopp, would encourage physicians to recommend suicide for patients whose care would burden the healthcare system; it had inadequate safeguards for patients who were suicidal because they were depressed; and it would force owners of nursing homes to permit suicide in their facilities even though they had religious objections to the practice.

On December 1, preparatory to the January 1 opening of the 1995 session of the Oregon legislature (which meets every other year), the state's Health Division convened a task force to write rules to implement the statute—no easy task, as Measure 16 had specified that only Oregon residents could request suicide, but hadn't defined residency; specified "medication" and "prescription" but not specific drugs and dosages; and specified that suicide be completely autonomous, which could be construed as discriminatory against the disabled terminally ill.

On December 7, 1994, Judge Michael Hogan of the United States District Court in Eugene halted implementation of Measure 16, saying that he needed more time to consider constitutional issues raised by the statute: "Death constitutes an irreparable injury, and I find that the possibility of unnecessary death by assisted suicide has been sufficiently raised to satisfy the irreparable harm requirement for a preliminary injunction." In August of 1995, Hogan ruled Measure 16 unconstitutional on the grounds that it did not assure equal protection under the law for the terminally ill—in essence, that the statute was not written carefully enough to obviate mistakes. Hogan's ruling was immediately appealed to the Ninth Circuit Court of Appeals in San Francisco, but the statute would languish in the appeal netherworld for three years.

When Measure 16 passed, the idea of assisted suicide changed in Oregon—it became reality, the law, normal, even as it languished in court. Suicide became part of the normal social, political, and professional discourse among Oregon's citizens. People talked about assisted suicide and quality of care for the dying in their workplaces, among friends, within families. Politicians were asked their opinions on assisted suicide in their campaigns and while they governed. Oregon's doctors started to focus on pain management, especially during the last months of life. Oregon soon was second in the nation in per capita consumption of morphine—a sign that physicians were not just discussing pain management for the dying, but were taking action to ease patients' last days.

So, from being a fringe issue in California and Washington, where political campaigns had succeeded in defeating ballot measures, assisted suicide entered into the mainstream of societal concerns in Oregon after 1994.

Meanwhile the state's legislators continued to grapple with the rules and regulations by which an assisted-suicide statute might actually be implemented in the life of the state, and finally—either with sensible caution or craven cowardice, depending on your reading of the situation—the legislature decided to throw the issue back at the voters, to be absolutely sure Oregon's citizens wanted to be able to commit suicide legally. Thus came about the 1997 special election, a statewide ballot on which would be only two measures: one about the use of state lottery money, and the other about suicide again (this time called Measure 51).

Between 1994 and 1997 the Catholic Church also continued to grapple with assisted suicide. The Oregon Catholic Conference lobbied energetically with the 1994 Health Division task force and in the 1995 Legislature, and the archdiocese paid for National Right to Life attorney James Bopp and his staff's legal appeals against Measure 16.

In March of 1995 Pope John Paul II issued an encyclical called *The Gospel of Life*, in which he said, "Suicide is always as morally objectionable as murder. 'Assisted suicide' means to cooperate in and at times be the actual perpetrator of an injustice that can never be excused, even if it is requested." Soon after this, Australia's Northern Territory approved a law legalizing assisted suicide and euthanasia for seriously ill patients, which caused such an uproar in the Antipodes that the law was subsequently revoked by the country's national assembly.

In October of 1995, Archbishop William Levada, who had led the Catholic fight against assisted suicide, was appointed Archbishop of San Francisco. Succeeding him in Portland, in April of 1996, was Francis George, who as Bishop of Yakima (Washington state) had helped craft and issue the 1991 Northwest bishops' "Pastoral Letter about the End of Life." George, familiar with the issue, familiar with the quirky independence of Northwest voters, and very able and willing to speak for the Catholic community himself, addressed the issue of suicide bluntly in the first hour of his tenure in Portland, at the press conference announcing him: "It's not a right to die but a right to kill," he said.

George also made two decisions in the next few months that shaped the Church's stance in the 1997 re-vote: to continue to discuss the issue on moral grounds, but to spend far more time discussing the medical and legal case against suicide; and to allow National Right to Life to play a significant role in the campaign. The archdiocesan-supported Repeal Measure 16 organization also reached outside the state for a fundraising director—Brooke Bodney, who had been instrumental in raising money for the Bob Dole/Jack Kemp presidential campaign—and a consultant, Chuck Cavalier of California, who had advised anti-suicide campaigns in California, Washington, and Australia.

In the legal world, early 1996 saw two signal events at the Ninth United States Circuit Court of Appeals in San Francisco, the body which establishes law and legal precedent in nine Western states, among them Oregon.

The first, in February 1996, was a brief filed by national and Western religious groups, comparing Measure 16 to legalized slavery. "Arguing that assisted suicide is a 'solution' to a problem is analogous to arguing that the poor and homeless should be 'free' to solve their plight by selling themselves into slavery," said the brief. "Oregon has instituted a system that is even more radical than 'voluntary' slavery because it results in the final and irreversible destruction of the human subject. Suicide is not a constitutionally protected act, and a person can no more 'consent' to ending his life than he can 'consent' to selling himself into slavery."

This brief, filed in the appeal of Michael Hogan's finding Measure 16 unconstitutional, was filed by a startling coalition: the U.S. Catholic Conference, the Catholic conferences of Oregon, Washington, and California, the Christian Legal Society, the Christian Medical and Dental Society, the Evangelical Lutheran Church in America, the Lutheran Church/Missouri Synod, and the National Association of Evangelicals. The range of the coalition was all the more noticeable because of a news item in national papers four days before: the Episcopal diocese of Newark, New Jersey, had issued a statement saying that suicide or assisted suicide "may be morally acceptable for Christians under some circumstances."

The second event came in March: the Circuit Court issued the remarkable ruling that there was a "right to die" inherent in the U.S. Constitution. The federal court, in striking down a ban on assisted suicide in Washington State, held that terminally ill adults had a right, not requiring special legislation, to end their lives with the help of a physician. Similar to the right to an abortion, said Judge Stephen Reinhardt, assisted suicide was an individual's decision and not something subject to state policy.

This issue, wrote Reinhardt, "may touch more people more profoundly than any other issue the courts will face in the foreseeable future ... the individual's interest in making [this] vital decision is compelling indeed, for no decision is more painful, delicate, personal, important, or final than the decision how and when one's life shall end. If broad general state policies can be used to deprive a terminally ill individual of the right to make that choice, it is hard to envision where the exercise of arbitrary and intrusive power by the state can be halted."

In November 7, 1996, the nine justices of the United States Supreme Court received a letter from a priest in Chicago.

"As one who is dying, I have come especially to appreciate the gift of life," wrote the priest. "Life is not simply a decision made between patient and physician. Because life affects every person, it is of primary public concern."

There is a great distinction, he wrote, between suicide and "choosing a life without the burden of disproportionate medical intervention"—as he had chosen, having decided to cease further treatment after being diagnosed with terminal cancer of the pancreas and liver.

"Suicide, assisted suicide, and euthanasia are wrong because they involve a direct attack on innocent human life," the letter concluded. "Creating a new 'right' to assisted suicide will endanger society and send a false signal that a less than perfect life is not worth living."

The author of the letter, Joseph Cardinal Bernardin, died twelve days later.

To fight Measure 51 in 1997, the Catholic community spent $4 million ($2 million from the Church directly)—four times as much as spent against Measure 16 in 1994. Again most of the money came from out of state, and again the Church emphasized the ethical issue, and again the pro-suicide forces had a field day hammering away at the Church as a brooding foreign authority itching to tell Oregonians what to do. "They're spending a fortune to repeal Measure 16 because they want to impose their views on the rest of us," went the most publicized pro-suicide ad.

The pro-suicide forces raised an additional $1 million of their own, and the more than $5 million spent for and against Measure 51 made it the third most expensive ballot campaign in the history of the state, behind only an anti-nuclear plant measure in 1992 (against which Portland General Electric desperately spent $5 million, and won) and a tobacco-tax measure in 1996 (against which the tobacco industry desperately spent nearly $5 million, and lost).

As usual, following the money trail was an interesting endeavor. Among the donors for and against were the Sisters of Saint Casimir in Chicago, who sent $1,000 to fight suicide; Republican presidential aspirant Steve Forbes, who gave nearly $8,000 to fight suicide; the Knights of Columbus, who gave $150,000 to fight suicide; the U.S. Catholic Conference, which gave $250,000 to fight suicide; archdioceses around the country, which donated $800,000 against suicide; and international financier George Soros, who gave $250,000 to support suicide. (Soros would also give money to a 1998 Oregon ballot measure decriminalizing small amounts of marijuana, which failed.) The extremist right-wing group Oregon Citizens Alliance, perhaps exhausted by two bruising defeats of its pet anti-gay ballot measures, gave $8.50.

But the Catholic community was missing a key weapon in the anti-suicide fight the second time around—an archbishop. In March of 1997 Francis George was appointed Archbishop of Chicago. George has said that he begged the Vatican to appoint his successor in Portland as soon as possible, given the imminent assisted suicide vote, but seven months passed before Bishop John Vlazny of Winona, Minnesota, was appointed Archbishop of Portland, and Vlazny was not inaugurated as leader of Oregon's 300,000 Catholics until after the election. George left Oregon in March, and Archbishop Thomas Murphy of Seattle died in June—so in the months before Measure 51, the more than 600,000 Catholics on the wet, green side of the Cascade Mountains, a region variously called Cascadia, Ecotopia, and the Far Corner, were sans shepherds.

The 1997 campaign was bitter and occasionally violent. Bishop Kenneth Steiner, Portland's auxiliary bishop, had a slab of concrete thrown through his office window and "SATAN" painted on the campaign signs on his lawn. Oregon Right to Die, the leading pro-suicide group, ran a series of television and radio advertisements punching the Church: "Don't shove your religion down my throat!" "The legislature [which had handled the issue like a hot potato and pitched it right back to the voters] is doing the bidding of the Catholic Church." "The Catholic Church is spending a fortune to repeal Measure 16 because they want to impose their views on the rest of us." Pro-repeal legislators "want to impose their religious views on you."

The anti–Catholic Church rhetoric even echoed in the august chambers of the state capitol, where supporters of Measure 16, furious at the legislature's May decision to put suicide to the voters again, offered these remarks for the record: "I don't care how many millions the Catholic Church spends . . . the raw political power of the Catholic Church has taken this political body hostage . . . this assembly has thwarted the will of the people and made every citizen conform to the dictates of the pope."

In June, the U.S. Supreme Court quietly ruled (unanimously) that while there was no constitutional right to die, and no compelling reason for legalizing assisted suicide since sufficient pain relief existed, the legality of assisted suicide was something for each state to decide. President Bill Clinton also weighed in that day with an uncharacteristically terse statement: "I continue to be against assisted suicide."

A week later Colombia's highest court legalized euthanasia for terminally ill people who have given consent.

In August, the Oregon Medical Association, which had been loudly neutral in 1994, came out against Measure 51—swayed in part, perhaps, by the increasingly vociferous Physicians for Compassionate Care, a group of more than one thousand Oregon doctors of various creeds who sponsored a much-publicized rally on the steps of the state capitol in Salem.

In early September, a poll of Oregon Catholics commissioned by the *Oregonian* found them split evenly on assisted suicide. A national survey released soon after (conducted by an ethics group called American Health Decisions and financed by the Johnson Foundation) found that Catholics and Protestants were evenly split about suicide, but Jews were more likely to vote for suicide than all other religious groups.

In mid-September, the University of Portland, Oregon's larger Catholic university sponsored an assisted-suicide symposium, which drew more than five hundred people to hear doctors, nurses, theologians, ethicists, judges, lawyers, and Francis Cardinal George.

In mid-October, the two hundred fifty Mormon congregations in Oregon—now encompassing 130,000 people, the fastest-growing religion in the state—heard a statement read to them from the First Presidency and Quorum of the Twelve Apostles, the church's highest offices, in Salt Lake City (where the Mormon Temple, the St. Peter's Basilica of that faith, is eight blocks from the Catholic Cathedral of the Madeleine): "One who assists in the suicide of another violates God's commandments." Mormons were "commended" to write letters to local editors, place anti-suicide campaign signs in their yards, and offer their services to the campaign. On that same Sunday Bishop Kenneth Steiner, acting administrator of the archdiocese in the absence of an archbishop, spoke in St. Mary's Cathedral, the seat of Catholicism in Oregon: "We entrust the battle of our state and our world to the late Mother Teresa."

A day later the United States Supreme Court refused to hear an appeal of Oregon's assisted-suicide law.

On October 27, 1997, one week before the election, the Ninth Circuit Court of Appeals in California lifted the injunction against Measure 16 that had been imposed by District Court Judge Michael Hogan in Oregon—making assisted suicide technically legal. The Circuit Court overturned the District Court on technical grounds—lack of legal standing by the plaintiff who had asked for a stay of the suicide law: a disabled Oregon woman who was not terminally ill, and so, said the Circuit Court, not personally affected by the law to which she objected.

On November 4, 1997, Oregonians resoundingly affirmed their 1994 decision to allow legal assisted suicide in the state, 60 percent to 40 percent. While Measure 16, proposing legal assisted suicide, passed by some 32,000 votes, Measure 51 (which would have repealed Measure 16) was hammered by some 200,000 votes.

Exit polls done for the *Oregonian* newspaper were revelatory: voter after voter told pollsters that the issues in the election were not ethics and morality, but autonomy and choice. Oregonians, as suspicious of outside influence and authority as ever, felt, as political analyst Jim Moore says, "that they had decided this issue for themselves in 1994, that they did not appreciate having to vote again on the issue, and that they damn well wanted to make their own decisions about the end of their lives. They wanted to be able to choose, period."

Even Robert Castagna, the director of the Oregon Catholic Conference who had fought ferociously against assisted suicide for eight years, acknowledged the nature of the election. "Oregonians," he said ("his head buried in his hands," as the *Oregonian* reported) "appear to have an exaggerated sense of personal autonomy at the expense of values of family, community, and the common good. Choice and personal autonomy have become the modern-day idols which Oregonians are worshipping."

"It's a different world today, November 5, 1997," said Dr. William Toffler of Oregon in the pages of the morning *Oregonian*. Indeed it was: assisted suicide was legal. But everyone was confused about what that actually meant: doctors, hospital administrators, legislators, lawyers, patients.

More confusion reigned late in the afternoon of November 5, when the news flashed in Oregon that the federal Drug Enforcement Agency had issued this statement: "The Controlled Substances Act authorizes the DEA to revoke the registration of physicians who dispense controlled substances 'without a legitimate medical purpose.' [Physicians prescribing deadly doses of medications] would be, in our opinion, a violation of the act."

For the next few days in Oregon, the papers and airwaves were filled with the angry or satisfied reactions of the state's elected representatives, summed up by, on one side, by the Republican U.S. Senator Gordon Smith ("I support this action") and on the other by the Democrat U.S. Representative Peter DeFazio ("The DEA is attempting to make criminals of physicians helping Oregonians with very personal, difficult decisions. They're way out of line, and they should just butt out").

The state's governor, John Kitzhaber, M.D., who had spent years working in an emergency room, tiptoed around the issue: "It's up to Oregon voters to determine what appropriate medical practice is, and they've done so." No further comment; he waited to see what would happen with the DEA. (One happening, according to the *Oregonian*, was that U.S. Attorney General Janet Reno flew into a rage; she hadn't been alerted to the statement beforehand, and it was the Justice Department that would have to defend the DEA in possible lawsuits from furious—and out of work—deregistered doctors.)

So everyone waited, in those first few days after the election: doctors, fearful of losing their DEA registration and unsure of their legal liability in assisted suicide; politicians, fearful (with the exception of Smith) of contravening a law twice voted in by their constituents; patients, unable to find doctors to prescribe lethal doses of medicine; and the Catholic community, rattled by an overwhelming political defeat.

News item, the *Oregonian*, November 14, 1997: Nadia Foldes, age seventy-four, of New York City, was reportedly assisted in her suicide in a Catholic church last week in the Archdiocese of Detroit. Foldes, suffering from liver cancer, inhaled carbon monoxide in an unnamed church "with a sympathetic priest," said Dr. Jack Kevorkian, who claimed to have assisted at Foldes's suicide and carried her body to a nearby hospital.

Physician–assisted suicide in Oregon, legal since 1997, entails these steps: A patient, at least age eighteen and an Oregon resident, diagnosed with a terminal illness (less than six months to live) and ascertained free of mental illness by her registered physician (a doctor of medicine or osteopathy, by law), requests help with her suicide. She must make this request orally.

Her physician enters her request into her written medical record, informs her that she can drop this request at any time, informs her of feasible alternatives ("including, but not limited to, comfort care, hospice care, and pain control," according to the statute), asks if she wishes to inform her family of the request, and refers her to a second doctor, who must confirm diagnosis, terminal illness, mental stability, and whether or not the request has been made voluntarily.

If these conditions are met, the patient presents a written request for "life-ending medicine." This request must be witnessed by two people who are not her doctors, and one of whom must not related by blood, marriage, or adoption, not entitled to any part of her estate, and not attached in any way to the health care center where she is a patient or a resident. This witnessed written request is then entered in her medical records.

Fifteen days after the oral request has been made, and two days after the written request, the patient can obtain the "medication." The doctor notes on the prescription that it is written in accordance with the Oregon Death with Dignity Act. The pharmacist (who has the same option as the doctors to decline to participate) counsels the patient on use of the "medication." Once the patient obtains the "medication" the formal involvement of the medical community ceases.

According to the *Oregonian*, doctors in assisted-suicide cases usually prescribe an overdose of barbiturates. Although Medicare and Medicaid programs do not cover assisted suicide because of a federal ban on spending for the procedure (signed by President Clinton), private insurers do because they are obligated to cover office visits and prescriptions. Oregon has the second-highest HMO membership percentage in America, behind only Maryland.

By August of 1998, the DEA had been forced off its stance by Janet Reno; the U.S. Congress was considering two bills prohibiting doctors from prescribing lethal doses of pills to their patients (sponsored by Henry Hyde in the House and Don Nickles in the Senate); Oregon had decided to cover assisted suicide in its statewide public health plan (which, eerily, covers 300,000 low-income citizens, the same number of people who are Catholic in Oregon); Archbishop Vlazny had written an article in the *Oregonian* objecting to state insurance coverage of "an immoral act;" and ten Oregonians (five men and five women) had obtained lethal prescriptions.

Eight had used them to die; the other two died of their illnesses. The average age of the ten was seventy-one years old. Nine different doctors wrote the prescriptions. Deaths came, on average, within forty minutes. On average the patients lapsed into unconsciousness within five minutes.

October 1999: Congressman Henry Hyde of Illinois, sponsor of the House of Representatives' Pain Relief Act, calls Oregon doctors who assist their patients in committing suicide "hangmen," "social engineers," and "messengers of death." His act, amending the federal Controlled Substances Act to forbid use of same in assisted suicides, passes the House 271–156. In the Senate, Don Nickles of Oklahoma readies a bill by the same name for a vote. Among its supporters is Joseph Lieberman of Connecticut, soon to be candidate for vice president of the United States. Senator Ron Wyden of Oregon announces angrily that he will derail the bill with a filibuster.

Nickles's bill never gets to a vote in the Senate, and has not to date come to a vote in the new Congress—shunted aside first by impeachment proceedings.

November 2000: The Dutch Parliament passes a bill which legalizes physician-assisted suicide in the Netherlands—a practice illegal but tolerated and never prosecuted. The law takes affect in 2001 and provides that Dutch citizens sixteen or over may request lethal medication on their own; patients age twelve to sixteen must have their parents' consent to die. The *New York Times* reports that an estimated five thousand Dutch citizens use assisted suicide to die each year.

February 2001: The Oregon Health Division releases its annual report on assisted suicide in the state. In 1998, the first full year in which suicide was legal, sixteen people killed themselves with the help of their doctors. In 1999, twenty-seven people killed themselves. In 2000, twenty-seven people killed themselves. For the third year in a row, "loss of autonomy" was the main reason patients sought assisted suicide. And for the third year in a row, the Oregon doctors filing reports on requests for assisted suicide noted that the number of patients who expressed "fear of being burdens on friends, family, and caregivers" continued to rise.

What are the national implications?

Many observers in Oregon consider the Oregon law essentially unique, on the theory that no other state has the combination of prickly independence, religious paranoia, relative lack of religious affiliation, vehicle for "direct democracy," and general suspicion of outsiders in any garb that Oregon does. In this vein it's interesting to note that a 1994 national voter survey paid for by the Our Sunday Visitor Institute found that only 43 percent of respondents said they would support an assisted-suicide initiative in their own states; polling of Oregon voters before, during, and after the 1994 and 1997 votes consistently show 60 percent support of assisted suicide.

It's also interesting to note how many medical authorities in Oregon and nationally said publicly that care for the dying improved markedly in the state even before the passage of Measure 16. Oregon Health Sciences University, the state's largest public hospital and medical school, expanded the teaching of end-of-life care to its medical students, who come from all over the nation. Referrals to hospice programs rose by 20 percent. Use of morphine in Oregon hospitals rose until it was second in the nation (behind Nevada—the other top states, interestingly, were New Hampshire, Vermont, Missouri, and Arizona, and the bottom states were Hawaii and Utah). Courses in pain control were developed by the Oregon Medical Association, the Oregon Board of Medical Examiners, and OHSU's Center for Ethics in Health Care. "End-of-life teams," first developed in Catholic hospitals in Oregon in 1993, spread first to the rest of the nation's 1,200 Catholic hospitals and then into the public sector.

Why have assisted suicide and euthanasia become more popular ideas in America in the last twenty years—so popular that organizations in Oregon, California, New York, Washington, Maine, Massachusetts (in a bill authored by a Boston College law professor), and Michigan have striven to make assisted suicide legal in their states?

I see four specific reasons: (1) a documented leap in suicide rates in America; (2) a documented leap in doctors informing their patients of terminal illness; (3) changes in medical technology that have made it easier to sustain life in the dying; and (4) the rise to legislative, judicial, and cultural power of Baby Boomers, a generation adamant about autonomy, independence, personal choice, and individual rights. It is no coincidence, I think, that *Roe v. Wade* and the rise of gender rights, ethnic rights, racial rights, and sexual preference rights movements have all come in the last thirty years, as the Boomers have come to adulthood, middle age, and now late middle age.

As for the suicide spike, a federal study of American suicides between 1980 and 1990 showed that there had been a 21 percent increase in suicides among Americans aged sixty-five or older. It is interesting to note a coincidence here: the Hemlock Society was founded in 1980.

As for the boom in informative doctors, a study by the *Journal of the American Medical Association* in 1961 showed that only 10 percent of the doctors surveyed nationally informed their patients of the patients' cancer—terminal or not. The same study in 1979 found that 97 percent of the doctors surveyed told their patients of their cancers, both terminal and not.

What did the Catholic community in Oregon do right and wrong in the assisted suicide debate in Oregon?

Right: Education of voters on end-of-life issues, pushing doctors and nurses and hospice workers to the forefront in public statements and appearances, recruiting hospital and healthcare and hospice spokesmen and spokeswomen to carry the campaign, making moral stance clear and unambiguous but not coercive or dismissive, building coalitions among other faiths and groups, using small-town newspaper op-ed slots, e-mail networks, encouraging and stimulating as much grassroots activity as possible in parishes, high schools, seminars, book groups, etc.—"Chicago-style ward politics," as Tyson of the University of Portland says.

Wrong: Shrill attacks on the immorality of other side, rising quickly like a stupid fish to anti-Catholic baiting (which only succeeds in making the church the issue at hand), recruitment of outside help and money (widely seen in Oregon, rightly or wrongly, as carpetbagging), laggard coalition-building, depending almost wholly on expensive television and radio advertisements, singularity of voice (in 1994 the Catholic anti-suicide campaign had few talking heads, foremost among them the archbishop, the director of the Catholic Conference, and the national bishops' spokesman, Richard Doerflinger; in 1997 far more local faces were seen, male and female, and doctors, nurses, and lay Catholics were far more prevalent in public discourse).

Perhaps the greatest irony here is that the Church, in my view, conducted a far more thoughtful and effective campaign against suicide in 1997 than it did in 1994, despite the far greater margin of victory for suicide proponents. The better campaign was hammered for two big reasons (I think): Oregonians' annoyance at a revote, and the fact that the Church was still a central issue, a stain left over from 1994.

Says Mary Jo Tully, the archdiocesan chancellor:

> If we were to conduct this campaign for the first time, knowing what we do now, I'd play the medical card far more than we did in 1994, and I'd recruit every voice possible from the hospice movement. Doctors and nurses and hospice workers are the people dealing with the dying. They know their patients and what the dying want and need.
>
> And I'd run two campaigns—one for Catholics, educating them on end-of-life issues and their faith's stance, and the other for non-Catholics, on end-of-life issues and ethics and personal stories from the front.
>
> We did not link with significant and respected individuals in Oregon in 1994, people with name recognition, with reputations as independent thinkers: writers, philanthropists, scholars, artists, historians, teachers, business leaders, scientists, politicians. We spent enormous effort trying to link to institutions, and that was a mistake. Voters don't care as much for official stances as they do for people speaking independently from the

heart. That's immensely persuasive in Oregon and I cannot imagine it would not be as persuasive everywhere. When we are moved or touched by a story, that's when our opinions change or are formed.

Last voices:

Archbishop John Vlazny of Portland:

I'm somewhat relieved that assisted suicide hasn't become common—we are averaging about twenty-three a year in Oregon. And there's been no state pressure on Catholic healthcare facilities to facilitate it. This may be one of those things that Oregonians want to be able to choose but don't actually use.

What concerns me most is that this will exacerbate the inconvenience of elderly women and men—like me—in our society. If you're old you're in the way. That's what we communicate to the elderly now. And such disrespect is a sign of failing civilization, I believe. This is a subtle but very serious problem, one we have attacked with many projects here in Portland, in large part to show the world that there are other ways to deal with the frail and dying elderly than to kill them. We cannot convert pro-suicide forces by arguing with them. We can only influence them by our example. That's our direction now. That's the influence we want to have on culture here. That's what the Church does at its best. That's what evangelization means at its best.

Bob Castagna, Oregon Catholic Conference:

The driving forces for assisted suicide are demographics and medical economics—a growing population, a population living longer, a large segment of the population aging at the same time. Those forces are not changing in the United States in the years to come. Assisted suicide is here, it is now legal, it has been voted on in several states, and it will not go away. Nor, I am afraid, will it be confined to Oregon.

David Tyson, C.S.C., president of the University of Portland:

The legalization of abortion has now led to the legalization of suicide, and I believe that twenty years from now we will be arguing about quality of life in Alzheimer's patients. Oregon will be voting on a ballot measure to decide who kills Grandmother: the family or the state?

In the same way that the U.S. Supreme Court decided that the fetus is not a person, so it—we—can say that Grandmother the vegetable, or the four-year-old vegetable child, isn't a person, and should die.

2

POPULAR CULTURE
AND LITERATURE

American popular culture and its sometimes outlandish, even surreal, images of religious faith and Catholicism, in particular, are often said to pose great challenges to Catholic civic engagement. James Fisher contravenes this typical view by asking in his opening paragraph: What if it turns out that our popular culture—as it is generally understood—is deeply rooted in the American Catholic experience? What if the real issue is not how the Church can more effectively engage the popular culture but what it thinks of its own role in creating and sustaining it? In its complex way, Mark Massa's lively rejoinder both confirms and challenges Fisher's argument.

High culture too poses a challenge to Catholics in the public square. European and English Catholics produced some of the great religious novels of the twentieth century; American Catholics have sometimes modestly, sometimes defensively claimed a place in that achievement. Assimilation, the end of a Catholic subculture, and a diffusion of religious identity make claims for a Catholic novel even more problematic. Can there be a distinct Catholic contribution to the contemporary American literary imagination? Paul Elie worries that the richness of the Catholic tradition does not necessarily lead to the freedom to write from that tradition—truth claims hobble the imagination. In contrast, Valerie Sayers offers two simple rules: "Question 1: What is the duty of the Catholic novelist? Answer: The duty of the Catholic novelist is to write a good story," and "Question 2: What is the duty of the Catholic novelist who chooses to write about the church? Answer: The duty of the Catholic novelist who chooses to write about the church is to write a good story."

Is anti-Catholicism a live issue in American culture? A former spokesman for the United States Conference of Catholic Bishops (USCCB) offers a case-by-case analysis of media coverage of important Catholic events in the 1990s. This "neuralgic" topic is taken up again part 3.

CATHOLICISM AS AMERICAN POPULAR CULTURE

James T. Fisher

Catholicism and American popular culture have generally been depicted as rivals, as competitors for the attentions of masses of people, the young in particular. If, as many seem to believe, the Church and the popular culture of the United States are wholly separate entities, then we might fruitfully inquire as to the nature of their interaction. But what if it turns out that our popular culture—as it is generally understood—is deeply rooted in the American Catholic experience? What if the real issue is not how the Church can more effectively engage the popular culture but what it thinks of its own role in creating and sustaining it?

Unlike the nation's civil and ecclesiastical traditions, there are few creation narratives for American popular culture that exclude a Catholic presence. Anti-Catholicism was deeply rooted in the imaginations of the nation's earliest religious and political leaders as well as in the institutions they created. Catholicism was proscribed at various times in several New England and Mid-Atlantic colonies, and as late as the 1850s a Republican orator could proclaim: "American civilization in its idea is historically, the political aspect of the Reformation." The development of a national popular culture proceeded from a very different story. As historian Russell Nye and others have argued, a truly popular culture requires the mass audience that only urbanization and technologies of mass distribution can produce—"a cultural condition," as Nye explained, "that could not have appeared in Western civilization before the late eighteenth century." In the United States those conditions did not exist until after the Civil War, though as early as the 1830s spiritually regenerated Protestant shopkeepers in brand new cities like Rochester, New York, would try in vain to control the scant leisure activities of an increasingly "foreign" (Catholic) workforce.

The notion of popular culture currently operative is clearly rooted in the rise of mass entertainment and leisure activities in the burgeoning urban centers of post–Civil War America, especially after the 1880s. By that time Catholics were the dominant numerical as well as political force in many of the booming cities of the Northeast and Midwest. The Germans and the Irish were soon joined by millions of eastern and southern Europeans who were often indistinguishable in the dwindling imagination of Anglo-Saxon privilege. Henry Adams's famous lament—in his 1905 autobiography—was inspired by Jewish immigrants but might have applied to Catholics as well. "Reeking of the ghetto" Adams wrote, these newcomers evinced "a keener instinct, an intenser energy, and a freer hand than he—American of Americans, with heaven knew how many Puritans and patriots behind him." By 1906 Catholics outnumbered Protestants by two and one half million souls in the nation's 117 largest cities. Henry Adams understood that these new Americans arrived at a moment of decisive social and economic changes that would yield a post-Protestant America. The birth of a mass popular culture was, as historian R. Laurence Moore has explained, "specifically a non-Protestant and ethnic working-class accomplishment. Immigrant Catholics, whether Irish, German, Italian, Polish, or Hispanic, carried to the United States a great variety of street entertainments, a zest for holiday and carnival rooted in folk traditions. Not only could these specific things be commercialized but they also reflected an untroubled acceptance of gaiety that made possible an enormous range of other commercial pastimes."

Mass circulation newspapers, nickelodeons, Coney Islands, vaudeville houses, movie palaces, and finally commercial radio broadcasting created a new language and a new culture whose initial exemplars were such urban Catholics as the writer Finley Peter Dunne—nephew of a prominent Chicago pastor—and boxing champion John L. Sullivan, an Irish-American national hero of the 1880s. On meeting the Prince of Wales, Sullivan declared: "If you ever come to Boston be sure to look me up—I'll see that you're treated right." If the Irish supplied the vocabulary of urban mass democracy, Italian Americans helped shape the sound of the city. Nick LaRocca of New Orleans led the first recorded jazz ensemble, while Philadelphia guitarist Eddie Lang (Salvatore Massaro) teamed with violinist Joe Venuti on legendary recordings of the early 1930s. Thousands of Irish- and Italian-American Catholics explored the boundaries of "white" and African-American urban culture in the early years of the twentieth century, shaping a popular sensibility that was enshrined nationwide in recordings and early films. The interaction of Jews and Catholics on the streets of New

York prefigured the almost reflexive tendency of Jewish producers in Hollywood "to synthesize the Christian religion," as Daniel Patrick Moynihan put it, "in the person of an Irish priest." Similarly, "when it came to playing a tough American, up from the streets . . . James Cagney was the quintessential figure."

Admittedly, as Moynihan noted, Cagney usually wound up dead by the end of his pictures, but the larger point is that American popular culture grew out of the interplay between Catholics and members of other urban minority groups. Pluralism was a creative fact of life rather than a theory in need of justification. Precisely at the moment when "Americanism" was drawing condemnation as a theological premise, it was being mastered in practice by the urban laity with little apparent spiritual damage. The same dynamic was at work during the "modernism" controversy. Scott Appleby has noted that theological modernism was hardly a "movement" in this country since fewer than two dozen priests were connected to the phenomenon in the late nineteenth and early twentieth centuries. While its condemnation by Pope Pius X as the "synthesis of all heresies" may well have dampened academic theology for decades, in the broader culture such Catholics as Eugene O'Neill and F. Scott Fitzgerald helped shape the contours of "the modern." But the real significance of modernism for Catholics was in the realm of mass production and mass consumption, where they played a leading role: on Henry Ford's assembly lines as well as in the industries of mass communications that flourished in the major urban centers.

In many ways Dorothy Day's conversion narrative marks a watershed in American Catholicism's encounter with both modernism and the popular culture it nourished. Day was the most influential Catholic of the twentieth century among elites in the Church, and she set a spiritual and esthetic tone that has been remarkably enduring. The "anti-modern" turn Day's life took upon meeting Peter Maurin in 1932 achieved its theological authority in direct proportion to the misery she presumably experienced as a Greenwich Village and Staten Island bohemian, friend to such quintessential modernists as Kenneth Burke and Malcolm Cowley. The Catholic Worker movement provided a theological model for resistance to mass culture—personalism—as well as an aesthetic of simplicity whose impact on American Catholic taste cannot be exaggerated.

These accomplishments were so significant that the wrinkles in the story are lost and may never be recovered. The canonical literature cannot even get the birth date of her daughter Tamar right (1926, not 1927), as though to do so would add an additional unaccountable year of wrestling with the decision to convert. Of greater significance for the present discussion is the period fully two years after her conversion when Day wrote scripts in Hollywood for Pathe films (she did not enjoy the experience, but who among the modernists in Hollywood admitted they did?). I belabor this issue to make a point: American Catholics have been denied the resources necessary for theological reflection on the potential value of Dorothy Day's career as a modern and pop culture maven. We have made compulsory a conversion model that proceeds from materialism to renunciation, from entanglement with the fearsome swell of popular culture to detached critique of its spiritual inauthenticity. And we have done so without acknowledging the partial sources for this move in what John Murray Cuddihy called "Protestant taste." We have severed theory from the experience of the urban, ethnic Catholics who invented American cultural democracy, the kind of people less likely to read the *Catholic Worker* than the *New York Journal-American*, a paper edited for twenty years by none other than Dorothy Day's brother Sam.

One indication of a thaw in this habitual Catholic intellectual response to mass culture may be found, surprisingly enough, in several recent studies of the Catholic Legion of Decency and the National Organization for Decent Literature. Without calling for a revival of these watchdog groups, scholars have found that they actually represented a major effort by figures in the Church to engage the popular culture in a meaningful way. Far from serving a merely censorious function, leaders of the Catholic cultural apparatus offered serious critiques of the film and popular literature industries, grounded in Neo-Thomism and the theology of the Mystical Body of Christ. They objected to the dissociation of art from morality and unfettered capitalist individualism without denying the democratic impulses of popular culture. Some even reveled in pop culture, including Daniel Lord, S.J., who drafted the Motion Picture Production Code in 1930, worked extensively in radio and theater and—according to my friend Steve Werner—may even have invented the lip-sync technique! The reappraisal of figures such as Lord has been prompted by the emergence of Catholic cultural studies, a field not often credited with inspiring theological reflection. Yet as historian Una Cadegan shows in a forthcoming article, the Legion and NODL generated meaningful discussion on popular culture both within the Church as well as without. For Cadegan, this provides sufficient evidence to claim that "American Catholicism was densely entangled in the web of mid-century culture, shaping the terms and conclusions of its debates even as it was shaped by them." Daniel Lord and his colleagues had limitations aplenty, but in recovering this story of the Catholic engagement with American popular culture, Cadegan and others provide models for a broadened discussion in our own time, with genuine theological implications.

The Catholic involvement in the culture industries was founded on an informal alliance with Jewish figures that generated tensions most evident in the 1930s and early 1940s. Then World War II generated a massive interfaith campaign, reflected in countless films depicting multiethnic multireligious platoons of men fighting for democracy. The postwar era witnessed a potent "spiritual front" whose magnitude had never been fully recognized. Beyond the spectacular conversions of ex-leftists to Catholicism and the mass appeal of Fulton J. Sheen to a national television audience, a more fundamental and lasting shift occurred in this period. The industries of popular culture became a powerful vehicle for both the formal teachings of the Church and a "practical Catholicism" that was all but synonymous with Americanism, and far from shallow or compromised. *On the Waterfront,* a collaboration between a Jesuit labor priest and a host of ex-popular front artists, won eight Academy Awards for 1954 and shattered the *Going My Way* priestly archetype in its explicit treatment of social injustice. Catholics reigned supreme on television in the 1950s, from Sheen to Jackie Gleason to Ed Sullivan. Sullivan was a premature multiculturalist who helped to transform popular taste on his Sunday evening variety show while using his powerful syndicated column to promote equal rights for all Americans. His Irish-Catholic rival in the gossip business, Dorothy Kilgallen, was an equally outspoken advocate of racial justice in the 1950s.

Cultural democracy was the central theme of the "spiritual front" and it was clearly grounded in the urban Catholic experience. This was the real "new frontier" of the period, since it introduced the nation to Catholics in action on the common ground of popular culture. Even the Hollywood "Rat Pack" did its part: two Italian Catholics, an African American, a Jew and an Englishman who qualified only due to his links to the Irish American they all hoped would become president. In many ways these characters showed the way to a "world made safe for diversity" that John F. Kennedy hoped to achieve, even as he was the greatest beneficiary of the vision. The Catholic cultural moment surely lasted longer than the political. Take a look some time at the video of Frank Sinatra and Dean Martin in performance at a 1965 benefit concert on behalf of St. Louis's "hoodlum priest," Dismas Clark, S.J. These men were no longer cultural outsiders, and the cause for which they worked was not incidental to their religious identity. In doing it "their way" they confirmed the triumph of the immigrant church in transforming the whole culture of a nation.

Few could have imagined in 1965 that thirty-five years later the prospect of a second Catholic president would be more remote than at virtually any time in the previous century. On the other hand, we do have a

Catholic president on TV, played by a man who changed his name to honor Bishop Sheen and is regularly arrested while serving witness to his religious convictions. Martin Sheen apparently insisted that his character on *The West Wing* be a Catholic and a Notre Dame graduate at that. It may not have been a very hard case to make at the network. Those who lament the ubiquity of the "secular media" would be hard-pressed to account for the presence of Robert Wright as President of NBC. Wright is a graduate of Holy Cross and Chaminade High School in Mineola, Long Island, where his Marianist teachers illustrated lessons on the social encyclicals with screenings of *On the Waterfront*. By the late 1950s, that is, some American Catholics were already becoming theologically educated, in part via the popular culture (one of Wright's Chaminade classmates, Pete Axthelm, went on to become an Ivy League educated, second-generation version of the streetsmart Catholic journalist, Jimmy Breslin variety). While I have no idea if there is a connection between Wright's background and Sheen's character on *The West Wing*, it is clearly much easier for a Catholic to head a television network than Harvard, Yale, Princeton, the American Historical Association, or the United States of America in "real life."

We might well ask if the power of popular culture to fulfill wishes grows as prospects in other spheres dim. The fragmentation of American Catholicism over the past three decades resulted in more than the demise of the Legion of Decency. It has also made it much more difficult to envision a scenario for Catholic engagement in the public square devoid of paralyzing internecine warfare. On the other hand, some might argue that if a Catholic influence or Catholic public presence had to be limited to one arena, popular culture is the place you want to be. The evidence there in recent years is incontrovertible: Catholic angles rule, from Gregorian chant and cloister walks topping the charts and bestseller lists, to the astonishing popularity of Frank McCourt's lugubrious memoir (admittedly more "ethnic" than religious, and with an anti-clerical twist), to Rosie O'Donnell and her pal Madonna, to the *Sopranos* and their more wholesome Jersey counterparts from *That's Life* (ditto the ethnic factor). "Religion" on TV shows has become virtually synonymous with Catholicism. The Catholic League's successful campaign to drive *Nothing Sacred* from the airwaves was accompanied by ritual incantations over "non-Christian" control of the media, but the real story was, of course, about the Catholic power on both sides of the issue, since the show was devised by a Jesuit. As sociologist of religion Robert Wuthnow has shown us, the truly contentious action today is within denominations, given the full cultural legitimacy afforded Catholicism and Judaism.

It's a wonder there is so little outcry over the Catholic dominance of the nation's popular culture. There are numerous obscure websites that offer whimsical or ominous arguments why Barney the Purple Dinosaur must be a Catholic, but they don't know the half of it. Barney is obviously a Catholic of the communitarian, diversity-embracing, pro-family variety. But it goes way beyond that. Richard C. Leach, the father of Barney's creator and the financial angel behind the Purple One's mind-boggling cultural hegemony among the toddler set, is a major impresario of Catholic television and theatrical programming. Leach bankrolled and produced the 1998 PBS documentary *Reflections on Vatican II,* and he underwrites religious education programs for public school children. Then there is Martha Stewart, the former Martha Kostyra from a Polish-American neighborhood in Nutley, New Jersey. I'm not a big fan or viewer of her programs but I'm told she does not discuss theology from her position atop a marketing and taste-making empire. She does, however, produce a magazine that features an extraordinarily if unofficially "sacramental" quality, from the faux-liturgical calendar of events to the highly ritualized approach to food preparation to loving reminiscences of her family life in Nutley. In one of the grossest misreadings of American popular culture, Stewart has often been critiqued as a purveyor of WASP values of genteel domesticity. Obviously no self-respecting WASP would share these bizarre secrets with an audience of millions. The Martha Stewart phenomenon is an instance of Catholic cultural imperialism: there's no domain we can't make our own, and share it with the masses; it's what Catholics do in making and remaking cultural democracy in America.

Sure, this is popular culture, skeptics may protest, but what does it really have to do with Catholicism? Well, we have been taught by some good priests that it has a lot to do with it. Father Andrew Greeley is the most prominent exponent of the "sacramental imagination" school that has "theologized" countless exemplars of popular culture. Greeley and those he inspires claim to discern a sacramental or "analogical" sensibility at work in a wide range of Catholic visual and literary art executed by figures with varying degrees of current formal allegiance to the Church. Greeley's work over the past fifteen years or so—deeply and openly indebted to theologian David Tracy, author of *The Analogical Imagination*—has helped to spark the emergence of Catholic cultural studies. Some are uncomfortable with ascribing "Catholic" stature to figures currently "outside" the Church, but who could object to suspending denominational credentialing if the results yield such pop culture luminaries as Bruce Springsteen, Madonna, Francis Ford Coppola and other avatars of Greeley's sacramental imagination? (I do not know if Greeley has caught up yet with Martha Stewart.) The problem with this approach is not its standards of membership but a kind of Catholic essentialism that ironically resurrects the specter of the dreaded "ghetto." Catholics are different, we are told, because they "imagine" differently than Protestants and others. Another wall of separation is just what we don't need.

Greeley's notoriety and his heavy reliance on Tracy's authority may help account for the obscurity of an earlier generation of works on the "sacramental imagination" that dealt much more concretely with the workings of the culture industries and were less partisan in spirit. In *The Image Industries*, published in 1959, a year prior to the appearance of his best known book, *Christ and Apollo*, William Lynch, S.J., argued that the explosion of popular culture (which he tended to equate with the "mass media" as was the custom) demanded a response in the form of a "creative theology." Lynch was less concerned with seeing Catholics win recognition for their creative prowess than he was with the role of the theologian in promoting "freedom of the imagination," the "preoccupation of the saint and of every true artist." Lynch worked out of the same tradition as his fellow Jesuit Walter Ong and Ong's former teacher, the Catholic convert Marshall McLuhan, who together provided much of the conceptual apparatus for understanding the rise of popular culture and mass media. For Lynch, it was not enough for Catholics to organize cultural watchdog organizations, because he doubted that "the Holy Spirit has ever operated" in such a fashion. The "creation of a really human world of beauty and sensibility," he insisted, "has never come from anything less than thousands of indeterminate forces."

Lynch also insisted that "the Catholic mind does not believe that some corners of life have a theological relevance (or a relevance for spiritual freedom) and others have not." In reading Lynch I could not help but recall one such corner on Route 36 in Leonardo, New Jersey, the site of a Quick Stop convenience store recast as a kind of sacred slacker's space in the film *Clerks*, Kevin Smith's 1994 directorial debut. I wrote at the time that this was a deeply Catholic film and that Smith would inevitably make a heavy-handed attempt to render his theological concerns more explicit. That prediction was borne out in *Dogma*, alas, but since Smith's religiosity has received some serious notice in recent years (in the *New York Times* as well as in *Commonweal* and *America*), I beg your indulgence (though a dispensation may be more accurate) as we return for a final time to the Quick Stop hard by Raritan Bay. The recent debacle does not diminish Kevin Smith's significance as a leading Catholic artist of a generation for which popular culture did not merely compete with religion, but shaped the form and content of spirituality itself. Smith wants us to see how much Catholic energy has been in-

vested in the materials of everyday life and how futile it is to seek boundaries between the sacred and the profane. The clerks (clerics) at the Quick
Stop engage in some of the most fervent verbal disputation this side of neo-
scholasticism, as distinctions between nature and grace are rerouted into a
virtuoso debate over the respective merits of *The Return of the Jedi* and *The
Empire Strikes Back*. The more conventionally spiritual messages in the film
are all encoded in mass culture detritus that viewers could easily overlook.
A headline on a news rack tabloid in the Quick Stop, for example cries out,
"Pray for Them," while a competing weekly weighs in with its own con-
soling response: "We're Saved!" Dante Hicks, one of the clerks, opens the
store for business with a set of keys affixed to rosary beads. Dante is of
course the guide to the netherworld of Jersey shore Italian and Irish America, mall rats, white ethnic "hicks."

The blackouts that punctuate each scene in *Clerks* bear such labels as
"vilification," "perspicacity," "vagary," "purgation," "lamentation," and
"catharsis." The spoken dialogue in the film is slightly less elegant. The jar-
ringly vulgar language that peppers the script of *Clerks* serves as a reminder
that grace will not always come wrapped in the mantle of good taste to a
generation that grew up on lewd comic books, blood-soaked video games,
and casual pornography. I taught history to members of this Catholic lost
generation (or is it children of the lost generation?) at the state university
just up the road from the Leonardo Quick Stop, and I spent far too much
time in barrooms with a just slightly older cohort. While the Dominican
chaplains stationed at Rutgers bemoaned the rampant secularism on campus, I felt the place was awash in Jersey Catholic spirit. It seemed that every
parish school found in the twenty-one counties was represented on campus
by a kid who embodied the home truth: all Catholicism is local. Yet we do
not train young people to appreciate this fact. In *The Image Industries*,
William Lynch noted that "it is amazing how many people will fly instinc-
tively to Italy or to Mexico for vacations within a Catholic style of the
imagination," yet no one ever thought of doing so within the United States.
Little has changed in forty years.

I wish to suggest that the suspicion with which many elite Catholics
continue to view popular culture is grounded less in theology than in the
nature of what sociologist Herbert Gans calls "taste cultures." For nearly
four decades the dominant American Catholic "taste culture" has been remarkably stable, comprised of individuals formed, or transformed, by the
experience of the Second Vatican Council and by the unofficial "canoniza-
tion" of influential spiritual figures and movements. The anti-materialist
spirituality fostered in various apostolates inevitably cast a shadow over

denizens of "mass culture" and its endless distractions. This has effectively disenfranchised an enormous cohort of Catholics under the age of say, forty-five, most of whom grew up amid a wholly separate "taste culture" that they are tacitly required to check at the door of the Church. As the former altar boy Kevin Smith complained to *Time* magazine, "Every week I go to church, and sooner or later the priest makes a joke! How come a priest can mix religion and jokes, but if I do it I'm anti-Catholic? That just burns my ass, because I'm out there trying to get people to think about God. I am working the good cause—and I'm anti-Catholic? I tithe! I don't bend down and tie my shoe when the basket comes around!"

Smith's jokes, of course, tend toward profanity and, some would suggest, "sacrilege." Yet for decades Catholic tastemakers have exalted the suave adulterers and booze-soaked priests of Graham Greene and other paragons of the "Catholic revival."

It's because they eventually take us to a place where we think we ought to be. Many younger Catholics have a different orientation, and this includes not only the "alienated" members of Generations X, Y, or Z but the neo-traditionalists among them as well, who often reveal a nuanced pop culture sensibility that belies their image as ultramontanist reactionaries. The American Catholic studies movement has made a contribution toward bridging the divide between these "taste publics," in recovering the material texture, for example, of immigrant devotionalism. The best of these works also provide rich material for theological reflection on popular culture that goes far beyond the celebratory mode. In *American Catholic Arts and Fictions*, Paul Giles showed how the thrice-weekly communicant Andy Warhol looked at such pop culture icons as Elvis Presley and Marilyn Monroe "through a pair of quizzical metaphysical spectacles that acknowledge how these American icons are like Catholic saints, but in the end really aren't. His works aggrandize American popular culture but also ironically detach themselves from their own (supposedly celebratory) premises." Giles places Warhol in the tradition of the "ironic imagination" limned by William Lynch S.J., which "works to 'de-absolutize' worldly objects by implying that they possess only a provisional quality in the light of higher truths."

Insights like these serve to enhance the Church's understanding of its own traditions. When we finally own it all, there will be no excuse for the kind of rub-your-nose-in-it antics of Kevin Smith and similarly talented but woefully unformed Catholics of his generation. The rest of the world knows America largely via a cultural machinery built by citizens of the immigrant church in collaboration with other erstwhile outsiders. We can acknowledge the magnitude of this achievement, while working to further transform popular culture in light of Catholic tradition unembarrassed by the resources it offers. In addition to asking "What would Jesus do?", we might ask with the Catholic author Jack Kerouac: "What would Jesus say if I went up to him and said 'May I wear your cross in this world as it is?'"

[handwritten: nice conclusion]

SELECTED READINGS

Una Cadegan, "Guardians of Democracy or Cultural Storm Troopers? American Catholics and the Control of Popular Media, 1934–66," *Catholic Historical Review* (forthcoming).

Bruce David Forbes and Jeffrey H. Mahan, eds., *Religion and Popular Culture in America* (Berkeley, Calif.: University of California Press, 2000).

Herbert J. Gans, *Popular Culture & High Culture: An Analysis and Evaluation of Taste* (New York: Basic Books, 1999)

Paul Giles, *American Catholic Arts and Fictions: Culture, Ideology, Aesthetics* (New York: Cambridge University Press, 1992).

Nathan Glazer and Daniel Patrick Moynihan, *Beyond the Melting Pot: The Negroes, Puerto Ricans, Jews, Italians, and Irish of New York City* (Cambridge, Mass.: MIT Press, 1964).

Andrew M. Greeley, *The Catholic Myth* (New York: Collier Books, 1990).

William F. Lynch, S.J., *The Image Industries* (New York: Sheed & Ward, 1959).

Colleen McDannell, *Material Christianity: Religion and Popular Culture in America* (New Haven, Conn.: Yale University Press, 1995)

R. Laurence Moore, *Selling God: American Religion in the Marketplace of Culture* (New York: Oxford University Press, 1994).

Nick Tosches, *Dino: Living High in the Dirty Business of Dreams* (New York: Doubleday, 1992).

"AS IF IN PRAYER": A RESPONSE TO "CATHOLICISM AS AMERICAN POPULAR CULTURE"

Mark Massa

When I was a newly ordained priest, serving in the wilds of North Cambridge, Massachusetts, in the working class parish of St. John the Evangelist—the parish, as it would turn out, of then Speaker of the House "Tip" O'Neill—I was initiated into the mysteries of popular devotion to the patron saint of hopeless causes, St. Jude. On the opening night of the novena to Saint Jude, the old Irish pastor of St. John's laid out the stage directions for the opening of our devotions: we were to go out into the sanctuary, genuflect in front of the blessed sacrament, and then walk over to the statue of Saint Jude especially constructed for the novena: we were to pause in front of the statue, the old pastor told me—and I quote—"as if in prayer." It struck me forcefully for the first time, as a newly minted cleric fresh out of seminary, that there might be quite a chasm between the academic theology I had been studying for three years, and the lived religion of the folks in front of me.

James Fisher takes as axiomatic the reality and the creative possibilities inherent in the chasm brought home to me that evening; further, he suggests that we take as our starting point the simple givenness of cultural pluralism, that we accept the popular mentality as a legitimate locus for authentic religious insight, and that we recognize the epistemological reality of "taste cultures" in writing about the relation between religious and popular culture. As a brilliant and creative founding member of the relatively new academic discipline of American Catholic studies, Fisher has provocatively asked us to reexamine the cultural location of an immigrant "ghetto faith" we thought we had pinned down—a faith we thought was located, as Lesley Woodcock Tentler once phrased it, "on the margins" of the landscape of American culture.

Quite frankly, I think that Fisher's proposal is an exciting and fruitful call for students of the American Catholic past to take responsibility for a lucid interpretation of the complicated history of cultural negotiations between Catholics and public culture in twentieth-century North America.

Fisher's framing of the relationship between Catholicism and popular culture offers us four important insights for discussing the location of Catholics in U.S. popular culture. First, he asks us to reconceive "center" and "margins" as fluid realities in cultural history; indeed, he implies that this very idea of center and margins is perhaps an outdated way of conceiving the relation of actual lived faith to the North American mainstream culture. One of the implications of this reconception might be that the model constructed by intellectual and institutional historians about "mainstream" Protestantism and "marginal" outsider faiths like Catholicism is perhaps no longer helpful in understanding how most Americans live their lives in the public square. In this, he is the inheritor of several generations of brilliant insights offered by social historians and *annales* scholars. What his paper asks is that we deal intellectually with the insights of scholars like R. Laurence Moore and Andrew Greeley in understanding how Catholicism has been a cultural player in North America for several generations. This point is the most obvious and most important in his paper: the real question in the world of Simpson family values is not "how can we make Catholicism more culturally relevant?" but rather, "how can we more effectively frame models to understand the considerable cultural power it already has, and continues to have?"

Second, (and related to the above), Fisher is asking that students of American religion simply "get with the social scientific program." As social scientists have realized for almost a century, human culture is a constantly renegotiated lived reality that includes consumer economics, demographic and ethnic loyalties and class relations. Given these rather old truisms ("old" at least for cultural anthropologists and sociologists), Fisher asks us to take seriously the long-known fact of the numerical dominance of Catholics in twentieth-century North America, the cultural and political power of Catholics in urban enclaves, and the reality of a "post-Protestant America" recognized a half century ago by Reinhold Niebuhr, and celebrated thirty years ago by the magisterial historian of religion Sidney Ahlstrom. The inside is the outside, as Ahlstrom pointed out in 1968, and vice versa. As Cher said when she slapped the face of Nicholas Cage in *Moonstruck*, so Fisher seems to be saying to the old consensus historians of American religion: "Snap out of it!"

Third, with Robert Orsi and David Tracy, Fisher asks us to face squarely the idea that the "religious imagination" might be far more decisive in shaping lived faith than doctrine, worship, or ecclesiastical norms. Implicit in this insight is the recognition that the history of ideas, which largely defined the field of American religious history for fifty years, can't get at the whole truth of lived religion. Thus, as he correctly observes in his paper, "Americanism" and "modernism" as systems of theological ideas—whether successfully condemned by the Vatican or not—can't explain the engagement on the ground of American Catholics with modernity and the dynamics of American culture.

And fourth, Fisher asks us to consider the largely ignored role of class in understanding the relation of Catholic elites to the "great unwashed" immigrant-shaped piety of American Catholics. With Lawrence Levine, Leigh Schmidt, and Colleen McDannell, Fisher asks us to utilize ideological suspicion to unmask the disdain of elite groups like Catholic theologians toward large portions of North American popular culture. He is undoubtedly correct in pressing the fact that the "anti-materialist" rejection of mass culture by such elites as theology professors, editors, and clerics represents a profoundly anti-sacramental, un-Catholic stance which must be examined more carefully to discern the non-theological, class-ideological impulses informing it.

At the same time that I would confess that Fisher has offered us remarkably fruitful insights for reconsidering the relation of Catholicism to mass culture, I would like to raise some questions about some of his points; more specifically I would like to raise five questions. First, I would propose that perhaps Catholics were far less important in crafting the twentieth-century mass-culture vision than second- and third-generation American Jews. Certainly R. Laurence Moore was correct in arguing that the birth of mass popular culture in the United States was an accomplishment of "non-Protestant, ethnic working-class immigrants." But I wonder if Catholics had pride of place on that list, as most of the engines of that culture—especially the engine operating out of Hollywood—were in other than Catholic hands, however much Hollywood bowed the knee to Catholic sensibilities. If Fisher is perhaps overly sanguine about the leadership of Catholics in mass culture during the course of the twentieth century, then I would like to pose an alternative question: Why have Catholics fairly consistently been successful as "players" in popular culture, but have left others to write the scripts and direct the action? Why has so much Catholic participation in the cultural world of films, radio, journalism, and television been "second storey" rather than seminal? Why have the children and grandchildren of other immigrant ethnic groups—Jewish Americans, for instance—been so successful in crafting, directing, and producing films, books, and television sitcoms, as well as symphony orchestras, book publishing houses, and journals, while Catholics have tended not to be? The standard characters presented as objections to this "second storey" interpretation—F. Scott Fitzgerald, Ernest Hemingway, Martin Scorsese, and Madonna all tend to be what we used to call *lapsed Catholics*. Why is this?

Related to this first point, it is possible to read the Catholic role in mass culture by applying the ideas of Ann Douglas. In *The Feminization of American Culture*, Douglas argued that the apparent gains made by marginal groups like nineteenth century women offer significantly less than we might think, on closer examination. Douglas's point was that the book publishing trade was allowed to cater to the tastes of religious women in the late nineteenth century precisely because both religion and the book culture itself lost significance for the culture as real centers of power. Ann Douglas's insight might be posed to us this way: Is it possible that Catholics were given cultural permission for more participation as players in popular, mass culture precisely at the moment when "nice people"—meaning white, Anglo-Saxon Protestants—took significantly fewer cultural cues from that culture, or much cared for its taste choices?

Can such an explanation of Catholic participation in popular mass culture help to explain why Catholic elites, both in the past and in the present, position themselves with such disdain vis-à-vis popular culture (at least partially in an attempt to gain a different kind of cultural legitimacy from the real arbiters of cultural power), and should Catholics therefore be worried about uncovering their participation in, and control over, very different loci of power and taste?

Second (and, as someone paid to do theology, this is my mandatory theological question): Is "a Catholic's view" necessarily "*the* Catholic view?" As every Catholic knows, there is a tensive quality between what Tracy and Greeley call the "sacramental imagination," and institutional loyalty to the Roman Catholic Church. Not everyone with an analogical imagination is necessarily Roman Catholic—for instance, the category may include Anglicans, Lutherans, and certain Reformed Christians. And the reverse is equally true: not all practicing Roman Catholics understand the cultural implications of their beliefs, and therefore live out of an "analogical" or "sacramental imagination."

The explicitly theological component of this question has to do with models of Christ and culture, more specifically with H. Richard Niebuhr's models of Christ and culture: What relation between transcendent belief and human culture is most fruitful for the flourishing of both religious faith and human culture? It seems to me that Fisher is proposing as normative for understanding Catholicism's role in American popular culture what Niebuhr labeled the "Christ of culture" model. In this model, religion's role is primarily to support, nourish and shape human culture on the culture's own terms, or at least according to terms fitted to meet cultural tastes.

This was, of course, as Robert Handy pointed out three decades ago, the privileged model of the Protestant establishment in the United States throughout most of the nineteenth and twentieth centuries. Handy's point in his great book *A Christian America*, however, is that this model of the "Christ of culture" betrayed mainstream Protestantism in its hour of need, during the gilded age, leading directly to its current position of cultural disarray.

It seems to me that a more fruitful and vibrant long-term model both for assuring Catholicism's integrity, and for fulfilling its duty of conversing with North American popular culture in understandable ways, is the model Niebuhr termed "Christ and culture in paradox." This model glories precisely in the fact that a Catholic's view is not necessarily *the* Catholic view, because transcendent values transcend all human cultural norms and tastes. From a theological perspective, the "Christ and culture in paradox" model asserts that religious faith best serves human culture, including popular mass culture, when it judges it and holds it to account as falling far short of faith's vision of the "good society."

The "Christ and culture in paradox" model is most assuredly not a popular one in any sense, in that it asserts that the very real, permanent tension between faith and culture is not, and should not be, relaxed. Indeed, faith's very purpose vis-à-vis culture is to make cultural participants anxious—anxious unto salvation, as it were. As John Wesley observed so well in the eighteenth century, in religion, nothing fails like cultural success, a point he made about Quakers. He observed that they came to Pennsylvania to do good to others, and ended up only doing very well for themselves.

Therefore, my second (theological) question is this: While it's important—no, probably vital—for religious faith to have its fingers on the pulse of popular mass culture, is success as participators in that popular culture the best means for gauging Catholicism's appeal or success in eliciting and retaining the loyalty of ordinary folks? Further, does Catholicism's success or failure in that arena tell us anything normative about what it should be doing in conversing and converting that culture in the future? From a theological perspective, quite honestly, I'm not so sure.

Third: Is "Catholic essentialism" a bad thing? Fisher's paper voices the fear that using ideational constructs like the analogical imagination to explain a Catholic take on culture raises the specter of the "ghetto mentality" that most of us are very glad to be free of. Perhaps. But is essentialism related to ethnicity in a positive and fruitful way, thus setting Catholics off from at least some mass culture values? I'm pretty convinced by folks like Marty, Greeley, and Moore that ethnicity has been an extraordinarily successful way for groups to navigate the rapids of North American culture, providing identity and direction for various social groups, especially in the face of prejudice and cultural suspicion.

The ancient and revered tradition of anti-Catholicism in the United States has a place in the discussion here—an anti-Catholic cultural impulse that Arthur Schlesinger once termed the oldest intellectual tradition in the United States. My question is this: Was "Catholic essentialism" something that developed as much from the anti-Catholic "outside" as from the Catholic inside in North America, and has the resulting sense of "ethnic essentialism" that—until very recently—has cut Catholicism off from many sources of popular culture been completely a bad thing for the health of North American Catholicism? Might it have given American Catholics their own, distinct, reading of ethnicity that has served them well for quite a while? And further, has that ethnic sensibility in the twentieth century— part of which was undoubtedly a sense of being outside the popular mainstream on issues like sexuality and reproduction, education, and family life— cut Catholics off from mass cultural tastes in fruitful ways?

Fourth: All Catholicism is, most certainly, "local in part." Indeed, I suspect that most Catholics are really Congregationalists, valorizing or demonizing their local parish as the sacrament of the true company of all faithful people. But my fourth question has to do with being part of a tradition that calls itself "Catholic" in every sense: It seems to me that being part of an international community of faith has saved North American Catholicism from the culture worship resulting from living in such an affluent country as our own—a country that G. K. Chesterton once termed "a nation with the soul of a church."

While more studies of the local church are certainly needed in the field of American religion to understand how the Catholic Christian tradition was and is actually lived in North America, is more localism exactly what we need in strategizing about the relation of Catholicism and North American cultural taste? Or, given the adulthood that American Catholicism finally entered several decades ago, is just the opposite the case? That is, should our membership in a transcultural institution make Catholics even more wary about entrusting their tradition to the vagaries of American mass culture? Is there a "transnational worldview" inherent in being a Catholic

Christian that militates against feeling completely comfortable in contemporary mass culture, with its appeals to therapeutic satisfaction, acquisition, and hedonism?

Related to this transnational sense, again, is the disdain of Catholic cultural elites toward American mass culture. Might this sense of being "catholic" with a small "c" account in part for the disdain of many officials of the tradition toward a North American mass culture?

And fifth (and this is the new, postmodernist category of "alterity" rearing its ugly head): Is being an "outsider," or "on the margins" of popular culture, a bad social strategy? I don't know. I was pretty convinced by R. Laurence Moore's book, *Religious Outsiders and the Making of Americans*, that alterity has been a clever cultural strategy for religious groups that want to maintain some sort of long-term presence and group cohesion in a mind-bogglingly open and free society, where everyone experiences not only the opportunity, but the expectation, that they will define themselves in their own way.

My sense, as a scholar who studies the experience of Jamestown to Jonestown, is that the American experiment is at least as communal as it is individualistic. One smart strategy for holding on to the Catholic communal identity over against the sheer force of mass culture, as Alexis de Tocqueville noted two centuries ago, is for groups to valiantly "be different," different in a way that defines them apart from popular culture and mainstream tastes. There is, of course, a price for such difference, both in terms of a ghettoizing identity and in terms of meaningfully engaging the culture. But do the benefits of alterity outweigh the hazards? I'm not sure, but I'd like to talk about this.

I still have the sense I had that evening in St. John's parish in north Cambridge—that popular culture and piety and Catholic theology are different, sometimes very different. I am pretty sure that I don't want to be a scholar who takes part in any communal activity "as if in prayer." But I also don't want to have my faith tradition reduced to exceedingly thin cultural props, as I think it was in films like *Dogma, Going My Way,* or *Truth or Dare*. What to do? What to do?

THE LAST CATHOLIC
WRITER IN AMERICA?

Paul Elie

A few of years ago, when he was still in Connecticut and some priests there were accused of sexually abusing children, Bishop Edward Egan testified in court that the archdiocese and the church shouldn't be held accountable for the priests' behavior. As far as the church was concerned, he said, the priests were "independent contractors."

When this testimony came to light I happened to be rereading *Death Comes for the Archbishop*. You've probably read it yourself: the story of Archbishop Jean-Marie Latour and his sidekick Father Vaillant, French priests and best friends who come to America and go west to hunt out the "lost Catholics" of the desert and call them back to the faith.

Because the novel is about Catholics, it is easy to forget that the author, Willa Cather, was an Episcopalian. And because it takes place in the nineteenth century, it is easy to forget that it was written in 1925. When we think of American Catholicism circa 1925, we usually think of the Catholic masses: packed city parishes, red-brick schools, armies of nuns, saint's-day parades. But there are no crowd scenes in *Death Comes for the Archbishop*. It is a novel about two men, their faith, and their companionship. The two priests are companions—they live in the same country; they eat the same bread—and their companionship comes to suggest the things that bind them in faith: the body of Christ, the life of the church, the communion of saints.

It would be easy to contrast those two priests with the so-called independent contractors of today. But what struck me as I read the novel again was that it is about Catholics who are, in their way, independents. The desert is vast. Other Catholics are few. Rome is far, far away. The priests must live according to their lights. Together, each is essentially solitary. Apart, they are lonely. When Father Vaillant gets an order from Rome to go to the Colorado gold rush, the archbishop is devastated. He passes his nights in the rectory longing for France while his friend goes over the mountains on a specially equipped wagon, big enough for one man to sleep in, with a portable altar hooked to the back of it.

The missionary efforts of the real-life Latours and Vaillants were successful. Today the Catholic Church is the largest church in the United States, and Catholic leaders miss no chance to say so. Yet companionship is sorely lacking. The individual Catholic feels not only independent but—fill in your adjective of choice—alone, lonely, ignored, alienated, solitary, separate, set apart, estranged.

The reasons for this circumstance are best left to other discussions and other experts. What interests me here is how this independence or aloneness affects the Catholic writer.

The other day I looked over the books on the shelves in my apartment, and I was struck by how many of them could be classified as "Catholic literature" or "Catholic writing."

There are big histories of Christianity in Europe and of Catholicism in the United States. There are scholarly books about Lourdes and Italian Catholic Harlem, which depict those places as worlds of wonder, where the religion was thicker and richer than it is today. There is a history of the Irish saints that reads like a novel, and a novel about an alcoholic Irish Catholic that reads like the life of a saint.

There is a Catholic's book about how one man—Otto von Schindler—saved Jews from the Holocaust, and another Catholic's book about how one man—Pope Pius XII—failed to save Jews from the Holocaust.

A trilogy on the moral life by a "philosopher's philosopher" who started out as a Marxist in Edinburgh and has wound up a Thomist in Nashville, Tennessee.

A book by a convert who became famous as a naturalist but sees herself as a theologian.

Several slim volumes of poetry, each of them dedicated "to the glory of God."

A big book of "all saints," one for each day, including Galileo and Gandhi as well as Baron von Hugel and Jacques Maritain, and a biography of Thomas More organized around the question posed to the nascent saint at his baptism: "Thomas More, what seekest thou?"

Book-length essays by the best liberal political commentator and the best conservative one, each of them a Catholic in his fashion.

A novel in which four Jesuit priests set out in the year 2019 on a mission of exploration to the planet Rakhat.

And half a shelf of books by the most acclaimed poet in the English language, a Catholic of Belfast. When this poet accepted the Nobel Prize, he described himself in Catholic terms, as a man "bowed to the desk like some monk bowed over his *prie-dieu*, some dutiful contemplative pivoting his understanding in an attempt to bear his portion of the world." To explain what poetry is, he told the story of Saint Kevin, a monk of old, who was kneeling with his arm stretched out when a bird made a nest in the palm of a hand—whereupon he "stayed immobile for hours and days and nights and weeks, holding out his hand until the eggs hatched and the fledgling grew wings, true to life if subversive of common sense, at the intersection of the natural process and the glimpsed ideal, at one and the same time a signpost and a reminder."

All this variety suggests that Catholic writing abounds and that Catholic writers are thriving. But in my own experience the Catholic writer feels strongly otherwise.

If you are a Catholic writer, you probably know the feeling yourself. It is as though you are the only person left who takes this stuff seriously—the only writer who cares about religion and the only Catholic who has any literary taste. You are the last Catholic writer in America, and you are afraid the species is dying out. That is one of the reasons you stick around.

Your independence becomes the linchpin of your faith, which is not held or practiced or prayed for so much as it is fostered imaginatively, through your reading and writing and your running conversation with the dead. You feel uncertain, even ashamed, to define yourself as a Catholic writer, but nobody is fighting you over it, so you persist.

And in fact in many ways you are indistinguishable from any other writer. The laptop computer. The grants. The symposiums. But you burn interiorly, like one of the French Jesuits of the seventeenth century, the North American martyrs.

You hear that religion is a "hot" category in the publishing world, yet you identify with those martyrs. In theory, they belonged to the church militant, a worldwide multiform communion headquartered in Rome. In fact, "they" were a priest who was alone in the forest trying to translate the Lord's Prayer into Huron in the hope of making himself understood by one of the natives before the others decided to cut out his heart.

If the Catholic writer's sense of aloneness is genuine, it seems a remarkable development, since it runs counter to all that we are told we should expect. By most reckonings, there should be a broad and lively Catholic literary culture.

You know the reasons. There are the numbers. Sixty million Catholics— one American in five—and many of them among the most literate and best educated, etc. Then there is the communal character of Catholicism: Here Comes Everybody and all that. Big families, big holiday meals, big crowds outside St. Peter's Basilica on Christmas Eve and Easter Sunday. Mass in thirty-seven different languages. Social salvation. The communion of saints.

And there are our predecessors. The era before this one was a remarkable one for Catholic writing. There were authors who were undoubtedly Catholic and unquestionably literary, who were read, understood, and appreciated by Catholics and everybody else.

So what makes the Catholic writer today feel so fixed in isolation? Why do we feel, each of us, that we are working alone in the dark?

I don't think there is any one answer any more than I think there is one kind of Catholic writer. But there are reasons, and they have to do as much with the nature of writing as with the nature of American Catholicism today. For one thing, much of the rhetoric about the communal character of Catholicism was just a theological stereotype, one half of a textbook comparison with Protestantism. If it was ever true, it is less true each day. And in truth, Catholicism and Protestantism seem to have switched places. The Evangelical Protestant megachurch is the successor to the urban Catholic parish where there was something going on at any time of day and all needs could be met. There is nothing more atomized than fifty suburban Catholics loping across the parking lot to fifty parked cars after Mass.

For another thing, if you are going to understand culture you can't go by the numbers. I work for a publisher, and when I get a proposal from an author who says there are sixty million Catholics and every one is a prospective reader of his book, I send it back. "It takes a lot of culture to make a little literature," Henry James said, but there is no guarantee that a lot of culture will make a little literature, or that the culture will want to read the literature that does get made.

Twentieth-century American Catholicism gave rise to half a dozen books that will last another century. This brings me to the point I really want to make. It is worth remembering that the great Catholics who wrote those books were independents. They started out alone. They chose solitude. They took trouble to maintain it. They considered their independence fundamental to their writing.

I'd like to dwell on that generation a bit. I have written a book about them, and about our relationship to them, as readers and writers. I would call their era a renaissance—a *Renascence*—except it was not a rebirth or revival. It was something new under the sun.

Here in the United States were four great Catholic writers at once: Thomas Merton, Dorothy Day, Walker Percy, Flannery O'Connor. (Yes, there were others, and I have had many a friendly argument about which names to add to the list, but concerning these four there is a high degree of consensus.) They knew one another just a little. But they shared aims and strategies to a remarkable degree. They all spoke the same language.

Their work is a kind of "wisdom literature." They were obsessed with the question of what it means to be a human being and how a human being ought to live. Their sense of the human person was Christian, so the question of how to live was, often, how the Christian ought to live.

A friend of theirs had a notion of "the School of the Holy Ghost," and that is what I call them. They had as much in common as the Bloomsbury Group, the Harlem Renaissance, the Inklings, or the New York intellectuals.

But what they had in common is not nearly as important as what made each of them unique. One of them issued a stern warning: "Today there are no good writers, bound even loosely together, who would be so bold as to say that they speak for a generation, or for each other. Today each writer speaks for himself, even though he may not be sure that his work is important enough to justify his doing so."

Yes, those four were great. Yet for the Catholic writer their greatness is cold comfort, even a reproach. It compounds your isolation. It suggests what you are not. If you try to identify with them, claim them, write the way they did, it just doesn't work.

Why? One reason, of course, is that the times were different. When you read their books you confront this again and again. Merton's autobiography implied that there was no salvation outside the church. O'Connor asked a priest for permission to read *Madame Bovary*. And here is Dorothy Day, in the confession scene at the beginning of *The Long Loneliness*: "Bless me father, for I have sinned," is the way you begin. "I made my last confession a week ago, and since then . . ."

Properly, one should say the Confiteor, but the priest has no time for that, what with the long lines of penitents on a Saturday night, so you are supposed to say it outside the confessional as you kneel in a pew, or as you stand in line with others.

That might as well be the week after Trent. Times have changed. So has the church.

We don't like to acknowledge it, but what we admire in them is not their books alone but the whole package—the books and the lives all together. We'd like to have them as companions. We'd like to be like them. We'd like to efface ourselves in them, to bury our unbelief in their belief, and in fact many of their readers have lost themselves in this sort of veneration.

But to want to be like them is to miss their point. If there is a single point all their work tends toward, it is this: God wants each of us individually. God calls us one at a time. We are on the same pilgrimage, perhaps, but each of us has to get to the destination. There are no proxies and no rain checks. No matter what church or culture you come from—Catholic or Protestant, in the monastery or on the Bowery—you finally have to believe or disbelieve for yourself.

Day, Merton, and Percy were all converts: the story of their lives is how they embraced the Catholic tradition and made it their own. O'Connor was a so-called cradle Catholic. But the drama at the heart of her work had to do with the moment when a person accepts or rejects the invitation to an act of faith—the moment of grace, she called it.

When somebody asked O'Connor why she wrote about Protestants and not about Catholics, she replied that Protestants had more interesting fanatics. If you are a Catholic fanatic, she explained, you disappear into a convent and are heard from no more, whereas if you are a Protestant fanatic "there is no convent for you to join and you go about in the world getting into all sorts of trouble and drawing the wrath of people who don't believe anything much at all down on your head."

Well, today Catholics as well as Protestants are staying away from monasteries in droves. We too go about in the world getting into trouble over matters of faith.

The Catholic writer might wish to identify with O'Connor, who claimed that the Catholic faith was so much second nature to her as to be the light she saw by, and who was confident enough of the truth of "Christian orthodoxy" to speak of her characters as people deprived of the sacraments and the fullness of truth—religious primitives, grotesques, freaks.

But the fact is that the Catholic writer today has less in common with O'Connor than with the primitives and grotesques she wrote about. Think of Hazel Motes, the evangelist in *Wise Blood*. Here is a young man, raised religious, who on the one hand is determined to show that Christ didn't literally redeem him, and who on the other hand would rather establish his own church than tolerate the imperfections, the blasphemies, the profanations of the church that already exists. He doesn't believe in Christ but still thinks the church has betrayed Christ's message. If he had written a book, it would be taught in the divinity schools.

O'Connor explained *Wise Blood* by saying that as far as she was concerned Hazel's virtue consisted in his integrity—in his refusal to let go of God without a struggle. That integrity is the closest thing to a virtue that the Catholic writer has today. This writer still harbors the suspicion that he or she was made in the image of God and that the Catholic tradition has something to say about it. But what does it have to say?

In his book on God and the American writer, Alfred Kazin said that Melville "retained faith even if he did not always know what and where and in whom to believe." He added, "An agony in the nineteenth century, wistful confession in the twentieth."

That seems to me a good description of the situation of the Catholic writer in America. The Catholic writer still has confidence in the value of the Catholic tradition—as a tradition. Catholicism is interesting. It offers good material. It is a storied history. It is a language we speak. Religiously, however, that confidence doesn't take you very far. And it won't take you very far if you are writing a book, either.

The Catholic writer envies, say, Jewish writers, who seem to have achieved a freedom to write about their tradition as their own without having to agonize over the literal truth of biblical and theological claims.

But our tradition compels us to regard statements about God as true or false. It insists, as Hazel Motes put it, that either Jesus was God or he was a liar. It urges us to look not upon the religious drama of our people but upon the drama of each individual person called to reckon this truth or falsehood—to accept or reject this God in faith.

The religious question of our time is whether religion itself is legitimate. The stumbling block to faith is religion, and even "the faithful" have to ask themselves constantly whether religion is a way to God or stands in the way of God—if God exists. The characteristic believer of our time is a seeker, and what this seeker is seeking is not God so much as a context where God can be sought authentically.

This is especially true of the Catholic writer. The Catholic writer tries to find that place, that context, in the work itself. In my experience there is no better or more excruciating way to find out what you really believe than to try to write about it.

Alice McDermott has said that she doesn't like novels in which Catholicism is a problem. She thinks it should be there in and through and behind everything, informing the way the characters see life and the world around them. I understand what she is getting at, but I think that Alice McDermott is just about the only writer alive who can write that kind of book. In anybody else's hands the Catholic background turns gauzy and sentimental.

I see the situation differently. In my own view, the Catholic writer today is in the same predicament as the person I'll call the "characteristic Catholic," and the best Catholic writing will be that which really confronts the problem that, for most of us, Catholicism is.

There are advantages to the Catholic writer's position. The characteristic Catholic feels independent, alone, estranged. Well, the Catholic writer takes independence as a precondition and an opportunity. Most books are written alone, and are still read that way. The Catholic writer, like that Jesuit priest in the forest, hopes to make himself or herself understood to one other only. A single convert will do. The reader must be persuaded personally, one at a time.

The Catholic writer's independence means, too, that this writer can focus on the individual person's struggle with the act of faith. When the life of the church is usually discussed in aggregate and demographically—the bishops, the declining numbers of priests, all the Catholics marrying outside the church, young Catholics, gay Catholics, Hispanic Catholics, disaffected Catholic women—the Catholic writer keeps in mind that every religious person ultimately must accept or reject faith for himself or herself. The best Catholic writing is the writing that honors, and probes, that act of faith.

Sixty-five million Catholics: sixty-five million acts of faith. The Archdiocese of Chicago once took out billboard space on the sides of the highways. The billboards say, "If you're looking for a sign from God, this is it." Well, the Catholic writer is interested in the story of the individual person driving on the Dan Ryan Expressway who sees one of those billboards and really does see it as a sign from God—and, say, winds up becoming a priest. How does that happen? What is that person thinking as he drives by? How does he overcome the bad pun, the shameless manipulation of the pitch, the knowledge that a hundred thousand other motorists have seen the billboard as well, and believe this is what the Lord meant for him?

Traditionally, the doubter is a solitary. We don't read about crowds of doubters. In art, doubting Thomas is set apart from the other apostles. He shows up late for the meal in the upper room where Jesus appears. He gets to the Virgin's bedside just after she dies.

A writer like Flannery O'Connor apparently knew doubt only secondhand and imaginatively. But the Catholic writer today knows doubt firsthand, from the inside. No matter how deep or assured your faith, as a Catholic writer you are perpetually unsettled. You are thrown back to first principles at your desk every morning. Everything must be plumbed, established again on the page. Nothing can be taken for granted.

So it happens that the Catholic writing of our time is often written not out of faith, but out of an aspiration. The act of writing is a kind of act of faith, similar to the act of religious faith but prior to it. The writer is testing the Catholic view of life to see what it looks like and whether it will suffice.

The writer would like for the Catholic religion to be true, indeed yearns for it to be revealed as such. So the writer adopts that point of view, someplace between revelation and projection. If it can be made believable in writing, maybe it really can be believed in.

There are consequences to this state of things. It means that there are many sincere books about Catholicism that are bad books—bad writing and bad faith. The writer tries to "correct" Christianity to make it persuasive. The writer unwittingly reduces Christianity to his or her own sense of things. The writer takes the supposedly robust faith of a past age as a subject and supposes that the subject matter makes faith plausible for the reader in the present. Or the writer mistakes a sincere act of inquiry for good writing.

This state of things also means that we can't confidently point to "Catholic writers." A writer will take a run at the act of faith once, then move on to the Civil War or sexual politics. Or a writer, having made a run at the act of faith, will go at it again and again, but the thrill is gone.

It means that there are Catholic books whose Catholic character is not immediately apparent. The successors to the two priests in *Death Comes for the Archbishop* are the two bums in William Kennedy's novel *Ironweed*, companions who hear the dead speak as they dig graves for spare change. The descendant of the Jesuit missionary in the forest is the essayist Richard Rodriguez on a tour of the California missions, a man whose aloneness is as vast as the Americas.

It also means that the authors of the best Catholic writing may not be known to us as Catholics. They may not be Catholics at all.

I think of Denis Johnson, who is known for his book of stories called *Jesus's Son* (the title is taken from the Velvet Underground song "Heroin"). His book *Resuscitation of a Hanged Man* is the best novel I know about the struggle for faith. The hero literally doesn't know whether he is a saint or is crazy. He goes to see a priest. It is Provincetown, Massachusetts, and he is wearing a dress. The priest asks him if he has sought help, and the hero says, "That's why I'm here, isn't it?"—a scene that seems to me to say it all about the mismatch between the religious impulse and the church's "resources" for dealing with it.

I think of Richard Bausch, author of a story called "All the Way in Flagstaff, Arizona." Walter is Catholic—a lapsed one—and the father of five young children. He is also an alcoholic, and at a family picnic he nips at a fifth of Jim Beam while the kids make a hash of the catechism. That night, he chases the kids around the yard—first playfully, then demonically—and his wife tells him she is leaving him. Haunted by memories of his own father, an alcoholic and child abuser, Walter sees a psychologist, but "there is no use talking about childhood drama and dreams: Walter is versed in the canon; his hopes are for something else." And so he finds himself in the back of an empty church in Flagstaff, wondering if he should tell the priest "how he walked out to the very edge of the lawn and turned to look upon the lighted windows of the house, thinking of the people inside, whom he had named and called sons, daughters, wife . . . trembling, shaking as if from a terrific chill, while the dark, the night, came."

A Catholic writer who isn't Catholic? This is not as unorthodox as it might sound. Chesterton's ideal Catholic writer was Charles Dickens. Flannery O'Connor said that "the Catholic novelist doesn't have to be a saint; he doesn't even have to be a Catholic; he does, unfortunately, have to be a novelist."

How else to explain that the best writer about religious life today is a Presbyterian laywoman who has found, in the disdained, uninhabited plains of the Dakotas, a correlative for the experience of monastic life today, and the setting of religious faith?

As an independent, the Catholic writer is especially clear on some things. The writer hopes the church will like the work, but doesn't count on it. The writer knows the old language of service and responsibility is provisional. This writer doesn't write on behalf of the church. But this writer also knows that the church doesn't believe on behalf of the writer.

Such a state of things isn't necessarily desirable. Most Catholic writers would like to be fully vested members of the church. That said, it is the situation. Catholics often make a fetish of the ideal. It seems to me that the most important thing is not to posit a shared system of values or to yearn for a Catholic literary community that doesn't exist. These things have to be earned, one believer at a time, not simply asserted.

The Catholic writer has to seek a companion in the reader first and foremost. Further companionship isn't strictly necessary. It might even hinder the work Catholic writers are trying to do.

There has been a run of memoirs of Catholic childhood. I'd give a hundred of them for one great memoir of Catholic adulthood, and I'd bet that such a book would mean more to the life of the church than a hundred polls.

As Catholics, too, we believe that we are bound together in ways that we do not realize, and that this binding is taking place in ways we cannot see. We are bound to one another, bound back to the dead, and bound to the future in hope in ways that are as yet unknown to us.

Perhaps in the future we shall be a community of writers—or we will be seen as such. But for the time being, the Catholic writer has to make his or her way independently. The work, and the life of faith, depend upon it.

BEING A WRITER, BEING CATHOLIC: SOMETIMES THE TWAIN CAN MEET

Valerie Sayers

Book editor, author, and journalist Paul Elie argues that the most distinctive thing about the contemporary Catholic writer is his or her "aloneness," and that any distinctively Catholic writing must come to terms with that fact. "What makes the Catholic writer feel so fixed in isolation? Why do we feel, each of us, that we are working alone in the dark?" Elie asks. The answer he gives is multifaceted and nuanced, but finally settles on the "nature of writing as much as the nature of American Catholicism today." Writing is first of all a solitary pursuit. The Catholic writer, like all writers, "hopes to make himself or herself understood to one other only. A single convert will do." Contrary to much of the communal rhetoric that attaches itself to the church, such an individual emphasis is not foreign to Catholicism. "The Catholic writer's independence means, too, that this writer can focus on the individual person's struggle with the act of faith," Elie says. "For many modern Catholics, the stumbling block to faith is religion, and even 'the faithful' have to ask themselves constantly whether religion is a way to God or stands in the way of God—if God exists."

My assessment of the problems facing the Catholic writer and my hopes for the future of fiction written by Catholics are slightly different from Elie's, although I do not fundamentally dispute his thesis. Let me begin with a little autobiography. I was raised in the deep South where Catholics banded together in large raucous groups, the better to flaunt our drinking and dancing in the Bible Belt; I spent a good chunk of my adult life in an equally social parish in Brooklyn, where even our little homeless shelter served as the site of all-night doughnuts and yacking; and I am currently employed by the University of Notre Dame, where I only have to holler down the hall to find another Catholic writer or two. And yet I think Elie's emphasis on the loneliness of the contemporary Catholic and the solitude of the Catholic writer is absolutely correct. Here we are in an age defined, simultaneously, as postreligious and hyper-religious. In such a time every writer is acutely aware, as Elie says, that "the religious question of our time is whether religion itself is legitimate." The very question, perhaps, is enough to make us feel alone.

At my university, as in other religious and political spheres, there is currently tremendous emphasis on answering that question by announcing religious identity repeatedly, by insisting upon it. I sometimes worry that the concern over self-identity obscures a far bigger problem. Easy enough to practice identity Catholicism, to say I am Catholic, or a Catholic writer; while that sort of name-tagging provides succor and support, as we Catholics in the Protestant South knew, it can also lead to the worst kind of front-pew breast-beating. Far harder to be a Catholic writer. Catholicism calls us to reimagine our lives by looking outward as well as inward, by identifying with the poor and the suffering and the least among us, and that is sometimes hard to remember in the comfy little enclaves of Catholicism, whether they be universities or jolly parishes. Certainly it is hard for the writer sitting alone at a blinking computer screen, engrossed in describing this glitzy world of ours in all its post- and hyper-religious manifestations. We can all recognize a piece of writing that uses Catholicism as subject, or even as background; far more difficult to define writing that is Catholic.

I don't believe that a Catholic writer needs to be writing about explicitly Catholic subjects, but I don't object to the most prickly of them either. I'm all for novels in which Catholicism is a problem, if that is where the writer must dig. It's also fine with me if a novelist chooses a religious crisis or an institutional crisis or abortion or the death penalty or parish scandals or all or none of the above. Writers choose their subjects in pretty much the same way all of us choose our dreams: subjects pursue writers, not the other way around, and often it is the least tasteful and/or the most threatening subject that insists on being explored. That subject may or may not be identifiably Catholic, but certainly a Catholic vision of the world will inform every word a writer chooses. If we aspire to Catholic writing, then we had better let the Gospels propel us. Let me invoke a non-Catholic, Eudora Welty, who says that the act of writerly imagination she holds highest is the act of identification with others: "What I try to do in writing of any character," Welty says, "is to try to enter into the mind, heart, and skin of a human being who is not myself. Whether this happens to be a man or a woman, old or young, with skin black or white, the primary challenge lies in making the jump itself."

This act of identification, it seems to me, is a writerly affirmation of the Gospels and their call to see ourselves in others. Christ's story, after all, is the ultimate act of identification, the narrative of God's willingness to take on human skin. Yet identification is useless if it is sentimental or deluded; writers have to be clear-eyed and they need to achieve that distance we know in literary terms as ironic. Perhaps the greatest danger for a Catholic writer is a projection of a personal spiritual struggle onto the subject at hand. But when a writer is able to simultaneously enter a subject's skin and see the subject clearly, from a distance—even when the subject is the self—then we have some hope of a connection between writer and subject and reader, a link, a shared vision which challenges the writerly solitude about which Elie spoke. Those are connections to be relished. Let me give an example. My eighty-two-year-old mother was hospitalized recently with heart fibrillations; when I called the hospital, she said (with some spirit): "I'll tell you what landed me here. I was reading Flannery O'Connor and, boy, she really set me off." (I am not making this up.) Naturally I asked which O'Connor she had been reading. *Everything That Rises Must Converge*, she said. "When they take the grandmother off to shoot her." She had confused *Everything That Rises* with *A Good Man Is Hard to Find*, but she said exactly what she needed to say to me, because it was I who recommended *Everything That Rises*, and that is yet another story in which an older woman dies at story's end. My mother's identification with these old mothers was so complete that her heart went a little wild; I think that would have pleased O'Connor, especially since my mother is one of those readers who not only won't miss the religious significance of the fictional physical crisis, she will take it upon herself. (Besides, O'Connor was uncharacteristically soft about that grandmother the Misfit shoots: "She lacked comprehension," O'Connor said, "but . . . she had a good heart." So, it seems, does my mother.)

Several years ago I spoke to the Catholic Commission on Intellectual and Cultural Affairs on the subject of the Catholic writer who chooses to portray the church. I ended that address with a little catechism for Catholic writers: Question 1: What is the duty of the Catholic novelist? Answer: The duty of the Catholic novelist is to write a good story. Question 2: What is the duty of the Catholic novelist who chooses to write about the church? Answer: The duty of the Catholic novelist who chooses to write about the church is to write a good story. I stand by those words, however much I recognize the wise-guy tone of my younger self. When the subject is the church itself, Catholic writers open their eyes wide and often find themselves describing—as O'Connor and J. F. Powers and Walker Percy did—the superficiality of much activity described in our culture as religious. We may also see unexpected images of the church: my Notre Dame colleague Sonia Gernes, for example, recently published a story in the *Georgia Review* about nuns on roller skates. Certainly we Catholics may have particular cause to concentrate on the physical, on the body—on the roller skates, perhaps—in our writing. My Protestant friends in South Carolina found it shocking that we kept Christ's body up there on the cross; we wallowed in suffering, they thought. Their own crosses were tastefully empty, the better to concentrate on Christ's triumph and not on his agony. But Catholics insist on the body, on the word incarnate, and that is just as likely to involve a depiction of suffering bodies as it is to involve suffering souls.

But most crucially, Catholic writers write knowing that, as Isaac Babel said, "No steel can pierce a heart so icily as a period in the right place." The Catholic writer's duty is not only to subject but to form: to affect a reconciliation between subject and form, to practice the art with responsibility and delight, to give fully of the writerly self in the service of the work. In that sense, we ask of the Catholic writer precisely what we ask of the Catholic carpenter or nurse or funeral director. There is certainly no guarantee that we as writers will give any clearer demonstration of what it means to be Christ-like than that carpenter or nurse or funeral director will; in fact, there is considerable evidence that writers, like the rich, may have farther to bend. Writing is not a higher calling; many argue that it's not much of a calling at all. The standard coy interview response to the question, "Why do you write?" is: "It's all I know how to do," but for many of us that's the sorry truth. When O'Connor was asked, she said: "Because I'm good at it," and then, she says, she "felt a considerable disapproval in the atmosphere. I felt that this was not thought by the majority to be a high-minded answer; but it was the only answer I could give."

But what, exactly, qualifies as "Catholic" writing? For many years a popular teacher at Notre Dame taught a course on Catholic writers whose reading list included Kafka. I think I understand what he was trying to do, and perhaps it's not necessary to be Catholic to be a Catholic writer, but I wonder then how useful the label itself is. There are Catholics who are writers, and there are writers who concern themselves with the church, and the intersection of those two groups sometimes looks tiny, especially since there are so many former Catholics ("bad Catholics," we used to say) writing about their institutional experiences. I find that I am a poor guesser about who belongs in what group: when, as a young woman, I first read Muriel Spark, I was astounded to discover that the possessor of that cold eye was a practicing Catholic. Ron Hansen's *Mariette in Ecstasy*, on the other hand, is so reverent a novel that I was certain only a non-Catholic was capable of achieving the distance necessary to describe ecstatic religious experience; that will tell you far more about my own cynicism than it will tell you about Hansen, who is indeed Catholic. Larry Woiwode's great American novel, *Beyond the Bedroom Wall*, is so suffused with Catholicism that I never would have guessed from its pages that its author would leave the church for Protestantism. The formerly Catholic—and here I think first of Robert Stone, Louise Erdrich, and (I guess) Maureen Howard—show us the church anew, sometimes in terrifying ways, and while it is fascinating to speculate about their current religious beliefs, the speculation isn't nearly as fruitful as the reading itself. Some writers—Tobias Wolff, Mary Karr—hardly give themselves away. In *Best American Short Stories*, Tim Gautreaux, who lately seems to be in the volume every year, has a story about an alcoholic priest and in his commentary mentions his own Catholicism: a delight to discover another from the fold, even though I didn't much like the story. One of the problems with discovering new Catholic writers is the problem with discovering writers at all: the consolidation of the publishing industry, the megacorporate bodies unwilling to commit to a novel they can't pigeonhole or guarantee to be an eye-popper.

When trying to define Catholic writing it's also impossible not to notice how many self-identified Catholic novelists—Spark, Waugh, O'Connor, Percy, Powers—have been drawn to comedy and how often that comedy challenges the limits of realism, as if our faith itself so challenges the limits of rationalism that realism becomes inadequate as form. I am working my way through the novels of Hilary Mantel, two of which, *An Experiment in Love* and *Fludd*, concern themselves directly with the Catholic experience. I am convinced (again, I'm guessing, and I'm a poor guesser) that Mantel is an ex-Catholic, but in *Fludd* the voice is so driven, the comedy so ecstatic, the form so enticingly close to surreal, that I see her literary connections to Spark and Waugh and I cannot but speculate. We should certainly also keep our collective Catholic eye on Latino and Latina writers— here I think of Cristina García, Junot Díaz, Ana Castillo. They offer us another vision of the way Catholicism makes its presence known in culture, and so too will emerging African and Asian writers.

One thing that a range of Catholic and once-Catholic writers from different cultures reminds us of is that it is a writer's formal impulses, and not just a writer's subject, that lead us to wonder whether Catholicism has a hand at the writer's elbow. For those of us who remember the Latin Mass, the effect of that liturgy on our formal concerns is a given. Among my undergraduate students, who've grown up on some pretty bad so-called folk music, I think I see the effects and I think they're pretty scary. They often include a fake sense of community, a gooey and repetitive blandness of voice that I find utterly depressing. And this is where we come full circle back to Paul Elie's insistence on the singular act of the writer, because much as we need community—Catholicism is community—the word comes out of one mouth at a time. For the writer the obligation is to make that word precise and pleasurable and challenging and true.

Elie also asks his audience to imagine what a great contemporary memoir of adult Catholicism might be like. I back off a little at the word memoir: the sheer volume of these self-reflections in the last decade or so has been overwhelming. When I think of the great spiritual memoirs, of Dorothy Day and Thomas Merton, I think of the communities in which they lived, the lice in the Worker houses which Day could use as the contrast to her own life story, the background of monastic life against which Merton could consider his own nonreligious upbringing. Those writers achieved a balance between the time spent looking inward and time spent looking outward. We, on the other hand, are living in the Age of the Self, and it appears to be harder for a memoirist to achieve that. In this age of the first person—look how shamelessly I have used it here—we can hope for a memoir of a spiritual life, but we might, if we are lucky, get other kinds of writing too, writing far stranger. Harold Bloom's whimsical notion that the great writers are also the odd writers seems tailored for contemporary Catholics, whose religion so often looks odd to the culture. If we look for idiosyncrasy from Catholic writers—and I think we should—we might get characters like Charmian Piper in Muriel Spark's *Memento Mori*, whose Catholicism is confused and imperfect but nonetheless unwavering and joyful, and not in the least perturbed by divine voices ringing up on the telephone. We might get the moral tales that Eric Rohmer gave us in two forms, story and movie, each unashamed to be Catholic and unashamed to be sophisticated and worldly and witty. We will get, I hope, a surprise, something that is as angular and gawky as *Wise Blood* or as starkly poetic as *Mariette in Ecstasy*, something as hard to believe and as inescapable as the Gospels themselves, something which makes its way to the self through an examination of other lives. I hope we get writing with forms that comment on this computer-video-comic-book-virtual reality age of ours. I hope we get writing that does not have to trumpet its Catholicism because it will be so Catholic. I hope we get writing created in isolation and loneliness that, as it reaches its readers, achieves communion.

THE PRESS AND THE CHURCH'S SOCIAL TEACHING: FRIENDS OR FOES?

Kenneth J. Doyle

When Pope John Paul II visited nine cities in the United States in 1987, more than 18,000 journalists were accredited to cover the trip—nearly twice as many as had ever covered any event in U.S. history.

In Miami, as the Pope celebrated the Eucharist in Tamiami Park, there was a huge thunderstorm; the Pope had to interrupt the Mass and ask the crowd to go home. (Some were standing in puddles of water, and lightning bolts were streaking the sky.) The Pope went into a small trailer and finished the Mass.

The press corps who had accompanied the Pontiff from Rome was transported immediately to Columbia, South Carolina, the Pope's next stop. As we entered the press center, we were besieged by the local press, seeking details. One journalist approached a colleague of mine and asked at what point the Mass in Miami had been interrupted. He was told that it had been during the homily, right after the reading of the Gospel. And the journalist asked, in all seriousness, "Does that part come before they sacrifice the virgin?" (It was then explained to the journalist that the sacrifice of a virgin is not a regular feature of the Catholic liturgy.)

I relate that incident simply to make this point: media personnel are not always religion-savvy, even when covering religious news. In fact, some studies would suggest that media personnel are often ill-equipped, by background, to make sense of religious news. In 1980, a survey by Smith College political scientist Stanley Rothman and Robert Lichter, president of the Center for Media and Public Affairs, discovered that among major media journalists, only 14 percent attended religious services at least once a month and that 50 percent had no formal religious affiliation. The same study, done in 1995, showed that journalists' church-going had doubled, to

30 percent. But that still means that major media journalists are less religiously observant than most Americans; a 1998 National Opinion Research Center (NORC) poll showed that 51 percent of Americans attend religious services at least once a month.

Those figures, I am quick to admit, prove nothing. But they suggest a lot. There is no iron-clad proof that a journalist's own religious practice makes him/her a better transmitter of religious news. (One even hears at times the reverse argument: that distance produces objectivity.) But most people would intuit—and rightly so, I believe—that a journalist who practiced some religion would—all else being equal—be more sympathetic to religious news and more comprehending of its importance.

So one might imagine, from the above figures, that Catholic teaching would not fare well in the media. But the fact that it is Catholic social teaching introduces another dynamic. The Freedom Forum and the Roper Center once asked 139 Washington bureau chiefs and congressional correspondents whom they had voted for in the 1992 presidential election; 89 percent had voted for Bill Clinton and 7 percent for George H. W. Bush. The same subjects were asked their political affiliation; 50 percent were Democrats, 4 percent Republicans. (Now this, of course, could simply mean that journalists who happen to be Democrats gravitate toward Washington, while Republicans remain elsewhere. More probably, it means that most of the media are Democrats.)

The nexus remains to be made with Catholic social teaching, and I am well aware, as the U.S. bishops' statement on political responsibility points out every four years, that Catholic teaching is not coterminous with any political party's platform. But central to Catholic social teaching, I would submit, is the thesis that government exists—in part, at least—to take care of people who are vulnerable in society and cannot otherwise provide for themselves (the poor, the elderly, the sick, the homeless). That political philosophy, I would further submit, gains a more sympathetic hearing among Democrats than among Republicans.

So one should perhaps look for the possibility that, in covering Catholic social teaching, the political philosophy of American journalists may help to balance out a religious aloofness. More, of course, remains to be done to demonstrate that hypothesis with any real certainty.

The overriding rubric in all of this is the media's penchant for the quick and the catchy. An anecdote will perhaps illustrate. In 1983, Pope John Paul II visited Austria. During that same week, a Korean airliner was shot down over the Sakhalin Islands, and more than two hundred people were killed. In one of his talks in Vienna, the Pope inserted a reference to that tragedy, lamenting the violence, praying for the victims. After the talk, I met a friend of mine who was covering the trip for a major international wire service; millions of people depended on him for their understanding of what the Pope was doing and saying that week. And he said this to me: "Thank God the Pope stuck something in about that plane. Otherwise we'd have nothing to write about. All the other stuff," he said, "was religious stuff." I laughed and said, "Well, he is the Pope, you know, and 'religious stuff' is sort of his business."

We are really a news generation that television has produced: it's the aberration, not the norm, the sensational not the sane, the controversial not the calm that tends to rivet the media's gaze. Today Catholic social teaching always has to be filtered through this lust for the sound bite; and, closely reasoned as it often is, it can suffer in that process.

Having set that backdrop, let us now see how the U.S. media has treated some of the church's social teaching over the last several years—with some observations, too, on how we can help to guide that coverage. My perspective on this comes from several angles: as a journalist in Rome covering the Vatican; as press secretary in Washington for the U.S. bishops; and now, in my latest incarnation, as a "simple pastor," on the lookout for what parishioners see in the media and how it strikes them.

PAPAL STATEMENTS AND COMMENTS

The papal encyclical *Centesimus annus* of May of 1991 is a case study in the inherent difficulty of covering a major document and how that difficulty sometimes can be surmounted. The encyclical, of course, is a lengthy and fairly "heavy" document—several thousand words, philosophically constructed and tightly reasoned. For many years, it was the Vatican's practice to spring such a document on the press corps unawares. Often, there had been rumors of its content and even of its release date, but never any solid information and certainly no advance copies. Occasionally, there would be a press conference to explain and expound upon the text, but generally not.

In part, at least, because of the strong pleas of the American bishops' conference, the Vatican modified its practice, and *Centesimus annus* was one of the earliest examples. Several days before its embargo and release, the encyclical arrived at the office of the U.S. bishops, so that bishops could have some grasp of its contents before being besieged by the press for a reaction. Upon receipt of the document, the U.S. bishops' press office took some proactive and unprecedented steps. First, an analysis was done by staff members specializing in social justice, and then a press release was prepared to coincide with the document's release in Rome. Then, without seeking the Vatican's permission ("always safer to apologize later than to ask in advance") the media office FedEx-ed the document (along with the release) to a handful of journalists in the secular press—journalists we knew could be trusted both to treat the text analytically and to honor the embargo.

The result was that, when the Vatican released the document two or three days later, the first stories by several major media outlets (Associated Press, UPI, *New York Times, Boston Globe*) had just the right perspective: the Pope notes the value of a free-market economy but cautions against making the profit motive supreme lest individuals be hurt in the process.

During the current pontificate, the bulk of the U.S. media's papal coverage—and ultimately the American reader/viewer's understanding of the church's social message—has centered on the Pope's travels. That, of course, has its virtues and its drawbacks. There is immediate access to headlines, but much of it is filtered through the journalists' bias toward the quick and easy. When the Pope visited Denver in 1993 for World Youth Day, much of what he told the young people (high school, college and young adult) focused on their responsibility for social justice—the ultimate test, he said, of your greatness is the way you treat every human being, but especially those who are weak, downtrodden, and defenseless. Several times, over the five days, the Pontiff returned to that theme. But much of that was lost on the media, who preferred to highlight instead the fact that some of the young people (a tiny fraction, actually) had suffered dehydration from the heat and the altitude.

A similar opportunity presented itself in 1987, when the Pope visited nine American cities, but with a different result. The Pope talked strongly on social justice, especially on the final day of the trip, in Detroit. There he spoke of poverty, discrimination, the loss of respect for human life. America is a country blessed with unmatched riches, said the Pontiff, and Americans are faced with a choice: you can choose to forget the rest of humanity, or you can choose to serve. And the "worthy national vocation" of the United States, said the Pope, is to serve the vulnerable.

It was a stirring, ringing talk, but the coverage, in my view, was fairly sparse, given the Pope's obvious intensity and the importance of the topic. However, on that trip there was a counterforce: there were many personal encounters which served as magnets for cameras and made the same point. (I think particularly of the Pope at Mission Dolores Church in San Francisco, a church filled that day with persons with AIDS, their faces drawn and disfigured by the illness. John Paul II walked among them embracing them, his hands stroking their cheeks. With his words he spoke of compassion and mercy, but words were unnecessary; the cameras caught the story, and America understood.)

Sometimes the media (at least the more responsible media) does a good job even with ideas. When the Pope came to the New York area in 1995, he spoke both at Giants Stadium and at Sacred Heart Cathedral in Newark about America's historical commitment to immigrants and to the poor. And he raised the question—quite forcefully, actually—of whether recent events were showing that America was, in fact, withdrawing from that commitment. The *New York Times'* headline the next day was right on target: "Pope to America: Live Up to Your Ideals."

THE SOCIAL MESSAGE OF AMERICA'S BISHOPS

We turn now to some of the social justice statements made by America's Catholic bishops and to the question of how faithfully and energetically they are transmitted by the American media.

My take on this is that the coverage depends on how well the media understands the topic and how well they like our position. Most of my presentation is anecdotal and subjective, but on one particular point there is even some objective research. In 1983, the U.S. bishops produced a pastoral letter on nuclear war, deterrence, and government policy. Andrew Greeley (as a sociologist with NORC) studied the attitudes of American Catholics before and after the pastoral. In 1983, before the pastoral was published, NORC's "General Social Survey" found that 32 percent of Americans (the figure was the same that year both for Protestants and for Catholics) thought that America was spending too much money on weapons. A year later—following the release of the pastoral—the percentage was still 32 percent for Protestants, but it had risen to 54 percent for Catholics. Greeley notes that this represents a reconsideration by some ten million Catholics, and he calls it "the most successful intervention to change attitudes ever measured by social science." (It remains, of course, for more refined research to make the causal link with the role of American media, but one can hardly believe that the media's effect was negligible.)

When, three years later, the U.S. bishops produced a pastoral on the economy, the media was more severely challenged. The pastoral made several points that seemed to me to be rather straightforward and easy to report: (1) American society has more material resources than any other in history, yet thirty-three million people live below the poverty line; (2) the burden of poverty is borne disproportionately by women, racial minorities, and the young; (3) the current level of unemployment is unacceptable, since it creates an intolerable economic and psychological burden; and (4) Americans have a responsibility to those who live outside our borders but not outside the reach of our economic policies, such as the poor in developing nations where U.S. business ties are strong.

But a fair share of secular media chose not to dig in on those issues, and to focus instead on the peripheral question of whether five bishops who are not economists had any business writing such a statement. And much of the media, in its quest for brevity, underreported two important points: (a) that the letter was the product of four years of hearings at which 125 experts were interviewed—including economists, business and labor leaders, representatives of the poor and disenfranchised, and officials from both Democratic and Republican administrations; and (b) that economics is not a technical field divorced from moral questions, and that an economic system must be judged first by whether it helps or harms the individual.

GUIDING THE COVERAGE

There are ways, of course, to (shall I say?) "help the media understand," and what follows is an example. In 1991, the U.S. bishops' conference issued a document on political responsibility, as it does every four years, during the year before the presidential election.

That document in 1991 (and this seems to be true quadrennially) was a treasure trove of Catholic social teaching as applied to the American scene. First of all, it fired a broadside at Americans for the laziness of their voting patterns; the statement pointed out how ironic it was that Eastern Europeans were thrilled to have recaptured the right to vote after decades of struggle, while in the United States in 1990 only a third of eligible voters went to the polls.

Then the document made the important point that the bishops were not interested in fashioning a voting bloc, or in directing Catholics as to which candidate to vote for. Instead, said the document, the bishops wanted to create a "community of conscience," lifting up the moral and human dimensions of public issues, testing public life against central values, asking how particular government policies or programs impact on the human person.

Finally, the statement indicated seventeen issues that were of concern in the public debate because of their moral and human consequences, and it noted the common thread that links them all: the notion that every person counts. The refugee to our shores, the family who is homeless, the woman who is poor, the man who is handicapped, the person with AIDS, the child in the womb and that child's mother, the patient who is elderly and fragile—each one of those people is sacred and deserves attention and help.

The statement decried the fact that our nation seems so often to turn to violence to solve society's difficulties—to abortion to solve problem pregnancies, to the death penalty to combat crime, to euthanasia to deal with the burdens of age and illness, to military force to confront international injustice.

So there the document lay—a gem of a statement, but a literary exercise only, unless it could make its way to the homes of America. I will detail now what the bishops' press office did to generate attention to the document—not, certainly, to boast, for there was surely more that could have been done, but to prompt some thinking on techniques.

The conference issued a press release about the statement, of course, which was sent to our regular distribution list of some 140 wire services, major newspapers, and broadcast networks. But because of the nature of the document as a source for reflection and commentary, we sent it, too, to editorial page editors of the seventy top-circulation papers across the country. And we called around to people who cover religion in the secular press—to some of the more perceptive and analytical among them—to encourage them to read the document and report on it. An article in the *Boston Globe*, for example, with a large headline saying, "Catholic Bishops Say Apathy Threatens U.S. Democracy," was a result of that effort.

We also sent the document, with the news release and a covering note, to a dozen or so prominent political columnists and to editors of some of the most influential Catholic newspapers and magazines. Finally, an audio news release was produced, which included commentary on the document by Archbishop Daniel Pilarczyk, the then president of the bishops' conference, and sent to one thousand radio stations around the country.

EVENTS OUTDRAW STATEMENTS

The church's views on social justice get the widest hearing when they are connected to an event. Two illustrations follow.

In November of 1990, the Catholic bishops of America wrote to Secretary of State James Baker and to President George H. W. Bush expressing their point of view on the Persian Gulf War—asking for restraint in the use of military force, continuation of the diplomatic effort and consideration of the just war criteria. That action had an immediate impact: there were calls for appearances on all the broadcast networks, and the story was carried by wire services and by every major newspaper in the country. On the day on which the letter to the secretary of state was approved, there occurred a most striking example of the church's proper role in the public policy debate. *The MacNeil/Lehrer Hour* was then a program of considerable influence (it still is, though perhaps less so now with the explosion of cable commentary), watched by many of the movers and shakers in America. That evening, *MacNeil/Lehrer* had the following panel: Al Haig (former Secretary of State), Congressman Les Aspin (chair of the House Armed Services Committee), Jim Webb (Secretary of the Navy during the Reagan administration) and Jesse Jackson. In the center of the panel sat Cardinal (then Archbishop) Roger Mahony, chair of the Bishops' Committee on International Policy.

For thirty-five minutes, Robin MacNeil moderated the discussion, calling on the panelists to respond to each of the church's traditional six criteria for a just war (proportionality, last resort, etc.) with reference to the situation in the Gulf. And it occurred to me, as I watched, that this was exactly where the church ought to be—at the center of society, asking the ethical questions, helping to set the agenda for our nation's moral reflection.

A second example: As I write this paper, the execution of Timothy McVeigh, the Oklahoma City bomber, has been postponed for a month. The scheduled execution has produced a torrent of media coverage, much of it swirling around the issue of the morality or wisdom of the death penalty. The views expressed by Pope John Paul II have been prominent in the ethical discussion; he has urged President George H. W. Bush to commute McVeigh's sentence to life imprisonment. So have the views of Archbishop Daniel Buechlein of Indianapolis, whose archdiocese includes Terre Haute, where the execution is scheduled to take place—he points out that the death penalty "feeds a frenzy for revenge . . . [which] neither liberates the families of victims nor ennobles the victims of crime;" and Cardinals Roger Mahony and William Keeler have asked how violence and killing—state-sanctioned or otherwise—can serve justice.

Knowing that certain events will generate considerable coverage, the church can also plan to make it more likely on those occasions for its point of view to be heard. In the summer of 1989, the U.S. Supreme Court issued the *Webster* decision, upholding the state of Missouri's right to say that human life begins at conception and to use public funds and facilities to favor childbirth over abortion. The U.S. bishops' conference had scripted in advance its response to the four possible outcomes of the case. On the morning the Supreme Court decision came down, within some thirty minutes Archbishop John May of St. Louis, the then president of the conference, had prepared a video news release (VNR) in response. In the VNR, Archbishop May said that "the biggest winners today are the tiniest people of all—children within the wombs of their mothers." The VNR was picked up by television stations across America and seen by more than two million viewers; Archbishop May's quote was the second item from the top on the Associated Press's schedule of stories sent to newsrooms around the world. (It seems wise to fashion abortion as a human-rights issue, as Archbishop May did in the VNR, thus establishing its consistency with the remainder of the church's agenda on social justice. Talk of politicians and ecclesiastical penalties, over which the media salivates, distracts the discussion, distorts it, and takes the focus off the child.)

Sometimes bishops unwittingly insure that their position on social justice issues is not heard. A salient example came recently when, in March of this year, Cardinal Edward Egan chaired a press conference in Albany on the church's legislative agenda in New York State for 2001. There were several "targeted objectives" on the agenda, and each of the goals was presented by a panelist: increased support services for the working poor, modification of the state mandatory drug sentencing laws, reimbursement for state-mandated intervention services in Catholic schools for low-performing students, etc.

But the topic which garnered nearly all of the press's attention was the church's quest for a conscience clause to exempt religious institutions from a state requirement to cover contraceptive services in employees' health insurance. In forty-five minutes of questions from the press, only one query related to anything other than the contraceptive issue, and the media coverage followed suit, with hardly a mention of any other topic on the church's wish list.

One would not have to be a longtime observer of media coverage to predict that outcome. The unfortunate consequence was that several worthy social goals were submerged. More effective planning would have separated the issues—as Bishop Howard Hubbard of Albany did earlier when he took the lead role in an ecumenical press conference on the Rockefeller drug laws and the wisdom of rehabilitation over incarceration.

Any anecdotal accounting, such as I have rendered, has value only insofar as it illustrates ideas. Lest the ideas give way to the images, let me summarize:

- journalists often have a marginal acquaintance with religious teaching, but there are some notable exceptions and these should be respected and cultivated;

- while hardly committed to the "consistent ethic," the media is sympathetic to many aspects of the church's social teaching;
- events get more mileage than statements, and the church's views get maximum attention when there is a natural "news peg;" and
- foresight and careful planning, while not guaranteeing productive coverage, can help to promote it.

I hope these points have been illustrated in my narrative.

ASSERTIONS, NOT REASONS:
A RESPONSE

J. Bottum

I saw the flash of steel in Father Kenneth Doyle's paper when he said that "central to Catholic social teaching is the thesis that government exists in part to take care of people who are vulnerable in society and cannot otherwise provide for themselves. That political philosophy, I would submit, gains a more sympathetic hearing among Democrats than among Republicans."

I don't understand what to do when faced with a proposition like that. I know what "expanding the community of care" means when I hear that phrase in Washington, D.C. It means abortion, homosexuality, and euthanasia —which, I imagine, are not the things Doyle means, exactly. In fact, the people in Washington, D.C., who best understand what he means by "expanding the community of care" are on the right, not on the left.

For opinion journalists in America, the parish church basically does not exist. The bishop in the cathedral and the diocese do not exist. The American bishops' conference basically does not exist. The Vatican does not exist. The Pope, well, yes, the Pope exists, but otherwise the structure of the Catholic Church is invisible. If our topic is the transmission of magisterial statements of social teaching, then the church in general and the bishops' conference have done a singularly bad—and I mean awful; really, really awful—job of transmitting those statements to opinion journalists.

Now, to a certain extent, of course, it was always thus. It's not as though there were some Golden Age in America where Catholic opinions got front page news coverage every time they were made, but I think we have a new situation that we need to face up to. Opinion journalists are the non-experts who fill the chairs in those talking-head programs on Sunday morning. They are the writers and editors of magazines with tiny circulations, but they actually have an impact on the discourse of things in America. To take an organization's position seriously, it strikes me that opinion journalists have to be convinced of three things.

First of all, the position has intellectual weight behind it. I don't mean that those opinion journalists have to understand those intellectual reasons, because usually they don't. But they have to have, somehow, the conviction that there are reasons behind it, if only ever they bothered to find out what those reasons are.

The second thing that they have to be convinced of is that the position has political consequences—which is to say that it isn't just a statement, that there are actually votes that may follow the statement, that it has actual force in the world.

And the third thing is that the position has political coherence—which is to say that it fits somewhere in the world that we did not make but happen to live in, that it doesn't simply come out of left field, that it belongs in the political world as presently constituted, that it's intelligible and coherent with a set of other positions.

By these three criteria, Catholic press officers and activists at every level have failed significantly. When I get calls from activists and press officers, when I get flyers, when I get statements interpreting papal documents, for example, I am consistently offered nothing but assertions, not reasons. I am never persuaded that there are people of deep intellectual seriousness behind it who will explain them to me if I ever do actually want to know what those reasons are.

So, too, I'm not at all convinced that there is actual political force behind these positions, that there are voters behind them. The statistics I've seen—and been worried about—suggest that the Catholic voter has basically disappeared into the general populace, indistinguishable from everybody else in America. *Crisis* magazine has made several attempts to distinguish an identifiable group of Catholic voters. I have been unpersuaded, primarily because even within their carefully selected groups, the Catholic voters again disappear. Catholics who go to church every week do have a distinct voting pattern—but it is nearly the same as the general population of people who worship publicly once a week, whether they're Jewish or Protestant or Evangelical or Catholic.

But the most telling problem in the transmission of Catholic statements is the massive failure of political coherence. In part this derives from a misunderstanding, it seems to me, of just how settled a negative view of the Roman Catholic Church there is on the American left. The primary effect of a Catholic statement denouncing, say, welfare reform, is to provide an occasion for columnists in the *Nation* and the *Progressive* to say that even the patriarchal and homophobic Catholic Church is opposed to this—which thus proves the hypocrisy of people like pro-life Congressmen Henry Hyde and Chris Smith.

Hypocrisy is the sin, of course, which left-leaning intellectual journalists believe that every religious conservative politician automatically commits, simply by his very existence. But you'd never know it from Catholic position papers. Take a look at the rhetorical gestures of the statements that come out of the bishops' conferences. Take a look at the rhetorical gesture that Doyle made, for that matter, when he said Catholic political philosophy is more properly Democratic than it is Republican—as though the fact that the media knows nothing about religion is counterbalanced to some degree by the fact that they are in imperfect communion with the Roman Catholic Church by being members of the Democratic Party. These rhetorical gestures are all apologetic gestures to the left. And, it seems to me, they are ineffective in bringing the left on board, while they alienate the right.

Think about a series of issues: the death penalty, for instance. I would submit that Republicans in Congress and conservative intellectuals and opinion journalists are far softer on support for the death penalty than Democrats in Congress and left-leaning intellectual journalists are on abortion. A producer of *The McLaughlin Group* was trying to put together a death penalty program. Did I want to be on? She asked me, "What do you think about the death penalty?" So I said, "I think that it's an outrage and a crime and a failure of civilized society." She sighed and said, "You know, we're looking for a conservative talking head who will actually defend the death penalty." If support for the death penalty is one of our measures, than the right is more educable on the Catholic position than the left is educable on abortion.

The same is true of cloning. Richard Doerflinger of the bishops' conference has offered the interesting proposition that we're going to see realignment or, at least, potential realignment: those patriarchal and homophobic Catholic bishops on the same program opposing cloning as good leftists from the Green Party. I think, in fact, that it's not true. As soon as abortion enters the equation, as it does in a lot of the discussion about cloning, things clog up. In fact, if right at this moment, you wrote a petition to ban all human cloning, you could get on it the signature of every major right-wing think tank and activist organization short of the Cato Institute and the Libertarians. You could not perform anything near as complete a feat on the left, even among the far-left green organizations, precisely because abortion gets in their way.

The same pattern holds with the issue of trade with China. It holds with euthanasia. It holds with faith-based initiatives and the role of

Catholic-oriented charities. It holds with the school voucher issue, which gets much more support among Republicans if one presents it in terms of giving to the poor what has been heretofore a middle-class entitlement. In fact, in the world as presently constituted, the right is far more educable on Catholic issues, far more malleable on Catholic thought, and far more able to take the church as a moral tutor than the left is.

Now, I mean "left" and "right" here within the range of opinion journalists. But think about that realignment that Doerflinger talks about, of the far left with Catholic social thinking and pro-life conservatives. If that coalition comes together, we will have an interesting new realignment in American politics. It only gets frightening when you start thinking about what that means on the other side. For the other side would get a brand new coalition as well—a brand new coalition consisting of the pro-choice Democrats and the pro-business Republicans.

If that coalition were to emerge, it would be a bloc on which Catholic moral teaching would have no purchase at either end. Finally, the emergence of that bloc would be contributed to, significantly, by the unwillingness and inability of Catholic activists and Catholic press officers to shake off the dead weight of old politics and seek their natural audience and constituency in American politics for the transmission of magisterial statements on social teaching.

3

ANTI-CATHOLICISM: THE LAST
ACCEPTABLE PREJUDICE?

Mark Massa

Several years ago while teaching the "Faith and Critical Reason" course that Fordham requires of all of its freshmen, I asked my eager students to write an essay on what they understood the relationship of "Christianity" to "church" to be. One especially astute undergrad began her essay by noting that "going to church does not make you a Christian, any more than standing in a garage makes you a car." I very much appreciated both her point and her wit, but I wrote at the end of her paper that while her point was undoubtedly correct, the question of the exact relationship between the Christian message and Christian institutions was, nonetheless, more complex and more deserving of study than her amusing answer seemed to allow.

I think that an analogous point to both my freshman's point and my rejoinder can be made about anti-Catholicism in the United States: criticizing the Catholic Church does not make you an anti-Catholic. But the question of the exact relationship between "critique of" and "prejudice against" Catholic belief and practice in the United States is more complex than such a quick observation can unpack—especially if one considers the long (and often unpleasant) history that has informed the history of Catholicism in North America, from the observance of "Pope Day" in colonial Massachusetts, through the activities of the Ku Klux Klan, to the more urbane humor directed against Mother Theresa of Calcutta by Christopher Hitchens in the pages of *Vanity Fair*.

It was precisely to explore this knotty cultural and theological question that *Commonweal*'s "American Catholic in the Public Square" project and Fordham's Catholic Studies Progam decided to cosponsor a one-day conference on "Anti-Catholicism: The Last Acceptable Prejudice?" on May 24, 2002, at Fordham University. The day opened with a welcome and some observations by Joseph O'Hare, S.J., then president of Fordham, who noted that our conference had to be situated within the context of the clergy sexual abuse crisis, revelations about which were just then at full tide. Father O'Hare further observed: "It seems to me that present attention being paid to the Catholic Church and the very, very genuine crisis in which we're involved is a kind of Rorschach test. Everybody can find in it whatever they particularly choose to find in it."

O'Hare's metaphor of the Rorschach test might prove useful—in part, at least—for understanding the presentations of that day: the four texts that follow, chosen from a rich and diverse group of presentations, offer glimpses of the varying presuppositions and disciplinary starting points of our participants. These texts enrich and (fruitfully) complicate our understanding of perceived—and real—anti-Catholic impulses in U.S. culture by witnessing to the fact that students of this phenomenon (many of them Catholics) are themselves divided on precisely what anti-Catholicism is, where it is to be found in North American culture, and how it is to be interpreted as an American, or even as a religious, phenomenon.

Historian John McGreevy opened by observing that anti-Catholicism was, from the standpoint of cultural history, "integral to the formation of the United States." But Professor McGreevy also observed that this culturally integral distrust of things Catholic had evolved into two quite distinctive strands: the intensely religious form of the animus had peaked in the nineteenth century, so that today it "continues with a whimper, not a bang, with anti-Catholic asides on the website of Bob Jones University." But the cultural strand of anti-Catholicism—"what our organizers termed the 'last acceptable prejudice'"—is both more virulent and more complicated at the beginning of the twenty-first century. And while allowing that the "overlap between religious and cultural anti-Catholicism is significant," McGreevy also argued that "we can make distinctions." The historical distinctions drawn by Professor McGreevy offered a rich starting point for the presentations and discussions that followed.

Sociologist Andrew Greeley offered intriguing data on the persistence of anti-Catholic presuppositions and stereotypes held by non-Catholics in contemporary American society. Father Greeley's reflections on what he described as his "pre-test on Anti-Catholicism in America" represented a social scientific complement to McGreevy's historical discussion by bringing quantitative data, recently compiled, into our consideration of anti-Catholicism.

In his questionnaire that sought to uncover how anti-Catholic prejudice might (or might not) have changed since the presidency of John Kennedy, Vatican II, and the emergence of Catholic ethnics into the verdant pastures of middle-class affluence, Greeley offered a battery of statements to

550 non-Catholic Americans for agreement or disagreement. The questions in Greeley's "pretest"—a kind of sociological "report from the field"—as well as his interpretation of the data the questionnaire generated are included here in the essay "An Ugly Little Secret Revisited." Greeley said that this "field report" contains both good news and bad news regarding the persistence in contemporary American society of the kinds of negative Catholic stereotypes outlined by McGreevy. The audience there—and our readers here—are offered several possible responses to Greeley's data, ranging from despair to renewed efforts by Catholics to educate their fellow citizens about their beliefs. But in the meantime, he says, "at least they have given up burning convents."

Media analyst Mark Silk began his consideration of the media treatment of Catholics by observing that from the standpoint of several other acceptable prejudices current in American society (most notably anti-Semitism) the dangers posed by anti-Catholicism were perhaps overdrawn. Catholics, he noted, now make up a quarter of the general population in the United States, while Jews make up less than two percent: "I dare say we'd accept an extra measure of anti-Semitism for numbers like that!"

Describing one earlier study of coverage of the Catholic Church by the *New York Times*, the *Washington Post, Time* magazine, and CBS News, Professor Silk drew attention to the fact that prejudice is not "just a numbers game. It is also about how people are represented in the central arteries of the culture." Drawing on his own work as editor of *Religion in the News* (a tri-annual publication that reports on how the media covers various religious topics), Silk offered several provocative interpretations of both the perception—and the possible reality—of the media's "hard line" on Catholicism, including the cultural rule of thumb observed by most journalists: "the media expect large and powerful groups to be able to absorb more criticism than small and powerless ones. The church may consider itself a minority school in a sea of Protestant and secular fish. But that isn't the way Catholicism is viewed by outsiders."

Newsweek's religion editor Kenneth Woodward followed Silk, and opened his presentation with a series of questions that set the stage for his paper: Did he think anti-Catholicism exists? "Yes I do." Has anti-Catholicism in America been as virulent as anti-Semitism, to which it has often been compared? "Not then. Not now. And likely not ever." Is anti-Catholic prejudice as important for maintaining Catholic group identity as anti-Semitism has been for American Jews? "Not by another long shot." Glossing some examples of what he took to be obvious anti-Catholicism (for instance, an ABC TV news special on clergy sexual abuse) as well as some less obvious ones,

Woodward addressed head-on the alleged anti-Catholicism of that newspaper most often accused of nurturing the bias—the *New York Times*—"in its own secularist fashion a kind of church, complete with its own hierarchy."

Deftly sketching the tensions between "Catholic" and "secular American" beliefs, Woodward suggested that "there will always be anti-Catholicism, enduring but intermittent in its manifestation. Speaking for myself, I am always nervous when too many people agree with me, which doesn't happen often. I think the church should be the same way, or else it will cease to be the church."

O'Hare's metaphor of the Rorschach test in the day's opening remarks proved apt for our conference (and was more than fully represented by the final panel, "Voices from the Field")—but not a metaphor without remainder. For while each of our panelists contributed to the discussion of anti-Catholicism in ways that reflected diverse (and sometimes conflicting) viewpoints, certain threads of continuity were nonetheless woven throughout all of the presentations that offer insights into the phenomenon of anti-Catholicism in the United States that transcended "point of view." The importance of these threads of continuity has struck me with special force during the year since the conference, as I completed my own book-length study of anti-Catholicism in U.S. culture since World War II (*Anti-Catholicism in America: The Last Acceptable Prejudice*, Crossroad, 2003).

Thus, going back to the presentations of the conference after constructing my own narrative of anti-Catholic impulses in our culture, certain themes seemed especially salient and durable for understanding a notably slippery phrase like "anti-Catholicism." I would posit that McGreevy's insight that anti-Catholicism was integral to the formation of U.S. culture is crucial for understanding why Catholic Christianity is perceived to be different from a number of mainstream values in U.S. culture: the historical answer for that perceived difference is that it is different. Further, I think that the distinction McGreevy draws between the religious and cultural expressions of the animus is a helpful one in unraveling densely-packed impulses often manifested in non- or even anti-religious parts of our culture. But I would also say—reflecting my own conclusions about the animus—that the cultural expressions of anti-Catholicism (admittedly more common today than explicitly theological ones) are in fact more deeply rooted in explicitly theological values and religious beliefs (broadly defined) than were perhaps appreciated at the conference.

Similarly, there are good indications that the troubling findings of Greeley's "pretest on anti-Catholicism" are very reliable indeed: while the animus is far less virulent today than in earlier periods in our history (as he remarked, "they have given up burning convents"), there are nonetheless persistent negative stereotypes and biases directed against Catholics in American culture at large that are by no means confined to undereducated, non-urban, or low-income populations. Greeley's announcement of both good and bad news on this score is grounded in persistent demographic data stretching over decades. Thus, the celebration of Catholic arrival into middle class acceptance—much like the reports of Mark Twain's death—is perhaps both premature and exaggerated. But I would also add that many Catholic leaders in the United States have not helped their community's cause when they play the anti-Catholic card in response to charges of authoritarianism, lack of accountability, and hostility to democratic values.

Mark Silk's point about the comparative virulence of the anti-Catholic bias is an important one that students of the animus should bear in mind: compared to other biases (anti-Semitism, homophobia, misogyny, etc.) that lead to vandalism, physical violence, or job discrimination, anti-Catholic impulses are comparatively mild. Slanted editorials in newspapers of record against an admittedly large and powerful institution (while hardly fair) are not the same as the desecration of worship spaces or the loss of income. At the same time, most Americans would—publicly, at least—label such biases and vandalism as unacceptable or immoral; I am not as certain about the social unacceptability of believing that Catholics have authoritarian proclivities, or that the Catholic Church poses a threat to democratic values. That word *acceptable* in our conference title remains questionable for me.

Ken Woodward is correct, I think, in arguing that there will always be anti-Catholic impulses, "enduring but intermittent," in American culture; he is likewise prescient in asserting that that fact is not in itself the bad news. As he rightly observed, "the challenge for any tradition that claims to be Christian is to be disliked for the right reasons. On this view, some anti-Catholic prejudices are not only acceptable but welcome." But prophetically accepting the "persecution for righteousness's sake" that Jesus prophesied for his disciples should not be construed as passively acquiescing to biased perceptions, or allowing a hostile dinner remark to go unchallenged. Catholics, like all Christians, are called by St. Paul to be able to "render an account for the faith that is in them." But rendering that account will sometimes be loud and disquieting to those around them: that's part of the "good news."

The conference at Fordham offers several satisfying results to participants and readers of this book: the complexities and nuances of the anti-Catholic impulse in U.S. culture were explored with exemplary dispassion and serious scholarly insight, and often with humor as well. Likewise, the presentations nicely balanced interdisciplinary and personal points of view with significant areas of agreement and interchange. And the nuances and complexities of Catholic tensions with areas of U.S. culture were allowed to remain nuanced and complex: there was no effort to oversimplify or explain away uncomfortable or disquieting realities. I would concur with the sentiment expressed in one of the exit questionnaires completed by members of our 500-plus audience that day (a sentiment shared by most of our audience): "It was a day of intellectual excitement, stimulating interchange, and 'stretching of boundaries.' We need more meeting of minds like this."

ANTI-CATHOLICISM IN THE UNITED STATES: THE VIEW FROM HISTORY*

John T. McGreevy

Two questions: How should we understand the history of American anti-Catholicism? And how should history help us understand the controversies of the current sexual abuse scandal raging with a passion that none of us could have predicted?

In a certain sense, of course, anti-Catholicism is integral to the formation of the United States. The men and women who founded the British North American colonies in the seventeenth century lived within living memory of Martin Luther and John Calvin. When William Brewster sailed for the New World on the Mayflower in 1620, he lugged along the just published English translation of Venetian historian Paulo Sarpi's slashing attack on the Council of Trent and the papacy. In 1775, Thomas Paine doubted that inhabitants of the "popish world" would ever enjoy "political liberty."[1]

The alliance with Catholic France during the Revolutionary War and the heroism of such figures as Lafayette briefly made anti-Catholic statements impolitic.[2] Alexander Hamilton urged the New York State assembly to allow Catholics full voting rights in 1787. Hamilton emphasized the "little power possessed by the Pope in Europe" and the needless "vigilance of those who would bring engines to extinguish fire which had many days subsided."[3]

Hostility to Catholicism began to swell again in the 1820s and 1830s on both sides of the Atlantic, as German- and, especially, Irish-Catholic immigrants made their way to Liverpool, Glasgow, New York, Philadelphia, and Boston. John Adams complained to Thomas Jefferson about the Jesuits

---

*Much of the material for this essay was extracted from a book entitled *Catholicism and American Freedom: A History*, published by W. W. Norton, 2003.

in 1821, and in Boston, in 1834, a mob destroyed an Ursuline convent. In 1836, a group of reformers arranged for the publication of Maria Monk's *Awful Disclosures of Hotel Dieu Nunnery,* a salacious (but wholly fictitious) exposé of life in a Canadian convent that nonetheless became the best-selling book of the nineteenth century ahead of *Uncle Tom's Cabin.*[4] In the 1850s, an explicitly anti-Catholic political party, the American party, became the most important third party in the country's history—the modern Republican Party emerged in 1856 only after the American party's popularity had shattered the prospects of the Whigs.

It's here, in the mid-nineteenth century, that we can begin to disentangle two strands of anti-Catholicism in the United States. The first is an intensely religious anti-Catholicism derived from the Reformation era–polemics that shaped American cultural life through the nineteenth century. Here Catholics are suspect because they are perceived to take orders from the Pope, who himself might be the anti-Christ. Here Catholics believe in self-evidently ludicrous doctrines such as purgatory and transubstantiation.

This religious anti-Catholicism does not vanish in the mid-nineteenth century. It informs the activities of the American Protective Association in the 1890s, the Ku Klux Klan in the 1920s, opposition to Al Smith in the presidential election of 1928, and modern Evangelicalism throughout much of the twentieth century. It continues with a whimper, not a bang, with anti-Catholic asides on the website of Bob Jones University.[5]

The second strand of anti-Catholicism, which has been termed the "last acceptable prejudice," is more complicated. Here Catholicism is troubling not as a set of religious beliefs per se, but as a hierarchical and authoritarian institution whose adherents are incapable of recognizing the importance of human autonomy. Call this a cultural anti-Catholicism. Listen to Theodore Parker, one of the most important American liberals of the 1840s and 1850s: "The Roman Catholic Church claims infallibility for itself, and denies spiritual freedom, liberty of mind or conscience, to its members. It is therefore the foe of all progress; it is deadly hostile to Democracy. She is the natural ally of tyrants and the irreconcilable enemy of freedom."[6]

The overlap between religious and cultural anti-Catholicism is significant, but we can make distinctions. Parker was a radical Protestant minister, but he was also a representative figure of nineteenth-century North Atlantic liberalism, religious or not. Like John Stuart Mill in England, Giuseppe Mazzini in Italy, Jules Michelet in France and others, Parker had become convinced that freedom or liberty meant an autonomous self, exempt from external constraint. The individual as negotiator of contracts, as voluntary (and equal) marriage partner and as owner of himself and his labor must serve as the starting point for a progressive social order. In the United States Ralph Waldo Emerson famously extolled "self-reliance" (and Emerson not coincidentally complained of "Romish priests, who sympathize, of course, with despotism").[7]

Parker and Emerson, I should emphasize, were not simply bigots. If nineteenth century liberals idealized human autonomy, Catholics habitually invoked communities. This meant that Catholics offered acute criticism of the new industrial economy, and how the right to contract for an individual might mean very little to workers unable to find jobs at more than subsistence wages. But the same Catholics only belatedly joined the first great human rights campaign of the modern era, against slavery. Again, Theodore Parker: "The Catholic clergy are on the side of slavery. . . . They love slavery itself; it is an institution thoroughly congenial to them, consistent with the first principles of their Church."[8]

Even so, Parker, Emerson and many of their nineteenth-century successors did cross the line from legitimate criticism of Catholic views on particular subjects, such as slavery, to a cultural anti-Catholicism. Like many American liberals in the nineteenth century, they too casually equated Catholic belief with opposition to the most precious achievements of modernity, notably individual autonomy and the political democracy and experimental science that came in its wake. Max Weber's link between Protestantism and the capitalist ethic is one version of this story, and Weber himself was shaped by fierce debates between liberals and Catholics in late nineteenth-century Germany. In the United States, the American pragmatists recently sketched by Louis Menand, including Charles Peirce, William James, and John Dewey, habitually framed against Catholic intransigence their own philosophical tributes to contingency.[9]

Differences of opinion between Catholics and American intellectuals did not always result in political battles. In the early twentieth century, American liberals and Catholics found much common ground in their criticism of laissez-faire capitalism, and their support of Franklin Roosevelt's New Deal. During the 1930s, especially, American liberals focused on modest attempts to redistribute wealth and support for trade unions—policies that had deep resonance within the still largely working-class Catholic populations of the urban North. When Franklin Roosevelt quoted Pius XI's papal encyclical on the social question, *Quadragesimo anno*, Catholic intellectuals responded with giddy shivers of delight.[10]

In the 1940s the tempo shifted. Prominent intellectuals such as Reinhold Niebuhr, Talcott Parsons, John Dewey, and others, appalled by Catholic support of Franco during the Spanish Civil War and worried about the possibility of government aid to parochial schools, offered lacer-ating criticism of Catholicism as incompatible with American democracy. Here, too, as in the nineteenth century, many intellectuals moved from le-gitimate criticism of a powerful institution to a cultural anti-Catholicism— many of these figures shared an unspoken assumption that any hierarchical institution, any organization making truth claims was morally suspect. One prominent contributor to the *Atlantic Monthly* insisted in 1948 that "[T]he clear implication in our Constitution [is] that religious truth is an individ-ual quest, that authoritarianism and religion are contradictory terms."[11]

These particular fears about Catholicism faded in the 1950s, and John Kennedy's election in 1960 and the Second Vatican Council seemed to mark a new rapprochement. Instead, since 1965 we've seen renewed, per-haps even more intense, conflict between Catholics and liberals around is-sues of sex and gender.

Let me make three observations:

First, no one in 1965 could have predicted that abortion would be-come a cornerstone of American liberalism, that a woman's right to choose would become so valued that the 1984 Democratic platform would call le-gal abortion a "fundamental human right." As late as the mid-1960s, the Democratic Party, often led by Catholic politicians, was arguably more con-servative on sexual ethics than the Republican party of Nelson Rockefeller, Gerald Ford, and even a California governor named Ronald Reagan.

Second, the Catholic Church was the single most important opponent of legal abortion in the 1960s and 1970s. This guaranteed renewed conflict between Catholics and liberals. It also meant that many liberals began to insist that so-called religious views had no place in the public sphere. Lau-rence Tribe, perhaps the country's most influential constitutional lawyer, argued before Congress in defense of *Roe v. Wade* in 1974 that only "ways of reasoning acceptable to all" should inform public debate, and branded Catholic arguments on abortion as impermissible efforts to legislate "reli-gious faith upon which people will invariably differ widely." Involving the State in a woman's decision whether to terminate her pregnancy, Tribe ar-gued, was as ill-advised as permitting governmental aid to Catholic schools.[12]

Third, the same decade, from 1965 to 1975, saw the birth of both the modern women's movement and the modern gay and lesbian rights move-ment. The combined effect was to weaken, perhaps fatally, Catholic credi-bility on all matters related to sex. The impact of the women's movement was obvious: even as women achieved positions of leadership throughout American society, they were prevented from doing so within the Catholic

Church. (And the sudden collapse in the number of women entering religious orders made the public face of Catholicism more male in the 1970s than it had been in the 1950s.) In itself, this gender hierarchy did not destroy the plausibility of the Catholic argument on abortion, as pro-life women attested. And yet the effect has been devastating: on one side, in a culture where personal experience seemed crucial to the assessment of moral problems, pro-choice women spoke of the terrors of unwanted pregnancy and the dangers of illegal abortions. On the other side, priests and (male) Catholic lawyers outlined in abstract terminology their opposition to the taking of innocent life. As one Catholic activist confided in 1967, the "impasse over [abortion] will not be broken by talking (as Catholics have been prone to talk) only about the right to life. If nothing else, that has been a principle which has precluded the need to look at the evidence, or listen to the testimony of women who want abortions."[13]

The impact of the modern gay and lesbian rights movement has become evident more recently. As we now realize, the gay awakening that came in the wake of the 1960s has had an immense, if largely uncharted effect on the Catholic priesthood. As sexual identity came to be understood as central to personal identity, many seminarians and priests came to understand themselves as gay, often in a clerical culture where bishops simultaneously denied the relevance of the issue publicly, and privately worried about a preponderance of gays in the seminaries.[14] Again the disregard of personal experience was central: how could Catholics credibly discuss sexual orientation (and important related issues such as the character of marriage) when Catholic leaders seemed incapable of acknowledging the issue's centrality to their own lives? All of this occurred in a society where the pace of change was breathtaking: in 1965 gays and lesbians were largely invisible, or at best understood as pitiful figures; now we watch *Will & Grace*.

My general point is this: some of the scorn heaped on official Catholic views on sexuality in the last two decades results from a cultural anti-Catholicism with enduring, if intermittent, strength in American society, one whose underpinnings I've tried to sketch here. A central assumption of this cultural anti-Catholicism in the twentieth century is that autonomy is the preeminent moral good, and that "abstract" rules cannot adequately guide the individual faced with complex moral decisions. In this context, prohibitions on abortion are unreasonable attempts to legislate morality, an awkward defense for liberals who also write checks supporting, say, Amnesty International's praiseworthy attempts to legislate morality throughout the world. Cautions against premarital sexual relations seem ludicrous. Celibacy, in a highly sexualized culture, is positively unhealthy. Priests, if we are to believe even such a distinguished figure as Garry Wills, too often enter the priesthood only to please their mothers.[15]

At the same time, the inability of Catholic leaders to offer a compelling vision of sexual ethics, one that takes women's experiences seriously, one that honestly acknowledges the importance of sexual identity for its leadership caste, invites criticism. If at times commentators on the current sexual abuse crisis have relapsed into stereotypical notions of Catholics as authoritarian and backward, or compared Catholic leaders with the Taliban, most of the analysis, from Catholics and non-Catholics, has rightly and appropriately focused on an appalling misuse of episcopal authority. None of this is pleasant. But Catholics at such a charged moment as our own should be especially careful not to mistake criticism for prejudice, acceptable or not.

NOTES

1. [Thomas Paine], "Thoughts on Defensive War," (1775) in *Paine, Common Sense and Related Writings*, Thomas P. Slaughter, ed. (Boston: Bedford Books, 2001), 68.

2. Charles P. Hansen, *Necessary Virtue: The Pragmatic Origins of Religious Liberty in New England* (Charlottesville: University of Virginia Press, 1998); Francis D. Cogliano, *No King, No Popery: Anti-Catholicism in Revolutionary New England*, (New York: Greenwood Press, 1995); Jason Kennedy Duncan, "'A Most Democratic Class': New York Catholics and the Early American Republic," (University of Iowa, Ph.D. diss., 1999).

3. Remarks on an act for Regulating Elections, January 29, 1787, in *The Papers of Alexander Hamilton Volume IV: January 1787–May 1788*, Harold C. Syrett and Jacob E. Cooke, eds. (New York: Columbia University Press, 1962), 30.

4. John Wolffe, *The Protestant Crusade in Great Britain 1829–1860* (Oxford U.K: Clarendon Press, 1991). John Adams to Thomas Jefferson, May 19, 1821, in *The Adams-Jefferson Letters: The Complete Correspondence Between Thomas Jefferson and Abigail and John Adams Volume II, 1812–1826*, Lester J. Cappon, ed. (Chapel Hill: University of North Carolina Press, 1959), 573. On the Ursuline convent, Nancy Lusignan Schultz, *Fire and Roses: The Burning of the Charlestown Convent, 1834*, (New York: Free Press, 2000). On Maria Monk, Jenny Fanchot, *Roads to Rome: The Antebellum Protestant Encounter with Catholicism*, (Berkeley, Calif., 1994), 154–61.

5. Donald W. Sweeting, "From Conflict to Cooperation? Changing American Evangelical Attitudes towards Roman Catholics: 1960–1998," (Trinity Evangelical Divinity School, Ph.D. diss., 1998), 1.

6. Theodore Parker, "A Sermon of the Dangers which Threaten the Rights of Man in America," July 2, 1854, in Parker, *Additional Speeches, Addresses, and Occasional Sermons, Volume II* (Boston: Little Brown, 1855), 241.

7. Ralph Waldo Emerson to Thomas Carlyle, September 26, 1864, in *The Correspondence of Thomas Carlyle and Ralph Waldo Emerson, 1834–1872, Volume II* (Boston: Osgood, 1883), 286.

8. Parker, 244; Dean Grodzins, "A Transcendentalist's Know Nothingism: The Anti-Catholic Thought of Theodore Parker," 6, paper in author's possession.

9. John T. McGreevy review of Louis Menand, *The Metaphysical Club, Commonweal* 128 (August 17, 2001), 22–24.

10. John McHugh Stuart to Ryan, October 29, 1932, file 12, box 35, John Ryan papers, Catholic University.

11. Agnes E. Meyer, "The School, the State and the Church," *Atlantic Monthly* 182 (November 1948), 50.

12. Lawrence H. Tribe, "The Supreme Court 1972 Term," *Harvard Law Review* 87 (November 1973), 25, 21.

13. Daniel Callahan to John T. Noonan Jr., September 16, 1967, Noonan.

14. Note Medieros letter of 1973 in recently released Boston documents.

15. Wills in *New York Review of Books* (May 23, 2002, 6–9). On liberals and human rights, Thomas Haskell, "The Curious Persistence of Rights Talk in an Age of Interpretation," in *Objectivity is Not Neutrality: Explanatory Schemes in History* (Baltimore: Johns Hopkins University Press, 1998), 115–44.

AN UGLY LITTLE SECRET
REVISITED: A PRETEST ON ANTI-
CATHOLICISM IN AMERICA

Andrew M. Greeley

Anti-Catholicism is as American as Thanksgiving, apple pie à la mode, and chocolate malts with two butter cookies. It has been part of American culture from the very beginning and, despite the election of John Kennedy in 1960 (which he won by a hundred thousand votes, having lost a half million because of his religion), it persists even today. Any Catholic who has walked down the beaches of the upper academy, the higher media, or the New York publishing companies will have been very fortunate not to have encountered it. The issue is whether elite bigotry is the tip of the iceberg or a tip without an iceberg.

For a long time I have felt that anti-Catholicism simmers just below the surface of American culture, relatively unchanged since the nineteenth century. Catholics cannot think for themselves, they do what their priests tell them to do, they are superstitious and idolatrous, when they have power they try to impose their beliefs on others, their politicians are corrupt, they really can't be good Americans.

Because they are concentrated in cities and in certain regions of the country, most Catholics rarely encounter this prejudice and are not harmed by it in their personal lives. Those who do suffer because of anti-Catholicism are not sufficiently numerous to fight back.

Since no one seemed interested in research on this last of the great unacknowledged American bigotries, I had set aside my concerns over it. Even Don Quixote had to choose which windmills to engage with his lance. Mark Massa's recent article in *Theological Studies* re-awakened me to the issue. The analogical imagination (an imagination which perceives God as aggressively present in the world in the Sacraments and the sacramentals and in all the objects, events of daily life), he suggested, makes Catholics different from other Americans. It is precisely this difference that turns off others—our statues, our stained glass, our communalism, our rosaries, our saints, our Madonna. They don't like our rain forest of metaphors. They fear the too-close identification of God with creatures. They would rather emphasize the distance of God from creation. Both imaginative perspectives are important, both face certain problems, neither is inherently superior to the other. But they are different. I had argued in both *Religion as Poetry* and *The Catholic Imagination*, against those on the right who lamented that Catholics had become like everyone else and those on the left who insisted that they should become like everyone else, that Catholics were and still are different and (implicitly) should and would remain different. Now Father Massa suggested that this difference might cause anti-Catholic feelings among those who were not Catholic. I consulted with David Tracy, who, if there were a copyright on the term analogical imagination, would own it. He agreed with me that Massa was probably right.

Then I was invited to participate in this symposium with a presentation on what social science data told us about anti-Catholicism. I could have done that with a four-word paper: "There are no data." The last study of which I know was done a couple of decades ago by Louis Harris for an organization which then called itself the National Conference of Christians and Jews. It showed that a substantial proportion of Americans thought that Catholics did what they were told and could not think for themselves. Surely, however, attitudes must have changed. Or might have changed. Or may not have changed.

So I decided I would sponsor what I call a "pre-test in depth"—a test of a battery of items which might discriminate among the target population and which would be of sufficient size to act as benchmark for future research, should there be any.

Since there is no repertory of questions on the subject, I had to make them up, relying sometimes almost literally on the anti-Catholic clichés of the nineteenth and early-twentieth centuries. I also wanted enough items to make it possible to falsify or verify Mark Massa's theory. Patently, as my friend Blackie Ryan would say, such a venture is necessarily preliminary and tentative. It is possible to nitpick any survey item to death if one wants to, particularly if it is a new item never before tested. Anyone who wants to attack my items is free to do so. I invite such a one, however, to invest their own money in creating and testing better items. The issues about a new item are whether respondents are capable of answering it and whether it discriminates among different groups in a population.

Here are the items I tested:

- Catholics really are not permitted to think for themselves.
- Catholic schools make an important contribution to education in the big cities.
- The statues and images in Catholic churches are idols.
- It is possible to be a good Catholic and a good American.
- Instead of worshiping only God, Catholics also worship Mary and the saints.
- Catholic politicians are about as honest as other politicians.
- Catholics do what the Pope and the bishops tell them to do.
- Catholics do not try to impose their moral beliefs on others.
- Catholic rosaries and holy medals are superstitious.

I checked the items with some of my colleagues and they could find no major flaws in them. Then I turned them over to Knowledge Network. The resulting sample of approximately 550 Americans who are not Catholic (numbers differ on specific items because of missing values) is a valid probability sample of the population.

(Knowledge Network has sampled a large number of television sets in the United States and installed a WebTV instrument on them. Anyone interested in a detailed description of their methodology should contact me at NORC/University of Chicago)

In the accompanying table the first column of percentages combines those who agree "strongly" and those who agree "somewhat" (the "soft core" perhaps of anti-Catholicism). The second column represents only those who agree "strongly," presumably the "hard core" of hostility to Catholics.

There is some good news in the table. At long last the overwhelming majority of Americans (93 percent) think Catholics can be good Americans, despite their idolatry and inability to think for themselves. Moreover, and much to my surprise, they (85 percent) also think there are good things which can be said about Catholic schools. Finally, Massa's theory about the problems with the Catholic imagination is stunningly confirmed.

The bad news is that the majority of our fellow Americans have preconceptions about us that differ very little from those of the nineteenth century. (See the table.) More than four out of five think we worship Mary and the saints; almost three out of four think we do what the bishops and the Pope tell us what to do (they should be so lucky!). More than half believe we worship idols and a similar proportion that we can't think for ourselves. Almost

Anti-Catholic Responses

	Somewhat or Strongly Agree	Agree Strongly
Worship Mary and saints	83%	42%
Do what Pope and bishops tell	73%	17%
Statues are idols	57%	24%
Not permitted to think for selves	52%	11%
Rosary and medals superstitious	46%	17%
Do try to impose beliefs*	48%	12%
Politicians not as honest as others*	27%	11%
Catholic schools not important*	15%	5%
Cannot be good Americans*	7%	3%

half argue that rosaries and medals are superstitious and a similar proportion rejects the notion that we don't try to impose our ideas on others. About a quarter are not willing to agree that our politicians are as honest as others.

I can concede for the moment the objection to exercises of the Catholic imagination as manifested in saints and statues and rosaries and medals. (They are still prejudices because they refuse after all these years to take into account Catholic explanations of these practices—we worship only God and believe that by honoring Mary and the saints we honor God through his creatures.) However, the notion that we cannot think for ourselves has hounded me and many others in our years in the academy and is damnable bigotry.

I conclude that, while my items doubtless can be refined, they work. (On the average, 80 percent of the respondents were able to answer the items.) Unless and until someone forces refinement and reanalysis of my data, I conclude that anti-Catholicism is alive and well and pervasive in American society, though they are not burning convents any more.

If I were to choose a couple of items to be used in further surveys, I would opt for "rosaries and medals" and Catholics "can't think for themselves."

In a factor analysis two clusters emerge, both of which correlate weakly with a number of background variables. Younger and better-educated respondents are less likely to be anti-Catholic. Blacks are somewhat more likely, as are those who attend church regularly. Political liberals, Democrats, and Gore voters are also less likely to be anti-Catholic, as are those who live in the Northeast. However, as a pretest the survey did not contain variables which might provide an explanatory model. Presumably the models that account for other prejudices would be useful. A society needs its inkblots. Authoritarian personalities need their scapegoats. People need to be shocked by transgres-sive behavior. As my friend the novelist Nanci Kincaid said in her charming account of the first Catholic family to move into her small southern town, they not only drank beer, but they drank it on the front porch! I leave to Fa-thers Massa and Tracy whether that is manifestation of the Catholic imagi-nation!

I confess that I was staggered by the extent of the persistence of anti-Catholic clichés among Americans. I had not anticipated that they would have gone away, but I did not expect that they would be as pervasive as they are.

There are a number of ways one could react to these findings. One could first of all say that they are truth. That's the way, regrettably, that Catholics are. Hence there is no prejudice or bigotry in the attitudes. Blacks don't smell, Jews don't cheat in business, gays are not effeminate, but Catholics are superstitious and idolatrous folks who can't think for themselves.

A second reaction would say that the findings are not and cannot be true. They should not be accepted because it is utterly improbable that such widespread attitudes could be invisible in American society. They cannot possibly exist or "we" (whoever "we" might be) would know about them. Therefore the findings should be rejected out of hand because of their ut-ter implausibility and because they are so completely counterintuitive.

Fine, say I, do your own research and refute me. However, until you do, I say—pace the late Jesuit sociologist Joseph Fichter—I have five hun-dred cases which say you're wrong!

Or it could be argued that anti-Catholicism isn't important because it is not as serious as anti-Semitism or racism or sexism or homophobia. All bigotries are serious. That some are more serious than others doesn't change the fact that a society which tolerates one form of bigotry tolerates them all, because its opposition to bigotry is not principled opposition.

Yet another reaction is to say that we Catholics are to blame for these reactions. We have to change our ways so that our separated brothers and sisters will correct their misunderstandings about us. In practice this means we must give up our saints, our statues, our rosaries, our medals, our Madonna. Cut back, in other words, on our noxious Catholic imagination and become more like them. In fact, since Vatican II, many of our liturgists, religious educators, theologians, and intellectuals have done just that. They have tried to deprive Catholicism of its color and texture and make it, as Fa-ther Robert Baron has argued, "beige." It hasn't done any good. Those who aren't Catholic still think we're idolaters.

How do we prove that we can think for ourselves? Obviously by leaving the Church! One of the great American cultural paradigms since the early-nineteenth century is that Catholics are in the process of leaving the church or about to leave or would certainly leave when they became more American and better educated. More recently, each time a Pope comes to America the networks run surveys which show basic disagreement on some issues between the Catholic people and the Pope. Therefore they hail a great Catholic crisis which implicitly is going to separate Catholics from the church. And nothing happens. Still the next time they do a survey, the same paradigm is used as the lead in the report. The paradigm was at work again during the feeding frenzy over priests who were sexual abusers. Daniel Schorr announced on NPR, for example, that Catholics were leaving the church—though none of the many surveys suggested that this was happening. Those who are committed to this paradigm cannot accept the fact that Catholics like being Catholic and that their faith does not depend on the wisdom of their bishops (though they are currently furious at them) or the virtue of their priests.

An obverse paradigm says that Catholics are more likely to vote Republican in this election (whenever the election is) because of the "abortion issue." As my colleagues Jeff Manza and Clem Brooks have demonstrated, Catholic voting has not changed disproportionately in the last half-century of the ebb and flow of American politics.

Moreover, even if we in the elite abandon our metaphors, there is solid reason to think that we cannot deliver our laity. Dean Hoge's study of the Catholic identities of those under forty establishes that the top four marks of that identity were care for the poor, the real presence of Jesus in the Eucharist, the presence of God in the Sacraments, and Mary the Mother of Jesus, the last three of which would be anathema to those who think we are idolaters—all four being quintessential manifestations of the analogical imagination: metaphors which are also doctrines.

Or Catholics could begin an intense educational campaign in which we would explain what we really mean by our devotions and try to prove that we can really think for ourselves. We can say on every possible occasion, "we are monotheists, we worship only God." Or, taking a slogan from James Carville we can say, "it's honor, stupid, not worship." In a less bigoted society, one would expect that the Catholic version of the role of the Mary and the saints would be listened to and taken seriously. In this country it is not even heard. Almost four decades of ecumenical dialogue have not changed the situation. After two centuries of nativist bigotry, no one could seriously expect dialogue to work.

Finally, there is the course I will follow—despair. There is nothing we can do about anti-Catholic bigotry. It is an intractable reality which will not go away no matter how much we may lament it. After four decades of propounding social findings I know losers when I see them. A "loser" is a research report which, while technically unobjectionable, is so clearly contrary to what everyone knows to be true that it can safely be denounced and ignored. (I remember what *Commonweal* did to my early research on Catholic scholarship and on Catholic schools). This report has "LOSER" stamped all over it.

Such despair is a reluctant judgment on American society and its culture. For all our self-righteous pride about our fights against racism, anti-Semitism, homophobia, and sexism, the structure of our presumed moral excellence collapses if the acid of an unacknowledged bigotry eats away at its foundation.

In the meantime, at least they admit we can be good Americans, even if we can't think for ourselves.

And, like I say, they have given up burning convents.

ANTI-CATHOLICISM: THE LAST ACCEPTABLE PREJUDICE? YES

Kenneth L. Woodward

I've been encouraged to speak personally and anecdotally, and will try to do so in the brief time allotted. I'll talk mainly about media.

Do I think anti-Catholicism exists? Yes, I do.

Can I define it? I can try. It's repugnance for things Catholic, both real and imagined. It's the sort of thing you recognize when you see it, among Catholics as well as others.

Is anti-Catholicism, historically, as virulent as anti-Semitism, to which it is often compared? Not then. Not now. And likely not ever. But in the American experience anti-Catholicism is older than anti-Semitism, and still the more acceptable prejudice among academics and their illegitimate off-spring in the chattering classes, among whom anti-Catholicism is less con-scious, less stigmatized, and therefore less noticed. In any case, why should anyone want to compare social pathologies?

Is anti-Catholicism as important to American Catholics as anti-Semitism is to American Jews for the maintenance of group identity? Not by another long shot. Jews are the least religious cohort in American society, if we ex-clude the Jewish Unitarians, Ethical Culturalists and Buddhists, and so the most in need of prejudice, real or imaged, for the maintenance of group iden-tity. Their only rivals are the Mormons, manqué Jews themselves. And I say that in full realization that my statement may be construed by some as itself anti-Semitic, if only because an outsider is saying it. Those at the American Jewish Committee and other communal organizations know too well that what I say is true. They are my sources.

Some manifestations of anti-Catholicism are obvious. For example, I think Daniel Jonah Goldhagen's diatribe in the *New Republic*—on Pius XII, the Vatican, and the Holocaust—was hard-core anti-Catholicism. But he is a known academic nut. More to blame, in my view is Leon Wieseltier, the magazine's powerful back-of-the-book editor and the man who decided to run Goldhagen's venomous piece, giving him more space than anyone has ever been allotted in the *New Republic.*

Do I think that some of the coverage of the current scandal in the Catholic Church is driven by anti-Catholicism? Yes, I think in style, intensity, and the unrelenting nature of the coverage some of it is. ABC's prime-time news special, "Father Forgive Me, for I Have Sinned," is a major example of what happens when producers choose a story line, and take from those they interview only what fits the points they want to make, thereby distorting not only what people say but the story itself. Peter Jennings, who is usually sensitive to religious nuance, should have known better. Similar examples could be drawn from *Vanity Fair* which, especially under Tina Brown, has been unblushingly anti-Catholic in a way that makes me think the editors automatically assume their readers are too.

And then there is the *New York Times.* Compared to the way the current crisis in the Catholic Church has been covered by, say, the *Los Angeles Times,* the coverage in the *New York Times* has been excessive and almost gleeful, revisiting old stories when no fresh revelations are forthcoming and even treating parish councils as if they were radical innovations. No editor in his right mind would have printed the recent rant by columnist Bill Keller, unless that editor (now former editor)—Howell Raines—were himself anti-Catholic. It says much about the newsroom culture of the *Times* that it finds the views of an ex-Catholic worth featuring. But then, compared to other national newspapers, the *Times's* op-ed page is the least diversified in its selection of columnists, most of them products of its own hothouse institutional culture, and in the opinions it will allow to outside contributors. For example, it is not unusual to find three or four pieces a week against abortion when that issue is in the news, but in thirty-eight years of reading the *Times* I can only recall—at most—three op-ed pieces arguing a pro-life position.

Anti-Catholicism comes in different packages. By its own reckoning, the *New York Times* is an institution, not just a newspaper: in its own secularist fashion it is a kind of church, complete with its own hierarchy and magisterium. For many of its readers, the *Times* defines what is real and what is not, what is acceptable thought and behavior and what is not, thereby setting the boundaries between the secular polis and the religious barbarians gnawing at the gates. In short, the *Times* evangelizes a wholly secular worldview, which bleaches out whatever—even in New York City—does not conform to that perspective. For instance, where a newspaper like the *Chicago Tribune* routinely includes parochial schools in its annual education supplement, the *Times* in its annual supplement has mentioned them only once in all the years that I've been reading it. Similarly, when it does its roundup of the year's notable books—at Christmastime, yet—there is no category for religion. Its news coverage of religion is spotty, though sometimes well-done, but it displays a noticeably unsure editorial mind in its judgment of what is important in this area. In short, to use David Tracy's categories, if the Catholic imagination is analogical and the Protestant imagination dialogical, the religious imagination of the *Times* is dermatological—that is, skin-deep.

It is common for defenders of the Catholic Church like William Donohue to substitute Jews or blacks or gays for Catholics, and ask those who smear Catholics if they would dare ridicule these other identity groups in the same fashion. In general, I think that is a fair test, and I am astonished to learn that his adversaries find his question repulsive. Clearly, Catholics are fair game, but why should this be so?

My guess is that most Americans—including most Catholics—do not know the history that John McGreevy has outlined for us. Harvard, to take but one example, has courses dealing with anti-Semitism, racism, misogyny, homophobia and the like, and you can be assured that in the nation's major divinity schools preoccupation with these sins is central to their not-so-informal curriculum. But I do not think that at any elite institution—including perhaps Notre Dame—you will find courses devoted to anti-Catholicism. In other words, our elites have been shaped by social constructions of reality that exclude anti-Catholicism as part of the American experience. Charitably, we might say that in some cases we are dealing with invincible ignorance, not outright prejudice.

A distinction has been made between religious anti-Catholicism and cultural anti-Catholicism. I can accept the former: there are doctrines and beliefs of various religious traditions that I find personally odious, and as a Catholic I am in no way bothered by the residual Reformation-style anti-Catholicism of, say, Bob Jones University—especially when I see that Bob Jones III, the university's putative heir-apparent, chose to do post-graduate work at Notre Dame. But I must say that I am struck by the fact that Protestants—including Evangelicals—have been noticeably sympathetic and non-judgmental toward Catholics during this time of scandal. As well they might be, since a recent story of child abuse in Protestant churches shows an average of seventy such allegations a week, though you won't find that mentioned in the *New York Times*.

As for cultural anti-Catholicism, I am surprised by the persistence of old stereotypes, such as those mentioned by Andrew Greeley today. One expects such crudities among academics, because the academy, particularly in the humanities, has become so ideologically driven and allergic to institutions and forms of authority other than its own. But I'd be surprised if it were prevalent in the business world—or even in country clubs—and I must say I have not found much of it in the environment of *Newsweek*. Quite the opposite.

Looking back over some 750 articles I have written for *Newsweek*, I find that less than 4 percent deal with mainline Protestants. Over these years, *Newsweek*'s top editors—all of them but one in the past forty years Protestant or Jewish by background—have manifested certain preferences in the coverage of religion. (Religion covers, by the way, have for twenty-five years always been among the annual bestsellers on the newsstand, though the biggest draws are usually cover stories about some aspect of the figure of Jesus.) In order of preference, what the editors have wanted from me are: First, stories about Catholics. Second, stories about Catholics. Third—at least since the rise of Jerry Falwell in the late 1970s—stories about Evangelicals. Fourth, Catholics. Fifth, everyone else. Yet Protestant readers, including clergy, very often compliment the magazine on it's coverage of religion—even though they never see their own traditions written about. In the words of the late Lenny Bruce, I think we have to ask why it is in the media, and not just *Newsweek*, that the Catholic Church is treated as "the only 'The Church?'" Here, I think, we can get into some of the ambiguities of cultural anti-Catholicism, ambiguities which make the Catholic Church at once attractive and suspect in a nation that is still, historically and numerically more Protestant than anything else.

Size: A quarter of Americans identify as Catholics. And, like Evangelicals, they are perceived as having political weight, at least in local elections. Reason enough to pay attention, certainly reason enough to worry if you don't like what the church teaches.

Authority: friends would say *authoritative,* foes would say *authoritarian,* and in the church you can find Catholics in both camps. *Authority* means the church makes truth claims, which some elites find onerous—including many Catholics. It also means there are moral norms, which some elites, especially those who came of age since the 1960s, find hard to accept—unless they are of their own manufacture. Hence the power of the word, "choice."

Authority implies hierarchy, another structural mark of the church that many folks find alien on principle. The irony is that Americans readily accept the need for hierarchy in corporations, the military and even to a degree in sports. But in religion most Americans are female in the sense that

Carol Gilligan uses the term: we like circles, not pyramids. That the Catholic Church is a pyramid that allows a lot of circles to be formed inside its space—that is, freedom within order—seems to escape most observers.

And then there is sex. The Catholic Church takes sex and gender seriously—maybe too seriously—which means it holds out norms to be observed. But on matters of sex and gender, we are well into a normless society, a society which, on both the popular and elite levels also takes sex too seriously, but for very different reasons. Here there really is a culture war, and institutionally the Catholic Church is the biggest, easiest target. I could go on, but I want to make sure two main points are clear.

The first deals with identity. Despite qualifiers like *liberal* and *conservative*, *progressive* and *reactionary*, *lapsed*, *collapsed* and *relapsed*, the public at large still thinks that the word *Catholic* has explanatory value in ways that words like *Protestant* or *Presbyterian* or *Episcopalian* or *Methodist* or even *Jewish* do not. The word may conjure stereotypes of the kind Andrew Greeley has mentioned, but at least Catholics and their church get noticed. Put another way, when was the last time—at least since the novels of Peter DeVries—you saw the rituals and symbols of, say, Congregationalists burlesqued? For the media, *Catholic* means, in words said of Willy Loman after his suicide, "attention must be paid."

The second deals with the church's noticeableness. It stands for something—many things—and is not afraid of the public square. The Catholic Church is certainly is not alone in this regard, but it is not in the nature of Catholicism to privatize religion in the ways that some others, especially secularists, would want. And when it fails, as its bishops most spectacularly have, when it resorts to secrecy—as all religious institutions do—its dirty underwear is there for all to see.

For both these reasons, there will always be anti-Catholicism, enduring but intermittent in its manifestation, as McGreevy says. What we see today is not as virulent as it has been in the past. Speaking for myself, I am always nervous when too many people agree with me, which doesn't happen often. I think the church should be the same way, or else it will cease to the church. Anti-Catholicism isn't always hatred and prejudice; sometimes it's being liked for all the wrong reasons. The challenge for any tradition that claims to be Christian is to be disliked for all the right reasons. On this view, some anti-Catholic prejudices are not only acceptable but welcome.

ANTI-CATHOLICISM: THE LAST ACCEPTABLE PREJUDICE? NO

Mark Silk

Let me begin by saying that, from a Jewish perspective, the problem of anti-Catholicism may not seem too severe. After all, there are a billion Catholics in the world today, as opposed to 15 million Jews. In America, Catholics are the largest religious body, representing a quarter of the population—as opposed to Jews, who represent less than 2 percent. I dare say we'd accept a fair extra measure of anti-Semitism for numbers like that! But prejudice is not just a numbers game. It is also about how people are represented in the central arteries of the culture. And so I will turn to the news media, with which, in one way or another, I've spent most of my time over the past couple of decades.

Are the American news media anti-Catholic? The only systematic effort to answer this question that I know of was a study conducted a decade ago by Robert and Linda Lichter and Daniel Amundson. It looked at coverage of the Catholic Church by the *New York Times,* the *Washington Post, Time* magazine, and CBS News during three five-year periods in the mid-1960s, 1970s, and 1980s. Commissioned by the Knights of Columbus and the Catholic League for Religious and Civil Rights, the study grouped stories into four coverage areas found to have dominated the coverage: sexual morality, power relations within the church, relations between the church and state authority, and relations with other churches. In all but the last area, the study concluded, the church was on the losing side of a policy debate. In addition, the authors assessed the media's use of descriptive language and found that the church was "overwhelmingly portrayed as an oppressive or authoritarian institution." The basic story line, they concluded, "increasingly . . . revolves around a beleaguered authority struggling to enforce its traditions and decrees on a reluctant constituency."

174

As striking as the study's conclusions were, they were immediately called into question by our friends at *Commonweal*, in a lengthy lead editorial in the May 17, 1991, number entitled "Thin-skinned." The editorial pointed out that of the 1,876 stories sampled by the study, only 115 used "emotive" words like *authoritarian, rigid,* or *emancipating* to characterize the church as either oppressive or liberating. That 98 of the 1,876 used "oppressive" terms hardly justified calling the media's portrayal of the church as overwhelmingly oppressive. The editorial had more to say about the inadequacies of the study, but you get the point. And from my own examination of coverage of the Catholic Church, I would agree with *Commonweal*.

For the past five years I have edited *Religion in the News*, a triannual magazine that looks at how the news media deal with various types of religious subject matter. In the course of a dozen issues we have published two dozen articles that look at coverage of the Catholic Church in some fashion—generally but not exclusively by U.S. news media. The stories in question include, among others: papal journeys to Cuba, the Holy Land, Greece, and the Ukraine; vouchers, international debt relief, and charitable choice; exorcism and Elian Gonzalez; *Dominus Iesus* and the *mandatum* for teaching theology at Catholic institutions of higher learning; the election of Vicente Fox as president of Mexico; a fight over a radical priest in Rochester; a fight over coverage of Cardinal Bevilaqua by the *Philadelphia Inquirer;* the fight over having a Catholic chaplain in the House of Representatives; the death of Cardinal O'Connor; controversies over the television show *Nothing Sacred,* the play *Corpus Christi,* and Chris Ofili's artwork, "The Holy Virgin Mary" at the Brooklyn Museum of Art; and, of course, the ongoing story of the church and pedophilia. I will not here attempt to run down how the coverage went in each of these cases. For all the details you can consult our Web site: www.trincoll.edu/depts/csrpl.

What I would say is that the treatment of the church—of Roman Catholicism—has run the gamut from the positively hagiographic to neutral to pretty negative, depending on the story. At the hagiographic end was coverage of Cardinal O'Connor. Also hagiographic, I might add, was coverage of the late Father Mychal Judge, the New York Fire Department chaplain who died giving last rites at the World Trade Center on September 11.

At the negative end, I'd cite the *Palm Beach Post's* religion writer Steve Gushee's 1998 characterization of the church as "the world's oldest totalitarian state and the quintessential old boys' club"—a crack made in the midst of the coverage of the resignation of Bishop Joseph Symonds for having molested several young men years earlier. The Catholic League could doubtless cite others. But so far as I have found, such comments are pretty infrequent.

Overall—and this will, I'm sure, come as a great shock—the church tends to look better in the eyes of the secular media when it takes positions that the media tend to find worthy—debt relief, ministering to the down-trodden, working for peace. On the other hand, when the church—or, let us say, its leadership—seems to protect child abusers, that's another story. When it comes to cultural productions like *Corpus Christi* or "The Holy Virgin Mary," there is tension between disrespect for a religion (something the press generally doesn't like) and the free expression of ideas (which the press tends to salute). When the Catholic League launches a protest, the balance tips towards free expression (now threatened by "censorship"), and the news media generally side with free expression.

Whether this is anti-Catholicism is a nice question. The claim is made that journalists would be a lot less tolerant of something that disrespects, say, Islam. Maybe so. But there is a cultural rule of thumb worth bearing in mind here. The media expect large and powerful groups to be able to absorb more criticism than small and powerless ones. The Catholic Church may consider itself a minority school in a sea of Protestant and secular fish. But that isn't the way Catholicism is viewed by outsiders.

In any event, it is hard not to notice how often controversies over Catholicism these days appear to be an intra-Catholic thing, with the rest of us kind of looking on with interest. *Nothing Sacred* and *Corpus Christi* and "The Holy Virgin Mary"—and, for that matter, the movie *Dogma*—are the creations of people who are Catholics or were Catholics. Maybe some would call them self-hating Catholics. But the point is, the controversies have the character of a commentary or critique or debate among insiders. This, indeed, can be said of a good deal of the discussion, in the media and outside it, of the current clerical sexual abuse crisis in the Church—especially in Boston, which is ground zero. Just about everyone weighing in, including the judges and the district attorneys, are Irish Catholics. The *Boston Globe*, which is filled with Catholics of different species, has of course led the journalistic pack. But, interestingly, the editorial line of the *Boston Herald* has been far tougher on Cardinal Law than the *Globe*'s, and indeed the *Herald* has had the better of the reporting from inside the archdiocese. Why? Because the *Herald*, from its publisher on down, is more connected to the church than the *Globe* is.

So where does this leave us? Is anti-Catholicism still an acceptable prejudice?

Despite the remarkable growth of acceptance of religious "otherness" in American society, there will, I believe, always be theological disagreement, an *odium theologicum* that shades into prejudice. The strongest hostility to Catholicism these days, I would venture to say, comes from the Eastern Orthodox, who fully share in the analogical imagination but have various historical and doctrinal bones to pick with Rome. If other Americans think that Catholics worship the Virgin Mary, it probably has as much to do with ignorance, invincible or otherwise, as prejudice. (I doubt many are aware of those who would have the church pronounce Mary to be co-mediatrix.)

But what the Jews have learned, more or less, is that the anti-Semitism that counts is not the *odium theologicum* per se but the anti-Semitism that has effects in the real world. I think that's a good standard. The fracas over the appointment of a Catholic chaplain in the House of Representatives was notable but, I think, far less notable than the election of Catholic governors in states like Alabama and Oklahoma. American Catholics themselves seem to me to be pretty at home in America—perhaps too much at home for some tastes, but there it is. There is no other explanation for their readiness to express their feelings about the church hierarchy as publicly as they have in the current crisis.

Consider the following exchange between Archbishop Elden Curtiss of Omaha and a local layman, Frank Ayers, who had written a letter to the *Omaha World-Herald* criticizing Curtiss's handling of a priest charged with viewing child pornography on the Internet. "Any Catholic who uses the secular media to air complaints against the leadership of the church, without dialogue with that leadership, is a disgrace to the church," wrote Curtiss to Ayers. "The clergy and the laity have been silent about this in the past, and it has not served the church well," Ayers told the newspaper. "We're going to discuss it openly and publicly. The bishops in the United States aren't going to be allowed to handle this quietly any longer."

From the peanut gallery of onlookers, I'd say that, for those worried about anti-Catholicism, there's a silver lining in the present crisis: It should disabuse all non-Catholic Americans of any residual belief that Catholics are people who follow the orders of the hierarchy like sheep. For this reason if no other, the revolt of the Catholic laity, evident on the pages of newspapers across the country, should gladden the heart of Father Andrew Greeley. I'd also advance the opinion that William Donohue's refusal to bash the media over the past few months has done more for the cause of anti-anti-Catholicism than all his previous protests. As we know from Sherlock Holmes, sometimes the most significant datum is when the dog doesn't bark.

VOICES FROM THE FIELD:
A PANEL DISCUSSION

Gail Buckley, Daniel Callahan, William Donohue, Paul Moses, Alan Wolfe

GAIL BUCKLEY

Is Anti-Catholicism the last acceptable prejudice? In May 2002, the answer might well be "Why not?" There is a caveat, however. It depends on which of the many aspects of Catholicism incurs the prejudice.

The Catholic religion is the biggest tent of all. The mandate is every race and nation. Add every opinion. The church is so utterly human and diverse that the tent is always being pulled in several directions at once, but the foundation of faith is solid. Thus, there can never be any justified prejudice against the Catholic faith or the Catholic faithful as a group.

As for intolerance of the Catholic power structure, as of May 2002, "Why not?" Sadly, the power structure seems to imitate the Pharisees more than it imitates Jesus. "Do as I say, not as I do," say the Pharisees. In the wake of the child abuse scandal, anti-Catholicism towards the power structure is now coming from inside the church as well as out.

As John McGreevy suggests, some anti-Catholicism is clearly criticism and not prejudice. Most of my non-Catholic friends are liberal; ergo, not prejudiced in their own eyes. They see the church as having a split personality: heroic on most social justice issues, but generally, to them, hypocritical and oppressive on reproduction and gender. "The Pope is good for the world," said an elderly Jesuit friend of mine, speaking of John Paul II, "but hard on Catholics." To a certain extent my non-Catholic friends would probably agree. They would surely agree with favorable responses to Andrew Greeley's Catholic education and care for the poor questions, but obviously be in the other camp on abortion. They can't deny the moral right of Catholics to be anti-abortion. They do, however, question the justice of sticking to the letter of the law against condoms in Africa, when the continent is dying of AIDS before our eyes and, according to polls, Catholics all over the first world are using them.

They've also questioned the justice of the power structure position on liberation theology. Catholic anticommunism is seen as morally correct, but supporting Central American oligarchs instead of the oppressed Catholic poor is seen as wrong. Even my non-Catholic friends know that the Catholic clergy, religious, and laypeople who were murdered in El Salvador and elsewhere weren't killed because they were spreading communism, but because they were spreading Christianity.

The rigidity and letter-of-the-law aspect of the power structure is what most arouses anti-Catholicism in people who aren't normally bigots. It has also, in the case of the child abuse scandal, aroused a form of anti-Catholicism among Catholics themselves, who feel betrayed by the hierarchy's refusal to admit that putting the structure ahead of the flock makes them very bad shepherds. The abuse, however, has also reinvigorated a "My brand is better than your brand" type of anti-Catholicism among Catholics themselves. I get e-mail from angry Catholic conservatives who berate me for a column in the *New York Daily News* criticizing the power structure, instead of what they see as the true source of evil—Vatican II—which they say permitted gay men to be ordained. To them, the issue is not child abuse and its cover-up, but gay men and, above all, Vatican II. Surely there were gay priests before Vatican II. Surely sin is in behavior, not orientation.

Many Catholic conservatives, against most current church liturgy, indulge another form of Catholic anti-Catholicism in bashing Vatican II. Vatican II bashers want to go back to 1870 in the worst way. "Traditional values, converts, and shedding your kind will be the way to renew this church," said an angry e-mailer, urging me to shed myself. "Get lost," he said, "find another religion, if they'll have you."

Liberals, like conservatives, are always going to be with the church. Neither of us can convince the other to leave and I, for one, wouldn't dream of trying. One of us seeks change, the other fears it; it's probably genetic. The truth lies somewhere in the middle. Vatican III, convoked by John Paul's successor, would be the perfect place to find it.

"We should not be uniform, we should be unified," said my friend, Father Vaclav Maly, when I interviewed him ten years ago for *America* magazine. What he had to say is relevant because he suffered another kind of anti-Catholicism as an ex-underground Czech priest, silenced and imprisoned under the communists. "We must recognize the living experiences of generations, but it should not just be the repetition of old customs," he said. "Christianity must be alive. Jesus always speaks in the present tense."

Unable to abolish the church, the communists hoped to make it die out by forbidding all public interaction between laymen and priests. Finally, banning all legitimate priests, they established a form of legalized Catholicism, with licensed priests sanctioned by the government instead of Rome. According to Maly (in my 1992 interview) certain banned bishops secretly ordained other priests, including some married men, and possibly even some women.

Perhaps because of his time in prison, Maly looked for a closer relationship between the people and the church. "We are given Jesus as a gift. Simultaneously we are gifts to Jesus from the Father—gifts; not property," he said. We are introduced into an almost equal relationship. Our relationship with Jesus and the Father represents our human dignity. Human dignity doesn't require the church to become a democracy, but Catholics can ask that it be democratized.

The child abuse scandal cries out for lay—especially parental—input. Why can't registered Catholic parishioners be permitted to vote from the Vatican-produced slate for their cardinal archbishops, for example? One name I would personally like to see on the Vatican slate would be that of Bishop Kenneth Untener of Saginaw, Michigan, who doesn't have a rectory, but apparently travels around the diocese basically living out of his car. The Little Books Committee of the diocese of Saginaw created the Lenten and Easter daily reading booklets sold at my parish for $1 each. Unfolding a new and wonderful mystery every day, they were a bargain at any price. "Our tendency to place Christ above and apart from us runs contrary to our faith," read an entry from May 17, 2002. "It is to take the incarnation too lightly." When I expressed the wish to a priest friend that Bishop Untener might come to New York, "Oh, he won't be going anywhere," my friend replied. "He's too good."

The Saginaw Easter readings included a six-part discussion on the virtue of hope and introduced some modern ecumenical saints, like Esther Wainio, religion unknown, the stepmother of Elizabeth Wainio, a passenger on United Airlines Flight 93 on 9/11. In a last fear-filled call home, Elizabeth talked to her stepmother awhile, then fell silent, apologizing because in the last moments of her life she couldn't speak. "You don't have to," said Esther, and possibly the last words Elizabeth heard, "I've got my arms around you."

Surely, one of the reasons that Catholics, as Andrew Greeley put it, "like being Catholic," is the knowledge that somewhere there are places like Saginaw, Michigan, where structure is unimportant and faith is radiantly alive. There, prejudice is irrelevant and a difference of opinion is resolved in friendship and the Holy Spirit.

DANIEL CALLAHAN

I feel I am here under odd auspices. As some of you know, but not all, I am what used to be referred as a fallen-away Catholic, or an ex-Catholic. But there are different types of ex-Catholics. I once wrote an article in the mid-1960s, when this was beginning to happen to me, distinguishing between those who left the church because they got mad at the church but remained religious, and a much smaller group who simply stopped being religious, but still loved the church. I fell into the latter category and to this day I remain fond of the church. Most of my friends are in fact Roman Catholic, but at the same time, I have not been drawn back. The Catholic Church seems to be a wonderful church except for its obsession with religion, but that's a separate issue.

I was cofounder of the Hastings Center in 1969, to examine ethical problems of medicine and biology. Very striking for me is that I went from an essentially Catholic world, as an editor of *Commonweal*, to an extraordinarily aggressive secular world. Over the years I had endless struggles in getting anybody with a religious background invited to be part of our research projects at the Center. The dominant group tended to be philosophers and lawyers. The philosophers, typically, were aggressively atheist, aggressively hostile to religion, and aggressively unwilling to even have that voice heard. That bothered me enormously. I felt there was much to be heard from the religious voice even if I was not part of it.

The case study I would like to use would be the stem cell debate. There is not an awful lot of anti-Catholicism around these days, though there might be some. But there is, among a certain portion of elite academics and intellectuals in this country, a very strong dose of anti-religion. The stem cell debate has brought that up in a very dramatic fashion, because the debate has essentially been cast as the religious right over/against the enlightened proponents of research, and particularly proponents of the saving of life and the relief of suffering. Religion is seen to stand in its way. Any number of statements by Nobel laureates and others in favor of the stem cell research dismiss all objections, and have a constant tendency to bring it back to the abortion debate.

Certainly the abortion issue is central to the stem cell debate, but there is another issue very close to it, and that is the standing one gives to scientific progress, and particularly biomedical progress. A characteristic of this secular world is that biomedical science, with the possibility of saving and reducing suffering, is itself a strong religion. And over/against this new religion—it's not exactly new; it's the religion of the Enlightenment—stand the churches, and particularly the very nasty coalition they see in the Roman Catholic Church and the fundamentalist Protestant churches. The *New*

York Times is a good example of this; it has never run one op-ed piece against stem cell research, though they have run many op-ed pieces on the subject. The editorials constantly speak of "them" as opposing it, and "they" are the forces of religion. Those of you who live in Boston may remember a column by Robert Kuttner, who talked about the religious ayatollahs and their objection to the stem cell research.

The Roman Catholic Church gets caught up in this in great part because it has been aggressively hostile, not only to stem cell research, but to cloning, both reproductive cloning and also to what is now called research cloning. It has thrown its weight around; it has acted like any other advocacy group in Washington, cultivating congressmen, sending letters, petitions, and the like, and perhaps even more so than some of the fundamentalist groups. The two together have made religion in general, but Roman Catholicism in particular, part of the enemy. I see a new kind of anti-Catholicism, but one which I would generically want to put under the rubric of anti-religion, and particularly politically aggressive religion, fighting what are seen as great and vital causes like cloning.

In the end, I see no particular resolution to this. I think it is a good thing. I happen to be a very weird character myself. I'm pro-choice in abortion and anti–stem cell research, and this particular combination is odd and would take me a few months to explain. But it seems to me that what has emerged in recent months with the stem cell debate is that there are now other groups being counted against stem cell research: some women's groups, some environmentalist groups, and in Europe you find the Green Parties opposed to much genetic research.

In this country, the issue has been cast as a debate of religion versus progress. I think that may change, but for a long time we're going to have this struggle. (I should add as a footnote that all of the secular people who know me don't make any distinction between a practicing Catholic and an ex-Catholic. Catholic is Catholic. They often say to me, "Well, of course you're against stem cell research, given your background.")

In the long run, if this debate is to be resolved in any satisfactory way, we are going to need a very strong religious voice. We're going to need the religious groups joining the coalitions of secular groups that also have reservations about much genetic engineering.

WILLIAM DONOHUE

I want to try and tease out some differences between what I consider legitimate criticism of the Catholicism and anti-Catholicism. But let me begin by talking about what I think is the core of anti-Catholicism today. I think it is the contrasting and conflicting visions of liberty.

The Catholic Church, the Catholic *Catechism*, and John Paul II teach that liberty is the freedom to do what you ought to do. I can't think of a single line that is more countercultural in our society today: "Liberty is the freedom to do what you ought to do." Contrast that with what the dominant elites have been arguing for some time, and I think quite successfully, that freedom is the liberty to do what you want to do. You can trace this back, as some people have, hundreds of years. You can go back 1859 to the little essay by John Stuart Mill, "On Liberty," with its one very simple principle. It is the idea of the unencumbered self—I am answerable only to myself—which has triumphed in our society. I much prefer the Catholic emphasis on community.

The idea that restraint is anathema to liberty is one of our greatest problems. I would much prefer sexual reticence as understood by the Catholic Church, as opposed to sexual libertinism as understood by our society at large. I think that you live longer and you're happier if you exercise restraint in your life. The fact of the matter is that sexual libertinism is what's driving broken relationships, unwanted pregnancies, AIDS, and herpes. It's not some little bug that came along and bit somebody. It's a matter of people breaking down in discipline, and that breakdown comes from an impoverished conception of liberty.

This idea that I am in charge of my own destiny even crept into the Supreme Court of the United States. Listen to this remarkable sentence written by Supreme Court Justice David Souter in *Casey v. Planned Parenthood* (1992). "At the heart of liberty is the right to define one's own concept of existence, of meaning, the universe and of the mystery of human life." I have never in my life read anything more preposterous, coming from the words of a Supreme Court judge. I am answerable to no one. I am the unencumbered self. I am detached from community. I can create my own moral existence. I would say this is madness.

Let me give you a contemporary example. Dina Wise has written in *New York* magazine (May 20, 2002) about Sylvia Hewlett's work on the biological clock. Once a woman hits thirty-five the fertility of her eggs starts to drop off. Some women are panicking: maybe they have to go out and find a husband. Now, here's what Wise says—she is distraught: "I don't like to hear the word can't. None of us do in New York. This city is all about can do and will do. You say I can't have a baby whenever I want. Well, I'll do it anyway, to spite you. But then the eggs," she says, "you can't really get around that."

Well, don't despair! Here's her answer. She says "Maybe I don't want to go there" [hunting for a husband]. I'm looking at a turkey baster." She must be liberated. "Or adopting a child from Cambodia. I'll figure it out. I'm a New York woman. I'm resilient. I know I can have it all."

Hubris is of course a staple of our society. As a sociologist, I think the idea that you can have it all is mad. The idea that limits are anathema to liberty is driving much of the problem. It's very hard to get a Catholic perspective out there when this seems to be the popular reigning idea.

When you get down to anti-Catholicism itself, I don't have a theological micrometer that I pull it out of my pocket and touch this cartoon, and all of a sudden it lights up "anti-Catholic." I have to make judgment calls like everyone else.

Let me share some contemporary examples because the sex abuse scandal in the Catholic Church ties to this. The fact is a lot of our priests haven't been able to put a harness on their libido. Certainly Paul Shanley couldn't. I wonder where he learned it—maybe from Father Anthony Kosnik, who wrote a book on human sexuality that was so popular in the seminaries in the 1970s. Maybe he learned it from Crooks and Bauer, the 1990s book, also called *Human Sexuality*, where even necrophilia is not regarded as a taboo. If you can accept that, then you can accept almost anything.

In terms of the situation with anti-Catholicism today, I think most of the hard news reporting has been pretty good. I have some problems with a lot of the cartoonists and with the essayists, but it's a different genre, I understand that.

Here is an example of a cartoon. I think it's fair, and I'll tell you why. Somebody's throwing a book at Cardinal Law, and it says, "Throwing the book at him." There are a couple of priests on the side, and one says "Whew, the Pope still has a good arm on him." First of all, it's cute; secondly, it's not against all priests. It's against Cardinal Law, who probably does deserve to have the book thrown at him.

Here's a cartoon that I think is despicable. It was in the March 22 *New York Post*. A kid's in the confessional. The priest is smoking a cigarette with his pants down around his ankles and a bottle of booze next to him, and the kid says to the priest, "Anything you want to confess to me?" That's a general thing. You can't go from the individual to the collective without getting into some problems with regard to bigotry.

Here's an example of a *New York Times* editorial that I certainly didn't have any problem with. They write, "Americans have become depressingly familiar with the sight of great men and woman dragged before a judge or grand jury and answering questions with an eye to the finer nuances of law rather than the grand moral questions of social justice," and they go on about Cardinal Law. They're putting it in context. How could that be anti-Catholic?

The *Boston Globe*: Kudos to columnist Eileen McNamara, who picked this up. Harvard University is making it more difficult now for a woman to prove that she's been raped. You have to have eyewitnesses. And they're not giving names over to the authorities. They are going to have a group with sophomore standing deal with this. Eileen McNamara writes, "Cardinal Bernard F. Law may not have come by his hubris naturally; he probably picked it up at Harvard," and goes on about comparing the two institutions in that regard.

The *Washington Post* talks about the Catholic Church, long a vital institution in American society, engulfed in a moral, financial and legal crisis, unthinkable only a few years ago. This is sympathetic. This is not hammering us. But why shouldn't you criticize the Catholic Church? I am concerned when dissent kicks over into distain into disparagement into insult. When you go from the individual to the collective like the cartoon I described. Or take, for example, KFI Radio in Los Angeles. Here's what they say: "Ten percent of priests are pedophiles; the other ninety percent are equally as guilty because they don't do anything about it. I always have heard that men have a calling to the priesthood, now we know the calling is in his pants."

We have people like Paul Vitello at *Newsday* who wrote a despicable column questioning the propriety of Denis Dillon, a practicing Catholic, investigating Bishop Murphy and the Diocese of Rockville Center. Can you imagine somebody saying, "Wait a minute, this guy's a Jew—he shouldn't investigate the Middle East; he may not be objective about it"? I resent that. Just because you are a Catholic that you would automatically assume that the man can't do the investigatory work.

PAUL MOSES

I was city editor of the New York City edition of *Newsday* for four years, and one of the great pleasures of that job was that I got to speak with the most persistent of the callers who wanted to tell an editor that some story in the newspaper was biased. One day a man called to complain about a story we had run about immigrants from Uzbekistan. I was totally lost because I hadn't read the story, and at that point, three or four years ago, I really didn't know anything about Uzbekistan other than it was a former Soviet Republic. The man said he represented a group called the Bukharan-Jewish Community and that he wanted to meet with me. And I said, "When would you like to meet?" and he said, "In ten minutes."

It turned out that there were thousands of Bukharan Jews living within a few minutes' walk of the office building in Queens where *Newsday* ran its city desk. So about three or four leaders from this community came up to the office within the promised ten or maybe fifteen minutes. They sat down at a table and laid out the newspaper story, an obscure story in the back of the paper, and they pointed to it. One of them said, "You called us Uzbeks." And I said, "Well, you're from Uzbekistan, right?" He went explained to me what many of you probably know now: Uzbeks are Muslims, and the Bukharan Jews were obviously Jewish. Yes, they were from Uzbekistan, but they were not Uzbeks, and our error was so colossal that they assumed that it was malicious, that we were somehow out to defame and insult them. I had to explain to them that it really resulted from ignorance and that it was not meant to insult them.

I bring that story up because any discussion of anti-Catholicism in the news media should begin with the understanding that we Catholics join a long line of aggrieved parties. It is astonishing to me that there is so little knowledge about the Catholic Church in newsrooms, given that Catholics make up so much of the population in major metropolitan areas—over 40 percent in New York City, I would say.

But are Catholics more misunderstood than Evangelical Protestants? I really don't think so. More than Muslims? Definitely not. And we are certainly better known in the newsroom than immigrants from Uzbekistan.

Editors, reporters and columnists often define the Catholic Church in terms of how its views differ from theirs. But then again, journalists tend to define everything that way. If you look closely, for example, at the New York City media's coverage of places like Staten Island, you'll see what I mean. The subtext is always that places outside of Manhattan are strange. They're not anything like the Upper West Side or Park Slope in Brooklyn, where most reporters live. There was a really good example of that on the front page of the *New York Times*, in which the reporter expresses real surprise that there are people in the city who take a long time to get to work. I read this story on my hour-and-fifteen-minute trip from the far reaches of Brooklyn. The news media does miss the boat in a lot of ways, not just with Catholics.

We Catholics get the same kind of coverage: the church is strange; it's against abortion and homosexuality and even condoms for people with AIDS. Since these are hot button issues, and since church leaders have emphasized these matters and sought to influence public opinion and legislation, the conflict is built in. But when does criticism or negative portrayal of the Catholic Church express bigotry? Maybe I'm just naturally contrary from working on a newspaper for so long, but based on what I have encountered in twenty-three years in the newsroom, I would have to say not nearly so often as some Catholics think. On that I tend to take a middling position between the excellent presentations by Mark Silk and Ken Woodward, which is, in some ways, a comfortable position to be in for someone who is a journalist—in the middle you feel that you're probably in the right spot.

Since I was known in the newsroom to be Catholic and not a lapsed Catholic or a collapsed Catholic, to borrow that phrase, but one who actually likes the church, I would often be asked about allegations of Catholic-bashing. And a lot of times I found them off base. When I was city editor, I used to get faxes almost every week about advertisers succumbing to a boycott of one of my favorite TV shows, *Nothing Sacred*, which was supposedly anti-Catholic. I thought it was a good and upbeat depiction of parish life, without having seen every episode. When have you ever seen a liturgy committee meeting depicted on television?

Then there was a song that I quite liked called "One of Us," sung by Joan Osborne, and I used it with my eighth grade confirmation class to get them to discuss the mystery of God. Here was something that was played constantly on the radio, and asked what the nature of God is—not a theologically perfect song, but it raised the issue well. Wouldn't you know that one of my students stopped me during this lesson and said she'd read in the newspaper that this was Catholic-bashing, and I found out what a long reach Bill Donohue has.

Similarly, I never understood the fuss made over the movie *The Last Temptation of Christ*. Without going into all the details, I thought it was spiritually uplifting and I was happy, a few years after its release, to read a piece in *First Things* that said the same thing.

Several years ago I was at a meeting with the Catholic Bishops' Conference for a discussion on the news media and clergy sex abuse. This was about four years ago. I was bothered by the reactions of some bishops, who wanted to complain about the news media and this issue: Well, they asked, would you do this with clergy from other religions? I told them—Mark Silk has addressed this very well—that I was surprised that some of the stories back in that period were not getting more attention nationally. I didn't think the news media was really that interested in the story, unless it pointed to an institutional problem in the church. In my experience, we were running tiny stories in the back of the paper during that period. I became skeptical of claims about Catholic-bashing, even though I knew that the church was often misunderstood and even disliked by some in the newsroom.

Of all the cases of alleged Catholic-bashing I encountered as a reporter or editor, the Brooklyn Museum's *Sensation* exhibit was probably the most interesting. I have to tell you, I was dismayed to see so little understanding among colleagues in the news media of why Catholics felt hurt that a museum would exhibit a painting of the Blessed Mother decorated with dung and with pictures of genitalia cut out from porn magazines. Articles on the subject often neglected that latter detail. But the cure was worse than the disease. Mayor Rudolf Giuliani tried to evict one of the city's great museums from its building. Here was a pro-choice politician ingratiating himself with the Catholic right to help his campaign for the U.S. Senate.

I wish that anti-Catholicism in China or in Sudan could one day get the kind of publicity that Mayor Giuliani generated over that painting. That said, I want to note that about two weeks ago I got a call from the Brooklyn Museum reminding me that my membership had long ago lapsed. Actually, to borrow a phrase again, I would say that my museum membership had collapsed. And I took advantage of this opportunity to tell the caller why I had no intention of rejoining any time soon.

ALAN WOLFE

Well, what can you possibly do when you're the last speaker of a long day and everything's been said. You have two choices, really. You can say, I relinquish my time; or you could say, I think that just about everything I have heard today is wrong. So I think I'll take the latter course and challenge the whole basis of much of the day, and that is of the predominance of anti-Catholicism in the media or in any other place in American society.

There are religions in the United States that have experienced tremendous prejudice. In the middle of the nineteenth century, believers of one faith were routinely killed, tarred and feathered, moved out of their towns by force and violence, constantly moving further west in order to find a home. One of the tenets of their faith was challenged in the American courts and declared unconstitutional by the United States Supreme Court, in the case of *Reynolds v. the United States.* I speak, of course, of the Mormons. Unlike Catholicism, Mormonism was an American faith from the beginning, born and bred in the United States. It experienced tremendous prejudice and hostility throughout much of our history, a hostility and prejudice that remains in some corners of contemporary America, in particular among certain kinds of Evangelical Protestantism. But these days Mormons are widely praised for their honesty and their probity. This is a dramatic transformation in the way in which the United States has related to one religion.

I think the history and evolution of Catholicism has gone along a similar track. I agree very much with the history as John McGreevy presented it. From the very founding of the United States there was a strong and persistent strain of anti-Catholicism. Indeed, I think the whole idea of the separation of church and state, which Americans are so proud of, was designed as a Protestant understanding of what the relationship of government and faith should be, and it was explicitly directed against Catholic Europe. In his letter concerning religious toleration, John Locke—one of the great political philosophers who influenced our culture—was explicitly anti-Catholic in his understanding of religious liberty and had terrible things to say about the Catholic faith. There's certainly a history here. There is absolutely no doubt about that. But it is a history that is long gone, in part because American religion has changed and in part because American Catholicism has changed.

We've heard a lot today about what the media think and about what Harvard University thinks and about what professors think. My own research is an attempt to discover how ordinary Americans practice their faith. I want to mention four aspects of the way religion is actually practiced in the United States that mitigate against the possibility of any strong forms of anti-Catholicism in everyday life.

The first is that there is a tremendous amount of religious switching in the United States, and it's increasingly unlikely that any adult will be of the same religion as their parents or grandparents were. This, I think, is responsible for a great deal of the increasing tolerance of all religions. It's almost like an insurance policy. If you don't know what your religion is going to be twenty-five years from now, let alone what cockamamie ideas your children are going to come home with, then, it seems to me, you are best off trying to be tolerant toward all of them. It's not a question of offending someone else; it's a question of offending where you might be. We don't know. Father Greeley mentioned that the drop-off rate from Catholics from birth to adulthood is from 31 percent to 25 percent. He minimized that. That's actually an astonishing drop in religious terms.

But I think it's much more important that every study I've seen of Evangelical Protestant organizations, like Promise Keepers and so on, show that there is a very large number of former Catholics in these Protestant organizations, and it goes both ways; there is switching in all directions. This is an enormously important aspect of how Americans practice their faith.

Second, there's an astonishing amount of theological ignorance in American religion. It's remarkable, because we're supposed to be a Bible-reading country, and we always hear—especially about Protestants—that they're Bible-believing people; but people don't know very much about the Bible at all. Actually, their knowledge of the Bible is as about as limited as their knowledge of American foreign policy. To think that people are going to make judgments about another faith based on ideas like the Real Presence of Jesus, or ideas about the liturgy and the role of the liturgy, is a misunderstanding. Most Americans don't know what the word liturgy means. Religious terms themselves are often confusing to people. Most people's approach to religion is not on the basis of ideas; it's on the basis of feelings, and what spirituality can do for me.

The notion that doctrinal disputes, especially the history of doctrinal disputes between Protestants and Catholics, are going to contribute to Protestant hostility toward Catholicism today is incomprehensible in the actual world. Most Calvinists don't know what Calvin stood for. They don't know what the word predestination means. Lutherans have very little knowledge of the writings of Martin Luther. They will talk about the idea of a priesthood of all believers, but they'll interpret it in ways that Martin Luther himself never interpreted it. Theological doctrinal differences between people have decreased dramatically in the United States.

Third, one thing that almost all Americans do know about the Bible is the one sentence, "Judge not, lest ye be judged." That comes up over and over and over again in all surveys. Americans don't want to make judgments about other faiths. You can't get students today to make a negative comment about anything. The idea that people are going to have a default position of negativity toward another faith runs against the grain of so much of what intellectuals, from Alan Bloom to William Donohue and even myself, find problematic in American culture. I wish my students would take their faith seriously enough to be critical of another.

In the aftermath of September 11th, teaching in a Catholic university, I could not get a single student to talk about whether Catholicism and Islam might in fact be different religions with different ideas. It was impossible to do. All faiths are good; we don't want to sit there and say anything negative about Islam. It took me to try to tell them something about their own faith and why it might have resources that other faiths might not have, and why its historical evolution included a Vatican II, and the historical evolution of Islam did not.

Finally, as with Mormons, there has been a dramatic change in the sociology of American Catholicism, an end to Catholic ghettoization, increasing suburbanization among American Catholics, increasing intermarriage between Catholics and non-Catholics—a completely different world on the ground of the reality in which most American Catholics live. The great controversy about what has happened in Boston involving Cardinal Law has not come from south Boston; it has come from Wellesley, Massachusetts. And I think that represents itself a symbol of the transformation of American Catholicism.

It's a new world. It's a world, I think, in which Catholics have rightly taken their place as one of America's great religions.

INDEX

191

ABOUT THE CONTRIBUTORS

J. Bottum is Books and Arts editor at the *Weekly Standard*.

Gail Buckley is the author of *American Patriots: Blacks in the Military from the Revolution to Desert Storm* and *The Hornes: An American Family*. She has written for *America*, the *New York Times*, the *New York Daily News*, and other publications.

Daniel Callahan, cofounder of the Institute of Society, Ethics, and the Life Sciences (Hasting Center), is now director of its international program. He has written numerous books in the area of bioethics.

Michele Dillon, associate professor in the Department of Sociology, University of New Hampshire, is author of *Catholic Identity* (Cambridge University Press, 1999).

Richard M. Doerflinger is Deputy Director of the Secretariat for Pro-Life Activities, U.S. Conference of Catholic Bishops, Washington, D.C.

William Donohue is the president and CEO of the Catholic League for Religious and Civil Liberties.

Brian Doyle is editor of *Portland Magazine*, University of Portland, Portland, Oregon.

The Reverend **Kenneth J. Doyle,** former director of media relations of the United States Conference of Catholic Bishops and former Rome bureau chief of Catholic News Service, is pastor of St. Catherine of Siena Parish, Albany, New York, and Chancellor for Public Information, Diocese of Albany.

Paul Elie, senior editor at Farrar, Straus & Giroux, is author of *The Life You Save May Be Your Own: An American Pilgrimage* (Farrar, Straus & Giroux, 2003).

James T. Fisher is codirector of the Center for American Studies, Fordham University.

The Reverend **Andrew M. Greeley** is professor of social science at the University of Arizona and the author of numerous sociological works as well as several novels.

Luke Timothy Johnson is Robert W. Woodruff Distinguished Professor of New Testament and Christian Origins at the Candler School of Theology, Emory University. He is the author of many theological books and articles, most recently, *The Creed: What Christians Believe and Why It Matters* (Doubleday, 2003).

Mark Massa, S.J., professor of theology and codirector of the Center for American Studies, Fordham University, is author of *Anti-Catholicism in America: The Last Acceptable Prejudice* (Crossroad, 2003).

John T. McGreevy is John A. O'Brien Associate Professor of history and author of *Catholicism and American Freedom: A History* (W. W. Norton, 2003).

Paul Moses, a former reporter and editor for New York *Newsday*, teaches journalism at Brooklyn College, City University of New York.

Susan A. Ross, is professor of theology and Faculty Scholar at Loyola University, Chicago. She is the author of *Extravagant Affections: A Feminist Sacramental Theology* (Continuum, 1998).

Robert Royal, director of The Faith and Reason Institute, was a codirector of the project, American Catholics in the Public Square.

Valerie Sayers, professor of English at the University of Notre Dame, is the author of five novels.

Mary C. Segers teaches political theory and chairs the Department of Political Science at Rutgers University, Newark.

Mark Silk is director, The Leonard E. Greenberg Center for the Study of Religion in Public Life, Trinity College, Hartford; he is editor of *Religion in the News*.

Margaret O'Brien Steinfels served as *Commonwael's* editor from 1988 to 2002 and as codirector of American Cathlolics in the Public Square project.

Peter Steinfels writes the "Beliefs" column for the *New York Times* and is the author of *A People Adrift: The Crisis of Roman Catholicism in America* (Simon & Shuster, 2003).

Barbara Dafoe Whitehead is the author of *The Divorce Culture* and co-director of The National Marriage Project, Rutgers University.

Alan Wolfe is a professor of political science and Director of the Boisi Center for Religion and American Public Life at Boston College. His most recent book is *The Transformation of American Religion: How We Actually Practice Our Faith* (Free Press, 2003).

Kenneth L. Woodward is a contributing editor of *Newsweek* where he was religion editor for thirty-nine years. He is the author of, among other books, *Making Saints* and *The Book of Miracles: The Meaning of the Miracle Stories in Christianity, Judaism, Buddhism, Hinduism, and Islam*.